Migration, Diasporas and Citizenship Series

Series Editors: **Robin Cohen**, Former Director of the International Migration Institute and Professor of Development Studies, University of Oxford, UK and **Zig Layton-Henry**, Professor of Politics, University of Warwick, UK.

Editorial Board: **Rainer Baubock**, European University Institute, Italy; **James F. Hollifield**, Southern Methodist University, USA; **Jan Rath**, University of Amsterdam, the Netherlands

The Migration, Diasporas and Citizenship series covers three important aspects of the migration progress. Firstly, the determinants, dynamics and characteristics of international migration. Secondly, the continuing attachment of many contemporary migrants to their places of origin, signified by the word 'diaspora'. Thirdly, the attempt, by contrast, to belong and gain acceptance in places of settlement, signified by the word 'citizenship'. The series publishes work that shows engagement with and a lively appreciation of the wider social and political issues that are influenced by international migration.

Also published in Migration Studies by Palgrave Macmillan

Bridget Anderson and Isabel Shutes (*editors*)
MIGRATION AND CARE LABOUR
Theory, Policy and Politics

Rutvica Andrijasevic
MIGRATION, AGENCY AND CITIZENSHIP IN SEX TRAFFICKING

Floya Anthias and Mojca Pajnik (*editors*)
CONTESTING INTEGRATION, ENGENDERING MIGRATION
Theory and Practice

Claudine Attias-Donfut, Joanne Cook, Jaco Hoffman and Louise Waite (*editors*)
CITIZENSHIP, BELONGING AND INTERGENERATIONAL RELATIONS IN AFRICAN MIGRATION

Michaela Benson and Nick Osbaldiston
UNDERSTANDING LIFESTYLE MIGRATION
Theoretical Approaches to Migration and the Quest for a Better Way of Life

Grete Brochmann, Anniken Hagelund (*authors*) with Karin Borevi, Heidi Vad Jønsson and Klaus Petersen
IMMIGRATION POLICY AND THE SCANDINAVIAN WELFARE STATE 1945–2010

Gideon Calder, Phillip Cole and Jonathan Seglow
CITIZENSHIP ACQUISITION AND NATIONAL BELONGING
Migration, Membership and the Liberal Democratic State

Michael Collyer
EMIGRATION NATIONS
Policies and Ideologies of Emigrant Engagement

Enzo Colombo and Paola Rebughini (*editors*)
CHILDREN OF IMMIGRANTS IN A GLOBALIZED WORLD
A Generational Experience

Saniye Dedeoglu
MIGRANTS, WORK AND SOCIAL INTEGRATION
Women's Labour in the Turkish Ethnic Economy

Huub Dijstelbloem and Albert Meijer (*editors*)
MIGRATION AND THE NEW TECHNOLOGICAL BORDERS OF EUROPE

Thomas Faist and Andreas Ette (*editors*)
THE EUROPEANIZATION OF NATIONAL POLICIES AND POLITICS OF IMMIGRATION
Between Autonomy and the European Union

Thomas Faist and Peter Kivisto (*editors*)
DUAL CITIZENSHIP IN GLOBAL PERSPECTIVE
From Unitary to Multiple Citizenship

Katrine Fangen, Thomas Johansson and Nils Hammarén (*editors*)
YOUNG MIGRANTS
Exclusion and Belonging in Europe

Martin Geiger and Antoine Pécoud (*editors*)
THE POLITICS OF INTERNATIONAL MIGRATION MANAGEMENT

John R. Hinnells (*editor*)
RELIGIOUS RECONSTRUCTION IN THE SOUTH ASIAN DIASPORAS
From One Generation to Another

Ronit Lentin and Elena Moreo (*editors*)
MIGRANT ACTIVISM AND INTEGRATION FROM BELOW IN IRELAND

Catrin Lundström
WHITE MIGRATIONS
Gender, Whiteness and Privilege in Transnational Migration

Ayhan Kaya
ISLAM, MIGRATION AND INTEGRATION
The Age of Securitization

Majella Kilkey, Diane Perrons, Ania Plomien
GENDER, MIGRATION AND DOMESTIC WORK
Masculinities, Male Labour and Fathering in the UK and USA

Amanda Klekowski von Koppenfels
MIGRANTS OR EXPATRIATES?
Americans in Europe

Marie Macy and Alan H. Carling
ETHNIC, RACIAL AND RELIGIOUS INEQUALITIES
The Perils of Subjectivity

George Menz and Alexander Caviedes (*editors*)
LABOUR MIGRATION IN EUROPE

Laura Morales and Marco Giugni (*editors*)
SOCIAL CAPITAL, POLITICAL PARTICIPATION AND MIGRATION IN EUROPE
Making Multicultural Democracy Work?

Eric Morier-Genoud
IMPERIAL MIGRATIONS
Colonial Communities and Diaspora in the Portuguese World

Aspasia Papadopoulou-Kourkoula
TRANSIT MIGRATION
The Missing Link Between Emigration and Settlement

Prodromos Panayiotopoulos
ETHNICITY, MIGRATION AND ENTERPRISE

Dominic Pasura
AFRICAN TRANSNATIONAL DIASPORAS
Fractured Communities and Plural Identities of Zimbabweans in Britain

Ludger Pries and Zeynep Sezgin (*editors*)
CROSS BORDER MIGRANT ORGANIZATIONS IN COMPARATIVE PERSPECTIVE

Helen Schwenken, Sabine Ruß-Sattar
NEW BORDER AND CITIZENSHIP POLITICS

Shanthi Robertson
TRANSNATIONAL STUDENT-MIGRANTS AND THE STATE
The Education-Migration Nexus

Olivia Sheringham
TRANSNATIONAL RELIGIOUS SPACES
Faith and the Brazilian Migration Experience

Evan Smith and Marinella Marmo
RACE, GENDER AND THE BODY IN BRITISH IMMIGRATION CONTROL
Subject to Examination

Vicky Squire
THE EXCLUSIONARY POLITICS OF ASYLUM

Anna Triandafyllidou and Thanos Maroukis (*editors*)
MIGRANT SMUGGLING
Irregular Migration from Asia and Africa to Europe

Vron Ware
MILITARY MIGRANTS
Fighting for YOUR Country

Lucy Williams
GLOBAL MARRIAGE
Cross-Border Marriage Migration in Global Context

Migration, Diasporas and Citizenship Series
Series Standing Order ISBN 978–0–230–30078–1 (hardback) and
978–0–230–30079–8 (paperback)
(*outside North America only*)

You can receive future titles in this series as they are published by placing a standing order. Please contact your bookseller or, in case of difficulty, write to us at the address below with your name and address, the title of the series and the ISBN quoted above.

Customer Services Department, Macmillan Distribution Ltd, Houndmills, Basingstoke, Hampshire RG21 6XS, England

---

Migrants, Work and Social Integration

Women's Labour in the Turkish Ethnic Economy

Saniye Dedeoglu

Muğla University, Turkey

First published 2014 by
PALGRAVE MACMILLAN

Palgrave Macmillan in the UK is an imprint of Macmillan Publishers Limited, registered in England, company number 785998, of Houndmills, Basingstoke, Hampshire RG21 6XS.

Palgrave Macmillan in the US is a division of St Martin's Press LLC, 175 Fifth Avenue, New York, NY 10010.

Palgrave Macmillan is the global academic imprint of the above companies and has companies and representatives throughout the world.

Palgrave® and Macmillan® are registered trademarks in the United States, the United Kingdom, Europe and other countries.

ISBN 978–1–137–37111–9

This book is printed on paper suitable for recycling and made from fully managed and sustained forest sources. Logging, pulping and manufacturing processes are expected to conform to the environmental regulations of the country of origin.

A catalogue record for this book is available from the British Library.

A catalog record for this book is available from the Library of Congress.

To my beloved family, Ayşe Defne, Sabriye and Murat

Contents

Tables

Preface

I have always aimed to bring out women's voices and views by using the research tools provided by interdisciplinary fields such as gender and migration studies. This pursuit has also tended to centre on women's work practices and gender relations, which shape the very nature of the practice of earning a living. Having this vantage point has also enabled me to analyse not only the life worlds of women, but also the ways in which women shape the political, social, cultural and economic changes taking place in the societies in which they live. Thus, it is always important to understand not only the socio-economic transformations of European societies through the lenses of gender and migration studies, but also the role women play in these grand transformations. That is why this book chooses to focus on one segment of economic life, i.e. ethnic economy, in which women seem to be quite invisible, with an aim to unleash the gendered aspect of habitus, even in the least expected areas. In this way, I have aimed to grasp the changing meanings attached to women's work and the major implications of immigrant women's roles in European societies. I claim that migrants have contributed enormously to the well-being of their host societies, and this is most evident in the case of Turkish women in London. While portrayed as the source of social exclusion and instability of their communities, and as the most disadvantaged group by political discourses, which try to put up entry barriers for immigrant women, especially for Muslim women, Turkish immigrant women find ways of positively contributing to, and socially integrating into, British society. By listening to the least heard voices of women, I have concluded that political discourses on the social integration of female migrants have essentially helped to conceal the most persistent structural problems, leading to inequality, poverty and discrimination, as well as persistent gender inequalities between women and men. Therefore, the policies addressing migrants as the cause for social ills only contribute to further escalating the negative perception of migrants, and to seeing them only as 'welfare spongers'.

Working on this book has led me to the fact that the act of migration is itself a journey lived not only individually but also collectively. At the individual level, it is a discovery of a new society, coupled with the realization of an aspiration to be in an advanced modern society.

The collective journey, on the other hand, is further characterized by a desire to be a part of that society and be recognized and accepted. This book is the story of the migration journey of Turkish people to Britain, told through the voices, lives and stories of women and written by a woman. Thus, this is the migration journey of 'other' voices.

Saniye Dedeoglu
Muğla, Turkey

Acknowledgements

The book is the result of a Marie Curie Fellowship supported by the Programme of Marie Curie Action (FP7-PEOPLE-IEF-2008: 237267). I am grateful to the European Commission for this funding. I would like to express my gratitude to Daniele Joly, the former Director of the Centre for Research in Ethnic Relations (CRER) at the University of Warwick, for her support and guidance throughout the research and publication process. Special thanks also to David Owen; without his support this research would not have been published. I thank my colleagues at CRER – Muhammad Anwar, Khursheed Wadia and Gülçin Erdi Lelandais – with whom I had lively discussions that broadened my perspective. Sam Hundal was always there to help, and I thank her. I must confess that this is a CRER book, showing that CRER is still alive, long after it was officially shut down.

Serap Özen in Muğla made plenty of time to listen to my progress almost every day and I thank her for her patience. I am grateful to Selmin Kaşka for her support and friendship. David Smith and Margaret Greenfield were a part of the research process; I thank them. Çisel Ekiz Gökmen took some of my day-to-day work off my hands to free up more time for writing. My student, Aslı Şahankaya, helped greatly with practical matters. The technical wisdom of Recep Kapar proved to be very handy. Gerard's offer to correct the English was a great relief. My utmost appreciation goes to all these people.

Finally, to the women in London who generously opened up their homes and hearts to me. No words of thanks are enough. I only hope that I have managed to remain somewhat true to their perspectives and stories, and that these perspectives will find their way into broader debates about the issues of immigrant women and social integration, and strategies for advancing women's interests in general.

1
Introduction

Work, Migrants and Social Integration is an account of the interaction between gender, labour in the ethnic economy and the social integration of migrants into their host society. With particular reference to the Turkish community in Britain, it investigates the relationship between Turkish women's work and their position in British society by focusing on how ethnically based employment affects their capacity to become socially integrated in the dominant society. The material presented here explores how women have been silent contributors to the expanding family-based establishment of the Turkish ethnic economy in Britain. It further shows how women's work in the ethnic economy and their role in social ties and networks on which this economy depends preclude their social integration within the wider society. The agency of women in maintaining community networks and representing ethnic/national identity has been essential in the establishment and success of the Turkish community, which places more emphasis on women's traditional gender roles as mothers and wives.

Sharing the basic premise of Floya Anthias, developed in *Ethnicity, Class, Gender and Migration* (1992), that the use of female kinship labour has even been considered a necessary 'building block' for the development of ethnic minority enterprises in Britain, my argument is that women's work in the Turkish ethnic economy has been central to its development and success, but that this work has resulted in the invisibility of women's economic contributions both to their households and to their community. Although the role and use of female labour has been seen as necessary for the development of ethnic minority enterprises in Britain, gender sensitive research, however, shows that ethnic economies do not necessarily support the professional advancement of women as much as they do for men and can keep them in a

1

subordinate position, thus preventing their integration into the host society. It is proposed that female immigrant workers are 'generally captive by other relationships than that of a wage' (Panayiotopoulos 1996:455). The predominantly male-controlled, labour-intensive nature of many ethnic economies are marked by 'social structures which give easy access to female labour subordinated to patriarchal control mechanisms' (Phizacklea 1988:22). In this framework, women are seen to be under the control of patriarchal and ethnic ties of their community. Therefore, gender divisions and the family are seen as central in understanding the forms of settlement and the economic and social integration of a migrant group in Europe. Migrants' interaction vis-à-vis the internal cultural and social differentiations within the group and the wider structural, institutional and ideological processes of the country of migration are affected by the very form of gender and family structures (Anthias 1992).

This research presents original findings in a number of ways. The dynamic nature of the relationship between women's work in the ethnic economy and their social integration has rarely been established in the literature. Most of the literature focuses on the social integration of women migrants who came to Western Europe in the 1950s, 1960s and 1970s and were able to integrate into regulated labour markets (Kontos 2009). However, today we observe a more diversified pattern of migrant women's work, mostly within informal labour markets such as domestic services, sex industries, agriculture and tourism. Therefore, there appears to be a need to investigate the integration of female migrants in the labour market and into their host society as the integration of migrants becomes even more important in the face of a changing economic and social structure in Europe. The empirical sections of this book document the complexities of the relationship between women's labour market position and their social integration in a community in which women represent ethnic and/or national identity and absorb the changing demands of their community with respect to their roles as workers, wives and mothers. These different roles pull and push women in different directions as they strategize their integration and survival in their host society.

Research for the book was conducted through a close examination of a single locality. The impact of the expansion of the Turkish ethnic economy on the role of women in the Turkish community and their social integration is investigated, and the book offers a fresh analysis of the contemporary trends in women, migration and labour in the ethnic economy in Western Europe. The empirical section of the book is based on 15 months of fieldwork, carried out in London, UK, and on the close investigation of the Turkish ethnic economy in London. Participant observation and in-depth interviews were conducted with women, shop owners, their families, community leaders and those engaged in the ethnic economy and community organisations. At a descriptive level, the book presents the lives of those women engaged in the insecure, invisible and low/unpaid end of the Turkish ethnic economy in London, and the Europe wide expansion of the Turkish ethnic economy and its role in offering employment opportunities to the Turkish community.

1.1 Migration and women's work in the Turkish ethnic economy

The feminization of international migration all over the world has gone hand in hand with the feminization of employment that has been a partial result of the increasing casualization of labour markets as a result of global economic restructuring. Saskia Sassen (1996) analysed economic and social developments in global cities and pointed out that the concentration of financial services in big cities results in a polarization of activities into highly qualified/well paid versus poorly qualified/devalued activities. The low qualified and devalued activities are for the most part performed by women and migrants, whereas the need for personal services for the highly paid opens up opportunities for small-businesses in global cities that are economically marginalized. However, there is little evidence of whether women's economic activities generated by their own ethnic networks offer chances to gain autonomy and foster their integration into wider society. The Turkish ethnic economy, through its kebab *döner* business, has been expanding all over Europe with its enormous employment generation capacity, and its small-scale family-based nature also implies that women's labour has been central in the expansion of the ethnic economy. Therefore, the book's first objective is to explore the nature of women's work in the Turkish ethnic economy in London, where Turkish women previously used to heavily work in the garment production industry until its demise in the early 2000s. It is highlighted that Turkish women are a major source of unpaid or lower paid labour for London's Turkish ethnic economy. They not only offer their labour as a family 'help', but are also the major source of low-paid wage labour. A similar situation is found in Light and Bonacich's study (1988), in which they show that 60% of all Korean firms in the United States relied on the use of nuclear family or extended family members in their businesses. Therefore, it is evident that the success of self-employed men is highly criticized as disguising the contributions and efforts of other family members, especially those of women.

The second objective of the book is to examine the structure of the Turkish ethnic economy in London and demand factors that condition women's ethnic work. The growing importance of the Turkish ethnic economy in Europe went hand in hand with the growing commercialization of *döner* takeaways, which led to a web of distribution and sales networks in Europe through large-scale factories owned and run by Turkish people in Germany. This resulted in the easy engagement of Turkish migrants in the production and sale of *döner* takeaways all over Europe, which generated a considerable amount of employment for Turkish migrants in Europe (Panayiotopoulos 2010). While there is clearly a Turkish economic enclave in the UK, the main economic unit is shops such as kebab houses, corner-shops and coffee shops, whose numbers have increased considerably in recent years. For Turkish migrants, employment opportunities are mostly limited to ethnic shops that offer not-so-decent jobs with low wages and long hours of work (Strüder 2003, Enneli et al. 2005). The operation of ethnic businesses is heavily based on the utilization of family labour and ethnic networks of support. The size of the community and the extent of ethnic economy are often dependent upon a constant flux of new migrants who are both an important source of clientele and labour supply for the ethnic economy. As more and more people seek to take advantage of the lucrative outcomes of ethnic business there is a growing demand for ethnic labour, which is usually met by newly arriving migrants and Turkish students who move to London mostly to learn English.

The dominance of small-scale, family-run shops in the Turkish ethnic economy provides the grounds for attracting women's labour from the same family circle into the ethnic economy, often informally and usually unpaid, while keeping their domestic identities as mothers, wives and daughters intact. The engagement of women in family-based business under the shadow of their domestic identities, without any public recognition of their work, casts doubt on the separation between women's public and private sphere activities. The entanglement between women's domestic and public activities provides a useful case study to show how difficult it is to separate one from the other. A very useful distinction was made by Elson (1999) between women's labour force participation, which includes all types of employment status (employee, self-employed and unpaid family labour), and labour market participation, which excludes unpaid family labour. Elson (1999) points to the measurable gaps that exist between women's labour force and labour market participation. Labour force participation, including all types of employment status or 'productive activities', is counted as a part of national production. On the other hand, the unpaid, unmarketed caring activities of women, the 'reproductive economy', are also crucial for the functioning of society as a whole and contribute to the reproduction of 'productive' labour, but are excluded from national accounts. Elson suggests that a large gender gap between labour force and labour market participation exists in every society (1999:614). The Turkish ethnic economy is the most ample example of the blurred line between the productive and reproductive activities of women's work.

Besides their (re)productive activities in the ethnic niche, women not only provide input to family-based establishments, but also to the continuation of Turkish culture, through their roles of motherhood. Migrant women are perceived to have a major role in the construction and reproduction of national ideologies and identities. As the symbolic figuration of a nation, women construct and reproduce particular notions of their specific culture, through their involvement in rearing children and in social and religious practices (Yuval-Davis and Anthias 1989). This representation is also found among the migrants from Turkey. Because of a strong emphasis on women's motherhood roles in the community, women not only care for their children and work in the ethnic shops, but also are representatives of their national and cultural identities. Moreover, women's maternal identities seem to set the foundation of national culture on which the Turkish ethnic economy rises. In this regard, this book pays special attention to the experience of migrant women, the ordeals to which they are subjected, but also their capacity to assume their destiny, to give it meaning and to represent it.

The focus of the enquiry of this book is on women's work in the Turkish ethnic economy in London, and it seeks to explore the structure of the ethnic economy, women's role in it and how women's work in the ethnic economy has an impact on women's position in their families, communities and their host society. Thus, my third objective is to provide an understanding of the implications of expansion of the Turkish ethnic economy as the sole economic activity of Turkish migrants in London on gender relations and women's perceived place in the society as well as their sense of inclusion and integration. This analysis is developed against a backdrop of transformations brought through migration and changing economic activity of the community which shifted from textile production to catering services. The transformation of the main ethnic economic activity has had a great impact on women's paid activities. In the heydays of textile production in the 1980s and 1990s in London, almost all Turkish migrant women were textile workers, but after the closure of the textile sweatshops women's economic activities remained limited. The growth of the catering based ethnic economy and family-based businesses has required women to be a part of the economy as family members and to focus on their roles as mothers and wives. In this regard, the prevailing culture of Turkish society is interlaced throughout as a necessary backdrop in analysing the changing position of women in economic activities. In traditional patriarchal relations, women's place in the society is defined as being home, and the portrait of women is thought to be 'women of their home' (*evinin kadını*). The justification for taking paid work is almost always connected with the aim of providing for their families, and before women can take up paid employment the consent (*izin*) of the male or senior female authority must be secured at all times. Despite the crises created over women's identity through paid work, women themselves very often make an extra effort to show that priority is always given to their domestic identities. Even their public demands and negotiations are voiced by the utilization of these roles and remain within their confines. Seemingly, women's internalization of traditional gender roles and identities allows them to move into the public arena and take up paid work without losing social protection and security. In this regard, women exchange their labour in the informal economy as a symbol of the manifestation of their community membership and identity in Turkey (Dedeoglu 2012).

Among the Turkish community in London, gendered relations are also mediated and renegotiated in relation to women's work in the ethnic economy. More specifically, the development of the Turkish ethnic economy in London is based on close family ties and the operation of family units, which provide safety as an institution and are the stimulator of change in the roles and positions that women have taken on as a response to the transformation in the community's economic activity. The themes addressed in the book are also highly relevant to debates concerning the impact of integration policies on migrant communities and gendered outcomes of engaging in ethnic economy, and women's roles and positions in a migrant community. By detailing the 'micro' level impact of 'macro' level changes, the book presents the consequences for women, gender ideologies and the structure of the Turkish community in London.

The growing importance of the ethnic economy not only has an impact on gender relations in the Turkish community of London, but also affects how the community constructs its social integration with the host country. Almost all EU countries hosting different immigrant communities have problematized these groups' social integration and labour market participation from the perspective of governments, and adopted social policies developed from a top to bottom approach. However, this research offers an insider view to inequalities in society and their consequences, and focuses on migrants' experience at the centre of the analysis with a theoretical and methodological reversal that shows how inequalities through social change are reproduced, as well as focusing on their economic and social consequences. Women's integration into the host society through their work and participation in the ethnic economy shows a zigzag way. This is because women's contribution to the Turkish ethnic economy enables the integration of their communities into British society. However, women's integration is not an individual affair, but one that traverses zigzagged pathways, based on their community's economic achievements and their role in the raising of second generation British citizens. Therefore, women are the invisible contributors to the survival and business success of their communities through their roles as mothers, wives and workers in the Turkish ethnic economy. In theory, this means only a weak integration and does not offer women the chance to emancipate themselves from their traditional patriarchal relations and roles.

The overall aim of this research is to render Turkish women's work more visible in London, by highlighting the role of women in the Turkish ethnic economy, and to represent a single account of the relationship between women's work and the ethnic economy in Europe. By placing gender in the centre of analysis, the formation of the ethnic economy and social integration are developed through migrant women's perspectives. Studies focusing on ethnic economy and gender usually date back to the late 1980s and 1990s, such as Annie Phizacklea (1988) 'Entrepreneurship, Ethnicity and Gender', in Sallie Westwood and Parminder Bhachu (eds) *Enterprising Women: Ethnicity, Economy, and Gender Relations* and also Felicitas Hillmann (1999) 'A Look at the "Hidden Side": Turkish Women in Berlin's Ethnic Labour Market', in *International Journal of Urban and Regional Research*. These studies take account of how the male-controlled and labour-intensive nature of many ethnic economies use patriarchal control mechanisms to have access to low-cost, easily accessible female labour. The examination of Turkish women's experience in London shows the way in which women have adapted to changes in the economic activity of their community over time, and the social and cultural resources that shape these adaptations. Moreover, the case of Turkish migrant women in London shows the result of economic restructuring of migrant communities in a multicultural society and the subsequent impact of these restructuring efforts on women and gender inequalities. The incorporation of theoretical perspectives on Turkish migrant women's social integration in Britain, together with gender sensitive evidence, allows this work to address the core concerns of migration studies and sociology.

1.2   Studying migrant women's work

Migration research is historically motivated by the need to measure and control migrant labour in a colonial or post-colonial context. Thus, its focus has been on 'male labour migration' and that became the central concern of policymakers. Until very recently, women were mostly invisible, due to normative assumptions that they were either totally absent from the migration process or present as passive 'family members' of male migrant workers. The most gender neutral research has explicitly appeared to reflect the experience of men. In the rare cases where the presence of women is acknowledged, their contribution to the economic and social realities of the host country is often ignored or underestimated (Kofman et al. 2000:3). When women are portrayed, they are often pictured as 'backward-looking...guardians of family unity and the culture of origin' (Council of Europe 1995:32). Metso and Le Feuvre (2006) show that some large statistical data is composed of genderless migrants. It is only when it comes to estimating levels of human trafficking that the statistics present a gender difference, thus making women appear exclusively the passive victims of forced migration for domestic servitude or sexual exploitation.

The use of feminist methodology is therefore important to further develop women's experience of migration from different angles. As Marjorie DeVault (1996) states, 'Feminist methodology provide the outline for a possible alternative to the distanced, distorting and dispassionately objective producers of much social research' (34). Feminist methodology is designed to shift the focus of standard research practice from men's concerns, in order to reveal the locations and perspectives of (all) women, seeks a science that minimizes harm and control in the research process, and will support research of value to women, leading to social change or action beneficial to women (DeVault 1996:32). Feminist methodology is mostly applied by using qualitative research tools, which is often thought to value subjective and personal meanings, and is said to be conducive to giving a voice to the most oppressed groups in society, while quantitative research is constructed in terms of testing theories and making predictions in an objective and value-free way (Metso and Le Feuvre 2006).

Given these concerns, a qualitative and biographical approach would be the most appropriate in exploring the relationship between women's social integration and their work in the Turkish ethnic economy, and the categories which women employ in their everyday lives and on the community networks that sustain women's social links. Chamberlayne and Rustin, advocating the use of a biographical approach, note that a biographical method, by contextualizing statistical data and demonstrating what they mean for individual lives, contains implications for social policy, and furthermore that such an approach can highlight the network of existing relations between the individual and others (1999:21).

> The point is that people live their lives within the material and cultural boundaries of their time span, and so life histories are exceptionally effective historical sources because through the totality of lived experience they reveal relations between individuals and social forces, which are rarely apparent in other sources.
>
> (Lummis 1987:107–108)

In-depth, open-ended, non-structured interviews and oral narratives were the methods utilized to give voice to the women whose experiences of ethnic-based work are at the centre of this study. Using these methods is the most suitable way of describing and analysing women's experiences from their own perspectives and making sense of their place in the world. These methods also capture interactions and interconnections between people and events, as they provide flexibility for explanation and allow space to the narrator to express himself or herself by reducing the control and direction of interviewer over interviewee (Borland 1991, Gluck and Patai 1991). In addition, open-ended and in-depth interviews, according to Anderson and Jack, represent a shift from asking the right questions to focusing on process and 'the dynamic unfolding nature of the subject's viewpoint' (1991:23).

My interest in exploring the connections between the expanding Turkish ethnic economy in London and women's work in the small-scale family businesses and the implication of women's ethnic work in their social integration into the wider society and their role in their community meant that developing a more situated understanding of the interactions between gender relations and women's changing work practices in London's Turkish ethnic economy involved locating myself within the communities where the Turkish migrants lived in London. Wolf has pointed out that researchers need to locate themselves and their personal objectives and experiences within the context of their research (Wolf 1996). The inequalities and power relations between the researcher and the researched are always depicted in the literature as distorting research results. Given the increasing self-awareness among feminist researchers of their limitations, many are focusing on the reflective mode or simply depicting women's voices rather than representing their own (Wolf 1996). In producing a more situated knowledge of women's ethnic-based work and reflecting these women's voices it was felt that my background as a former migrant student who lived in London would prove to be a valuable asset while conducting this research. I spent almost ten years in London as a student supported by the Turkish government to pursue higher education, and when I arrived in Britain I had very little knowledge of English. I know what it means to not be able to comprehend the language of the society in which one lives. During my prolonged study years in London, I had extensive connections with the Turkish community and migrants in London and other parts of Britain. I had the opportunity to know some families who migrated to London in the mid-1980s and 1990s; some of these people were highly educated but others were simple kebab shop workers or owners. This research was the result of my experience of the Turkish community in Britain. Each time I had an interaction with a Turkish family during my study years it was like going back home and it helped to ease my homesickness. Thus, conducting this research was my duty and small contribution to the community which nurtured me during my student years and helped me become an academic. During the fieldwork I moved to North London and lived in Green Lanes, which was a good location to observe the Turkish community in London and their day-to-day experiences. This was vital in accounting for factors particular to the locality and to broader structural factors in understanding how women's work has been shaped by gender relations, as well as the community's social relations.

Gaining access to a sample involved utilizing personal connections and was guided according to the nature of the information sought. This approach is a snowball or chain-referral method, in which friends and associates in London introduced me to people I could interview. Community organizations such as Day-Mer and CemEvi contributed to finding more informants. Snowball sampling is especially appropriate where populations are hidden and no sampling frame is available. It involves random sampling of the population, which was a very suitable method to collect information on women's work in the Turkish ethnic economy as it is highly family-based and invisible (Faugier and Sargeant 1997). For this purpose, I conducted interviews with 60 migrant women in the Turkish community in London over 15 months in 2010 and 2011. Having a few key informants from different segments of the community later branched out into meetings with other respondents. Gaining access to connections and networks improved my relationships with the women and their families, and thus, I traced my way into their households and to the locations of various social networks and livelihood activities. I also interviewed a limited number of men. These were mainly ethnic shop owners and community leaders.

My sample was a purposefully composed one, which did not aim at ensuring the statistical representation of women. It was rather intended to select categories of individuals using lifecycle and employment criteria. 'Theoretical sampling' involves sampling on the basis of concepts that are relevant to the study (Glaser and Strauss 1968:47). As a consequence it tends to promote a sample that is homogeneous in its attributes, rather than providing linkages to groups whose social characteristics are different (Lee 1993). Moreover, a homogeneous population was itself advantageous in exploring the nature of women's work in the ethnic economy; the relationship between their social integration and their work in the Turkish ethnic economy in London; how individuals and households respond to the migration process and the different work patterns of their community in their host country; the implications of the migration process on women's position in their community and gender relations; and the importance of ethnic networks and community organizations in maintaining migrants' day-to-day survival.

Besides visiting ethnic shops and interviewing women individually, I attended women's social gatherings on different occasions, such as marriage ceremonies, religious meetings, afternoon get-togethers (*kadın günleri*) devoted to chatting and rotating savings associations. These meeting were particularly useful for observing women's relations with each other away from the patriarchal domination of men in the public sphere such as in the workplace or in the household. I listened intently to gossip as a form of communication that transmits information about customs, change and ideas, as well as the opinions of women. Gossip is a powerful tool not only to ensure women's conformity to social customs and ideas, but also to release information on issues that otherwise would be impossible to reach. Moreover, I recorded Turkish proverbs pertaining to gender and family relations that reflect the families' perception of immigration and their survival strategies. I recorded both those that emerged spontaneously in the course of an interview or conversation and also the proverbs that provide an accurate description of reality. Women often used these idioms and proverbs to articulate their views, and to describe their work and daily life. As tools for filtering how women conceptualize their social situations and their own reality, these idioms are a resourceful way to 'map out a field of meaning based on local categories, and give people a language to talk about differences, as well as providing local definitions and understanding of concepts like values, status, power, equity, injustice and domination' (El-Kholy 2002).

Conducting research entailed collecting a mass of data, only a small proportion of which is presented in the book. This process inevitably entails the omission of a large quantity of data that may represent a significant aspect of the respondents' lives, highlighting the central tensions between the complexity of social life, and the textual strategies and techniques available for representing it (Hammersley and Atkinson 1995). The explanatory framework will also depend upon the researcher's interpretation of the ways in which individuals' perceptions, experiences and behaviour intersect with cultural, social and economic forces. It shows that women's work and lives can only be understood in the context of a complex web of social relations in which social dynamics and available economic opportunities to migrant communities shape women's roles, economic activities and social integration in their host country.

The selection of examples was guided by the research objectives, which seek to explore the lives of Turkish immigrant women in London. The book does not offer an exhaustive account of women's lives, but focuses on the economic and social strategies that are deployed, and the 'cultures of solidarity' in response to the problem of their survival in a new home country (Fantasia 1988:14). Giddens argues that an individual's sense of 'ontological security' is the confidence that people have in the continuity of their self-identity and in the constancy of their social environments (Giddens 1990). The data presented explores the way in which women attempt to maintain their lives and also try to better them through their motherhood, work and community memberships.

1.3   Structure of the book

The structure and content of the book reflect the fact that it analyses the relationship between migration, work and the social integration of Turkish female migrants in Britain and the situation of migrant women in London's Turkish ethnic economy. Chapter 2 analyses the emerging issues in gendering social integration, ethnic economies and the gendered nature of migration, and wider debates concerning the increasing significance of women in the migration trends and migrant communities of Europe. The chapter outlines the major theoretical and empirical perspectives of gender, ethnic economy and social integration of migrants, and shows how this book contributes to studying the way in which Europe is being transformed through a bottom-up process as a result of the economic activities of migrations and the ways in which they produce their own systems of social integration in their host society. A key aim of this chapter is to show that gender is a facilitator of this transformation from below, through its 'symbolic figuration' of identity and belonging.

Chapter 3 examines ethnic economies and the Turkish ethnic community of Europe in particular. The growing importance of the Turkish ethnic economy in Europe has become the focus of academic research, mainly in terms of its capacity to generate self-employment for the Turkish migrants and its contribution to the European economy. The growing commercialization of *döner* takeaways has generated a web of networks in Europe. The reference population of this book is migrants engaged in the Turkish ethnic economy in Britain. The context is one in which the Turkish ethnic economy has been flourishing and offering enormous employment opportunities to people in the Turkish community. This deepens our understanding of the way in which migrant groups living in Europe develop specific survival strategies.

Chapter 4 introduces the Turkish community of London and their migration patterns by sketching the particularities of their settlement in London. This contextualizes the ways in which the changing economic activities of the Turkish community over the course of their migration and the corresponding labour requirements influence their interactions with the wider society as well as women's role in it. The chapter presents the reader with a detailed account of the Turkish community in London. The literature examining Turks in Britain mostly pictures them as an invisible or silent community, and most of the literature is devoted to the heterogeneous nature of ethnic and religious backgrounds of people from Turkey, but what this book offers is the chance to build their visibility and economic contribution to the larger British society.

Chapter 5 explores the lives and motivation of a sample of women working in the Turkish ethnic economy. The chapter opens with an introduction of the discussion and debate over migration and gender that provide the backdrop to the potential implications of migration for changing gendered roles and relations. The ethnographic sections conducted with a sample of women workers explore the demographic characteristics and household structures of women who are engaged in

the ethnic economy. The attempt to introduce women here is significant, as there is no study conducted on this group and they largely
remain invisible to the academic interest. The chapter takes up other
important sociological contentions concerning household characteristics and women's domestic roles, as well as women's personal experience
of migration and how they conceptualize their lives in Britain as
migrants. Within this context, this chapter deals with the question of
how the process of migration has affected gendered roles and relations,
and how women themselves construct their work, as well as of the way
in which women set their priorities as 'the woman of the home'. The
relevance of sociological concepts, such as gender relations, patriarchy,
marriage and familial relations, are acted out in understanding the
change that takes place in the post-migration process through a care-
ful ethnographical study, which relates those theoretical debates with
women whose voices are the least audible.

Chapter 6 consolidates and develops the role of Turkish women in
the ethnic economy and the ways in which women's labour is being utilized in the family-owned ethnic business. The chapter contextualizes
the women's work in a historical perspective in which female migrants
in London have experienced a major shift in their economic activity,
which has changed from garment work to being unpaid family or low-
paid workers in their ethnic enclave business. This shift occurred with
the closure of textile workshops and the expansion of the ethnic catering shops. It, in fact, meant for a large number of women a move
towards economic inactivity. The expansion of the Turkish ethnic economy, on the other hand, confined women to the domestic sphere or
forced them to take up roles in ethnic shops corresponding with their
domestic roles as wives, mothers, sisters or daughters. Some of these
women worked as unpaid family workers in family-owned businesses,
but some became low-paid wage workers to provide additional income
for their families and children. Moreover, those men married to second generation immigrant women utilize their wives' knowledge of the
British system and language skills to run their businesses. The chapter
will also discuss the fact that there are many women who are unemployed and concerned more with child raising. This is because many
Turkish families have cut off relationships with the second generation
of their families, and this is seen as the result of mothers' work in the
textile workshops back in the 1980s and 1990s. This is the new injury of
the Turkish/Kurdish community in Britain, and women are generally
blamed for not being 'proper mothers' and for not paying sufficient
attention to their children. Now, for this generation of mothers, there is

the double burden of motherhood and raising children and the need to be involved in full-time work.

Chapter 7 presents Turkish women's views on integration. Women walk a zigzag path to social integration that is constructed on a communal way of social integration through their work in the ethnic economy and their role in child raising. This chapter challenges the assumption that first generation migrant women's way of child rearing feeds into social exclusion and non-integrations of the migrant community, and shows that Turkish women are working hard for their children to be well integrated into their host society. Turkish women's social value and contribution is measured against their children's success in education and potential life paths. This measure is imposed on women not only by their families and community, but the women themselves are judging their contributions in terms of motherhood and their children's success. Therefore, it shows the particular ways in which women construct their own integration.

Chapter 8 summarizes the arguments and themes developed in the main body of the book. Some general conclusions are drawn from the research concerning the potential of women's work in the Turkish ethnic economy in London to enable women's integration into the mainstream society. This book demonstrates that women have been the silent contributors to the expanding Turkish ethnic economy in Britain, and women's work in the ethnic economy and their role in social ties and networks on which this economy is built preclude women's social integration in the wider society. The agency of women in maintaining community networks and representing ethnic/national identity has been essential in the establishment and success of the Turkish ethnic economy, which has also led to the increased emphasis on women's traditional gender roles as mothers and wives. This has resulted in women's isolation within small community circuits and disabled women's connections with the larger community. This book is the first comprehensive research study focusing on the migrant experience of the relationship between work, gender and social integration among the Turkish community in Britain. This has enabled an insider view of the inequalities in society and their consequences. The Turkish community has placed changing demands on women's labour and roles in the community, resulting in women's exclusion from the wider mainstream society.

2
Women Migrants, Work and Social Integration

This book tells the story of the Turkish community's social integration into British society and economy. The Turkish communities of London have developed their own methods of social integration in Britain through the ethnic economy, community organizations. These methods include the ways in which the community reproduces its social ties, networks and familial relations in which gender plays a significant role. The debate over social integration is usually underlined by the theme of ethnic minorities' assimilation into their host societies. Although its emphasis has shifted slightly over time, from assimilation to inclusion, and then to multiculturalism, the recent debates often focus on moments of crisis and points of anxiety around cultural diversity, terrorism, race riots, ethnic gangs, ghettoes and so forth. While official multiculturalism is informed by older liberal notions of identity politics and group rights, social integration should have a grounded approach that examines context-specific relationships between ethnic minorities and the host society in which they live. Through this context-specific relationship, migrants may challenge the traditional notions of social integration, based on the assimilation of ethnic communities, but may generate an ethnic culture of interacting with the host society and the state that they are part of.

This study aims to introduce the efforts of London's Turkish community to achieve social integration, in which the ethnic economy and gender play a significant role in, and help to pave an original and grounded path to integration. Therefore, this chapter rests upon the three distinct areas of migration, work and social integration, and aims to analyse their relationships with each other through the lens of gender. Studies that analyse the intersections between work, social integration and female migrations are rare. In one such study, Verdaguer (2009) provides rich and meaningful evidence to examine the ways in which the intersectionality of ethnicity, class and gender profoundly influences immigrant adaptation processes, resource mobilization strategies, social embeddedness dynamics and actors' entrepreneurial behaviour. It demonstrates the intersectionality of structures of differences (class, ethnicity and gender) in the lives of Latino immigrant entrepreneurs, as well as how they reshape the terms of their opportunity structures. It further enriches our social imagination by linking structure to the individual and to public policy.

In outlining the major theoretical and empirical perspectives of gender, the work and social integration of migrants, this book contributes to studying the way in which Europe is being transformed through a bottom-up process as a result of the economic activities of migrants and their distinctive ways of social integration into their host society. The Turkish community in London is presented as a key example of an attempt to combine three distinct areas of literature on migration, work and social integration. A key contention of this chapter is that gender is a facilitator of this transformation through bottom-up processes, and through its 'symbolic figuration' of identity and belonging. This chapter analyses the emerging issues in the gendering of the social integration of migrant communities, and explores wider debates concerning the increasing significance of women in the migration trends and among migrant communities of Europe.

2.1 Immigrant social networks, social capital and ethnic economy

Social networks and ties among migrant communities have been seen as the sources of resource mobilization strategies and immigrants' economic and social incorporation into host societies. As a middle ground between individual and structural forces, social networks differentially mediate the adaptation of immigrant groups (Massey et al. 1987, Portes and Borocz 1989, Aldrich et al. 1990, Light and Bhachu 1993, Menjivar 2000). In this regard, social capital plays a significant role in explaining solidarity networks among disadvantaged groups and their role in providing employment and survival strategies. Bourdieu defines social capital as the realized or potential resources that result from network relationships of mutual acquaintances that are, to some degree, institutionalized. Coleman approaches social capital from an 'economic' or rational action point of view, indicating that social capital consists of social structures, facilitates actions within these structures and produces outcomes that would not otherwise be possible (McLean et al. 2002). However, these insights are based on comparisons between disadvantaged and advantaged groups. What they do not do is examine the dynamics of exchange within disadvantaged groups and how gender, as well as other factors such as age, disability and sexual orientation, plays a role in this.

Human interactions are bounded by a variety of institutional arrangements that can be characterized as informal, and different types of social capital facilitate interactions within social and ethnic groups. These insights may be applied to gender relations, because they embody human interactions that occur within racialized and ethnicized settings. Putnam (2000) and Narayan and Cassidy (2001) among others have delineated three types of social capital that refer to the nature of human interactions occurring within various institutional structures: bonding, bridging and linking. Bonding occurs among family members and ethnic groups, and the bonding capital facilitates the sharing of resources under the constraints of the norms and values defined by family, friendships or ethnic groups. Bonding is a social adhesive that promotes solidarity, trust and confidence. Bridging, which occurs among distant friends, colleagues and associates, promotes transcendence of one's narrow traditional (cultural) focus to that of broader society. In other words, bridging creates the social adhesiveness that leads to intergroup connectedness, communal stability and expanded configurations of trust that promote resource exchanges for economic and community development. Linking is an even broader concept of relationships, based on institutional arrangements that promote the exchange of power, wealth and status among different social groups. However, in applying these concepts to gender relations, we are exploring new terrain, because the most often cited texts on social capital are ungendered (Goulbourne and Solomos 2000, Lowndes 2000). By offering a gendered and ethicized analysis of social capital, this research shows how Turkish speaking women's bounding capital is appropriated by men and their ethnic community in London.

We have seen a growing body of literature concerned with the role of social networks more broadly in the migratory processes. Much of this literature focuses on ethnic bonds and ties and the part they play, on the one hand, in migratory paths and choice of residence and, on the other, in the process whereby migrants come to settle or 'integrate' into host societies, by facilitating access to social networks and knowledge. A particular strand of literature that has attended greatly to the role of ethnic networks concerns the study of ethnic entrepreneurship (e.g. Light 1972, Portes and Jensen 1987, Zimmer and Aldrich 1987, Waldinger et al. 1990, 2000, Zhou 1992, Phizacklea and Ram 1996, Werbner 1999, Ram et al. 2002). While households and wider social networks have important roles in migratory paths, some more recent literature has suggested that the changing nature of migratory flows and systems entails a need for a revised understanding of the mechanisms at play in relation to migratory decisions and processes. While there is a significant body of literature that emphasizes the importance and role of more or less informal social networks in migration and the making and sustenance of transnational links, another has developed alongside this, focusing on the institutional frameworks in both sender and receiving countries in relation to the increasing needs and wishes to migrate on the one hand and to restrictive immigration regimes on the other.

Feminist scholars have also examined how gender organizes social relations through networks, which unevenly circulate information, resources and belief systems that can give way to new aspirations among men and women. It is now widely accepted that women are central transmitters of ethnic culture; they reproduce the culture and tradition of the group, and its religious and familial structures and ideologies. They reproduce the group biologically, and are used as symbols of the nation or ethnic group. They are important as 'mother' of patriots, and represent the nation (Anthias and Yuval Davis 1989). Therefore, women are the bearers of cultural codes that reproduce group identity, and the social relations that stand at the centre of those cultural exchanges and reproduction.

In their study of the ethnic economy, Anthias and Mehta (2003) analysed the gender-related social resources available to migrant women in their endeavour to start a business. Family and other ethnic resources that are necessary to circumvent social exclusion through self-employment are discussed as being socially shaped and socially controlled. In the case of female entrepreneurs, Anthias and Mehta (2003) challenge the central assumption made in ethnic business research and economic sociology that family and community networks function as an indispensable resource for entrepreneurs. Anthias and Mehta (2003) argue that the family support roles are different for men and women in the self-employment process, and that access to ethnic community networks also differs. While the family of origin was a source of support for both men and women in business, the immediate family (in particular the spouse) and community networks constituted a resource for men only, there being a notable absence of emotional and practical help from husbands and partners for women.

In a similar argument, Hagan (1998) examined gendered networks among Mayan immigrants in Houston, and their role in mediating social and political incorporation outcomes. In looking at how immigrant networks facilitated and/or impeded men's and women's access to legalization opportunities, Hagan argued that social networks fluctuated over time, changing differentially for different segments of the immigrant community. Whereas men's networks expanded through their participation in more formal types of work, women's networks contracted as they became secluded in private homes doing domestic work. Ultimately, this isolation from information sources prevented Mayan women from applying for legalization.

There are other streams of research that focus on changes brought to gendered social relations in the post-migration process. For example, Menjívar (1997) studied Salvadoran men and women, and her research focused on localized conditions under which immigrant networks eroded. She argued that after an initial stage when immigrant networks facilitated members' migration and settlement projects, the lack of material resources in the immigrant community weakened such networks' effectiveness. Menjívar explored the differential effect of gendered networks among Salvadorans, concluding that whereas men's networks granted members access to larger financial resources, women's networks gained access to more diversified sources of information beyond the immigrant community. Because women were primarily involved in children's schooling and other social reproduction duties, they relied on social service agencies and had more contact with mainstream representatives than men. This bridging out beyond their immediate social circles increased the effectiveness of women's networks.

It is apparent in the evidence presented above that gender identity shapes the kinds of ties within networks, and that network characteristics and macro changes brought about through migration, in turn, influence cultural expectations about gender. This circular process shares the dynamism described by the theory of migration networks, while attributing more nuanced meanings and variable consequences to networks. Thus, it is possible to argue that gender inequality may be magnified, challenged or diminished through the influence of networks of meaningful social ties defined by identity, obligation and trust, via migration. The ethnic economy is also an area where migrants fully utilize social capital and networks, and below is an examination of the theories focusing on the ethnic economy as a manifestation of migrants' strategy of integration into their host societies.

2.1.1 Theoretical evaluations of the ethnic economy

Ethnic entrepreneurship is only one variant of immigrant economic adaptation, and mostly refers to any member of an ethnic/immigrant group who owns and operates a business (Auster and Aldrich 1984, Light and Bonacich 1988, Light and Gold 2000, Rath 2000). In this regard, ethnicity has an economic value through which migrants secure their livelihoods. Scholars offer two models for the interpretation of the economic value of ethnicity. On the one hand, immigrants possess a culturally specific toolkit with values, skills and attitudes derived from their ethnic tradition or historical experience (Waldinger et al. 1990, Light and Gold 2000). On the other hand, other interpretations high-light the value of ethnically derived sources of social capital marked, primarily, by boundaries in immigrants' social relations (Cornell 1996). When a group establishes social boundaries, cooperation and assistance among members ensue. Ethnic boundaries are, for the most part, effec-tive in promoting solidarity and cooperation among individuals given that ethnicity is a primary source of personal and collective identity.

Sociology, anthropology and the labour economics literature have each contributed to the development of theoretical frameworks address-ing the effect of ethnicity and race on entrepreneurship. Research into ethnicity and entrepreneurship can be traced back to classic works such as those of Weber and Simmel (Volery 2007). These scholars' concept of the stranger as a trader, called the middlemen theory, has influ-enced subsequent literature about and study of ethnic entrepreneurship (Volery 2007). As the most widely used cultural explanation, middle-men theory is a concrete example of a trade diaspora, but this group is an exception to the theory that most ethnic groups are seen to be disadvantaged and beneath the working class (Bonacich and Modell 1980). However, middlemen minorities are found to be in between classes, and fail to engage in the kind of activities characterized as modern capitalism; instead, they work as single units in which the dis-tinction between owner and employee is blurred. Weber termed this entrepreneurship 'pariah capitalism' because of the local unpopularity of the entrepreneurial minorities. Among the middlemen minorities, the Jews of Europe, the Hausa of Nigeria, the Sikhs of East Africa, the Chinese of South East Asia, the Armenians of the Near East and the Parsees of India were the most prominent (Light 2007). Light and Gold (2000) discuss the idea that the exceptional involvement of middlemen minorities in international trade arose in part because of the ethno-religious oppression to which they were subjected, but also because of the unique ethnic resources they enjoyed.

Two sets of factors, often referred to as the 'structure' and the 'resources' arguments, have been used to explain the emergence and development of ethnic economies (Ward and Jenkins 1984, Waldinger et al. 1990). The structural side refers to factors external to the minority group. The existence of a potential market is obviously a crucial factor. Immigrant entrepreneurs have often relied on their fellow immigrants' particular needs, thus creating a 'protected market', or have invested in sectors of the economy that were abandoned by native business-men because of their demanding working conditions (grocery stores and newsagents are classic examples). Government policies may or may not facilitate the creation of businesses by immigrants. High unemploy-ment and the possible discrimination a group endures on the labour market are also factors that push immigrants into self-employment. The resources side is composed of factors that are internal to the minority group. Its capacity to organize itself and to mobilize ethnic solidarity, and its cultural predisposition for business or a trade experience are some of the characteristics of a group that favours independent business activities. Ethnic entrepreneurship is the product of a successful interac-tion between these two sets of factors. In other words, immigrants must not only find themselves in an appropriate context, but must also be able to seize the existing opportunities (Volery 2007).

Most initial theories on ethnic entrepreneurship stem from soci-ology. The disadvantage theory and the cultural theory are two major theories that can be drawn from this field to explain ethnic entrepreneurship. Disadvantage theory suggests that most immigrants have significant disadvantages hampering them upon arrival, but which at the same time steer their behaviour (Fregetto 2004). Firstly, they lack human capital such as language skills, education and experience, which prevents them from obtaining salaried jobs, leaving self-employment as the only choice. Secondly, a lack of mobility due to poverty, discrimi-nation and the limited knowledge of the local culture can lead ethnic minorities to seek self-employment. This theory sees entrepreneurship not as a sign of success but simply as an alternative to unemployment. Therefore, it is probably more accurate to explain the development of informal and illegal activities, rather than to explain the widespread creation of immigrant businesses. This is because immigrant policies prevent newcomers from becoming legally self-employed in the first years of their stay, when the disadvantages would be the greatest.

Cultural theory suggests that ethnic and immigrant groups are equipped with culturally determined features such as dedication and hard work, membership of a strong ethnic community, economical living, acceptance of risk, compliance with social value patterns, solidarity and loyalty, and orientation towards self-employment (Masurel et al. 2004). These features provide an ethnic resource which can facilitate and encourage entrepreneurial behaviour and support the ethnic self-employed (Fregetto 2004). Ethnic people often become aware of the advantages their own culture might offer only after arriving in the new environment: 'Whether one is English, Albanian or Mongolian, the very act of transferring to a new society with alien customs and incomprehensible language is in itself likely to heighten awareness of one's own cultural and national identity' (Jones and McEvoy 1986:199).

The differences in ethnic resources also act as an explanation for the different rates of self-employment between equally disadvantaged ethnic groups (Waldinger et al. 1990). For example, cultural aspects are particularly popular for explaining the propensity of Asian people, for example, to become self-employed. The strong presence of Chinese people in the catering sector has many observers believing that a certain predisposition of the Chinese culture determines their participation in such economic sectors (Leung 2002). New studies, however, have attempted to illustrate that these assumptions fail to consider other critical aspects of the complex phenomenon, such as employment alternatives, immigration policies, market conditions and availability of capital. After a while, ethnic businesses can start to grow by engaging in trade with entrepreneurs from other ethnic groups. After reaching a critical mass and gaining acceptance within the indigenous population, they can become a viable and respectable business, by expanding into high-volume trade with the local population.

The business entry decision has had a strong impact on the development of theories in ethnic entrepreneurship. Much attention has been given to the question of whether cultural or structural factors influence the business entry decision and therefore are responsible for the rise of ethnic entrepreneurship. Supporters of the culturalist approach believe that immigrant groups have culturally determined features, leading to a propensity to favour self-employment (Masurel et al. 2004). The structuralist approach, on the other hand, suggests that external factors in the host environment, such as discrimination or entry barriers on the labour market due to education and language deficits, push foreigners into self-employment. More recent approaches which attempt to combine these two perspectives show that a differentiated view is necessary to understand this complex phenomenon.

2.1.2 Turkish ethnic economy in London

In recent years, Turks have emerged as self-employed entrepreneurs in almost all Western European countries, engaged in the *döner*-kebab business. The peculiarity of the Turkish ethnic economy is that its small-scale, family-based establishments spread to all of Western Europe and also those wholesale suppliers located in Germany. Wholesale production units and large-scale factories owned and run by Turkish people in Germany resulted in the easy engagement of Turkish migrants in the production and sale of *döner* takeaways all over Europe. This generated a considerable amount of employment for Turkish migrants in Europe. Since the early 2000s, in the UK, the Turkish ethnic economy has been expanding, and working in kebab-takeaways became the main economic activity of Turkish migrants after the closure of garment workshops in London.

The classic feature of the Turkish ethnic economy is its small-scale nature, through the pooling of family labour and other resources. Families usually used their own financial resources, especially savings accumulated through their informal work in the garment production industry in London, to open their shops. The degree of self-exploitation, coupled with harsh working conditions in the ethnic economy, leads to people forming partnerships within their own families so that they can share the workload and take turns to have breaks and holidays. The most common forms of business partnerships are those established between fathers and sons or close family members such as brothers or brothers-in-law. The second generation has played an important role in the expansion of the ethnic economy by virtue of their language skills and their knowledge of the British system. In almost all small-scale shops, the use of family and self-exploitation is observable in the long hours of work and harsh working conditions. Family members are the main source of labour that the Turkish ethnic economy depends upon, and whenever there is a need for extra labour it is brought in from the intimate circles of the ethnic community. In this regard, the word 'ethnic', in the ethnic business circles, translates into cheap, reliable and docile labour that is ready to work for long hours for very small returns and mostly on informal terms. This economic cooperation of migrants living in the margins of British society promises a successful ethnic economy only in extreme exploitation of labour and communal sacrifice for very small returns and marginal incomes.

2.2 Women, migration and work

Gender had been a silent issue in migration studies for a long time, even though it has always been at the centre of transnational movements. Men were considered to be the prototype migrants and were seen as the decision makers and bread winners. The main neo-liberal theory of pull-and-push factors separated the decision of migration from its structural factors and focused only on the rational choice of individuals. On the other hand, Marxist theory examined migrants as proletariats who were the bearers of the burden of the uneven development of capitalism. Such work has treated migrants as a reserve army of labour, subjected to the power of capital (Anthias and Cederberg 2006). However, these theories fall short in explaining 'how decision making takes place within the family and broader social networks, both within the sending and receiving countries, and the ways in which knowledge and communication channels and opportunities for work are mediated by social actors in specific social locations' (Anthias and Cederberg 2006:4).

Together with globalization and increasing transnational movements, the earlier paradigms that focused primarily on economic migrants, mostly men or families led by men, could no longer be used to explain new migratory trends. New migration has been diversified in regard to the profile of migrants and includes a large number of educated and skilled people. What is new about the current migration is the significance and visibility of female migrants and mostly women migrants moving across borders as solo migrants rather than a member of a moving family. Therefore, the diversity of migration has gone hand in hand with feminization. This diversity has also been in terms of migrants' motivations: some migrate for purposes of family reunification; others migrate mainly for work; a significant number of others are asylum seekers (Koser 1998).

Feminist theorists have contributed an understanding of migration with its gendered dimensions and proposed the importance of agency. In the analysis focusing on agency, women migrants become active in making choices and plans for themselves and their families. They are not only pictured as dependent migrants following their husbands. Rather, women are seen as an active agency, seeking an improvement in their own economic and social position, or hoping to help out family members left behind in their homelands (Anthias and Cederberg 2006). This approach enabled an analysis of women's experience of migration. For example, Kofman et al. (2000) show that women facing violent and oppressive familial or marital relations wish to escape them, and that the constraints of gender roles and normative expectations more generally may act as powerful factors in women's thinking of migration in terms of emancipation and greater opportunities.

Factoring in the agency of women has shifted the focus of migration studies away from the image of the rational individual migrant to the household as the unit of analysis (Anthias and Cederberg 2006). This also meant a move away from an analysis of the household as an unproblematic, homogenous unit. This led to the development of literature focusing on the household as a site of divergent interests and positions as well as of power and struggle of different kinds that also include gender ideologies and relations (Kofman et al. 2000). Moving beyond the limits of individual households, we have seen a growing body of literature concerned with the role of social networks more broadly in migratory processes. A particular strand of literature that has focused on the role of ethnic networks concerns the study of ethnic entrepreneurship (see chapters 3 and 6).

There is also a strand of literature dealing with the role that women play in the reproduction of national and ethnic boundaries (Anthias and Yuval Davis 1989, Wilford and Miller 1998, Charles and Hintjens 1998). Yuval-Davis and Anthias (1989) point out that gender divisions play a crucial role in constructing ethnic and racial divisions, an example being the central role played by women not only as biological reproducers of an ethnic group but also as its ideological reproducers, i.e. the transmitters of culture and the socializers of children; there is the familiar feature of women as the symbolic embodiment of ethnic/national identity and difference, constituted in no small measure by their sexual and social demeanour, and the traditional role of women as the supporters and nurturers of men. Anthias and Cederberg (2006) show that a central distinction to be made in theoretical debates on the social function of gender is between approaches that consider gendered relations of power as a distinct system, and those that find gender to be a function of the broader economic system. The notion of patriarchy has become central to the former approach: it helped an understanding of social inequalities residing primarily in the power relations between men and women that allocate social positions and resources.

While the focus of studies examining women's position in migration has changed considerably, this change has overlapped with the visibility of migrant women in the labour markets. The following section traces the main findings of the literature dealing with migrant women's work in labour markets and their involvement in the ethnic economy.

2.2.1 Migrant women's work

Socio-economic restructuring in Western countries has led to the steady rise of women's paid employment and a steady decline in full-time male jobs. Called the feminization of the labour force, this refers not only to the increase in the number of women in the labour force and paid employment but also to a deterioration of employment conditions the creation of flexible jobs associated with less protections, security and temporariness favoured the employment of mostly women. This process has overlapped with the increasing visibility of migrant women's work in the flexible service sector. A growing body of literature exploring migrant women's work shows that women are engaged in a number of economic activities such as domestic work, care work, sex work and ethnic business. Even though a great deal is made of ethnic minority women's 'lack of skills' and their 'language deficiencies' and, in some cases, their irregular legal status, we witness the greater visibility of migrant women's economic activities, albeit in informal and precarious jobs.

Migrant women's work in domestic and care work has gained visibility all over the world as a result of increasing job creation in the service sector. The domestic sector is regarded as potentially the largest informal sector employing migrant women. Aside from high levels of informality, another particular characteristic of this sector is the disrupted boundaries between the public/private and market/non-market relations (Anderson 2006). Domestic work can include different types of work and contractual relationships, and may range from full-time care for children or the elderly, to hourly paid cleaning. It also includes different types of contractual arrangements in which migrant women's work can be as living-in domestics or hourly paid workers. In relation to caring activities, private care homes for the elderly are a source of work for migrant women but in some cases the care takes place in private homes. Domestic work is not only gendered, but also highly racialized as white, middle-class women leave their primary caregiver roles in the household to migrant women from the global south (Anderson 2000, Ehrenreich and Hochschild 2003). While private homes can become a 'refuge' for undocumented migrants who fear deportation and who are at greater risk of detection in public workplaces, it entails a set of complex relations and, not uncommonly, cases of exploitation and abuse (Anthias and Cederberg 2006). Domestic work also offers ethnic minority women the opportunity to work and earn a cash income without losing their access to welfare benefit entitlements, and so emerges as a popular work option for many women.

Jobs in the service sector, such as cleaning, hotel work and catering, have emerged as one of the major areas employing migrant workers. As a significantly expanding sector it has a particular profile relating to the conditions of employment, such as low levels of security, flexibility and high levels of irregularity. This sector may be regarded as one of the weakest in terms of work conditions, pay and prestige. The sector is mostly associated with a flexible workforce pushed in and out of employment as and when desired by the employer, and the workforce of migrant women is heavily concentrated in this sector (Anthias and Cederberg 2006). Female cleaners are often employed in private spaces, such as private offices. More generally, cleaning is regarded as a particularly isolated occupation, in terms of the nature of the activity as well as the hours worked (Anderson and Rogaly 2005).

Migrant women's work in professional jobs such as nursing and care work has been receiving increasing attention. With the effects of increasing privatization of care services and the ageing population the need for overseas labour, including care workers, nurses and doctors, has been growing in Western countries. Studies on the living and working conditions of migrant care and health workers have pointed out higher levels of exploitation, such as higher workloads and excessive working hours (Buchan et al. 2006). At the same time, while deskilling is a common experience of migrant workers, skilled staff are frequently expected not only to do skilled tasks but also more menial jobs, such as cleaning. An important aspect of care services is the fact that migrant women in the public sector compete with indigenous labour, while, commonly, the labour force of private care homes consists largely of migrant workers (Anthias and Cederberg 2006).

Migrant women are mostly employed in flexible, low-paid and informal jobs with very little prospects of gaining skills or promotion. Harsh working conditions offer women little prospects for greater personal and financial autonomy. It also translates into severe economic need and vulnerability at home and in the labour market. Most studies that have questioned whether migrant women's wage work has generated a positive change on gender relations conclude with a bleak result by pointing out different directions that gender relations follow post-migration. While some women perceive work as an opportunity to raise the family's living standards, others indicate the enforcements of patriarchal ideology. In some cases, women gain power via their husbands' inability to fulfil their socially assigned role of bread winner.

2.2.2   Women's work in the ethnic economy

Much of the contemporary debate about the world of immigrant women and the labour market is marked by the strong demand of private households for domestic and caring immigrant labour (Lutz 2004) and ethnic women's self-employment (Phizacklea 1988, Dhaliwal 1995, Strüder 2003). Many studies (Phizacklea 1988, Anthias 1992) emphasize the importance of self-employment for immigrant women and the fact that extensive use of unpaid family labour has been essential for the formation of many ethnic economies. The literature questions whether the use of women in the family or ethnic economy has positive or negative implications for women. The research findings indicate that women's ability to gain resources in terms of social, cultural and financial capital in ethnic business depends greatly on their position in the business, the work they perform and the amount of power they hold (Anthias and Cederberg 2006).

Given that the division of labour in the ethnic economy is as gendered as in the general economy, a look at the role of family, personal and community ties in the operation of immigrant businesses reveals the persistence of a gender division of labour which remains critical for their success. The enormous importance of kinship and family ties for the functioning of the ethnic economy is also frequently underlined in the European context. The exploitation of female kinship labour is even considered to be a 'building stone' for the development of the entrepreneurship of ethnic minorities in Britain (Anthias 1992). It is proposed that immigrant women workers are 'generally captive by other relationships than that of a wage' (Panayiotopoulos 1996:455). The predominantly male-controlled and labour-intensive nature of ethnic economies tend to be most successful in ethnic groups which are marked by 'social structures which give easy access to female labour subordinated to patriarchal control mechanisms' (Phizacklea 1988:22). Female immigrant labour is considered to be essential in keeping fresh supply coming into ethnic economies that usually operate on a small-scale basis (Portes and Sassen-Koob 1987, Anthias 1992). These studies have also identified how gender exclusion operates to keep women in a subordinate position in the ethnic economy. Gender sensitive research shows that ethnic economies do not necessarily support the professional advancement of women as much as they do for men (Zhou and Logan 1989). Rather, they keep women in a subordinated position by defining them primarily as daughters, mothers and wives.

Research showing how women's involvement in ethnic economies as independent entrepreneurs, unpaid family labourers and employees affects immigrant women's social inclusion in their host societies is scarce (Phizacklea 1988). Ethnic women's social exclusion is encompassed in the general arguments and policy proposals on how to integrate socially excluded groups into mainstream society. The narrow meaning of social inclusion in the EU context is used to formulate the inclusion policies through paid work (Lister 2004). The European

Foundation defines social exclusion as 'the process through which individuals or groups are wholly or partially excluded from full participation in the society in which on lives' (European Foundation 1995:4). In contrast to the definition of the European Foundation, De Haan and Maxwell have a more narrow focus in their approach, suggesting that social exclusion is 'the failure or inability to participate in social and political activities' (1998:2). Levitas has described it as a performative construction of inclusion (1998:362). In the UK, the new Labour government has labelled it as a new contract for welfare in which social integration is achieved through paid work, what Levitas calls SID (Social Integrationist Discourse) (Levitas 1998). Inclusion in the labour market, through marginal, low-paid, insecure jobs under poor working conditions, is not a favourable inclusion and is referred to as unfavourable inclusion or a disempowering form of inclusion (Sen 2000). But these definitions are ungendered and do not consider the gender differences in the experience of social exclusion and poverty. Gender analysis provides a means of examining the claim that social and ethnic networks ease the lack of social integration of the most disadvantaged into the wider society. It is possible to argue that these networks are an indicator of social integration or the essence of social inclusion (Martin 1996, Spicker 1997, Gallie 1999). It seems that they act in this way only for some, mainly ethnic minority men.

In another study, focusing on Asian American families, Espiritu (1999) examined the impact of ethnic self-employment on gender relations and family dynamics. She concluded that, in most instances, immigrant entrepreneurs accrued low gross earnings and faced high risks of failure. Most of the meagre profits of these labour-intensive small-businesses came at the expense of the minimally paid labour of spouses, children and relatives, and of excessive work hours or what scholars call 'self-exploitation' (Light and Gold 2000). While in some accounts, examples of mutual cooperation and trust prevail, others emphasize the need to pay attention to the relations of power within families and communities, and warn of the risk of exploitation (e.g. Anthias 1992).

2.2.3   Women's work in London's Turkish ethnic economy

Women's work has been a central element of the success of London's Turkish ethnic economy. There are many other categories of women involved in the ethnic business. However, their contribution remains invisible and is subsumed as domestic work or reproductive activity. The most common businesses Turkish people own in London are *döner*-kebab houses, off-licence shops and coffee shops. There are different ways in which the ethnic economy utilizes female labour. The most common form is women's 'help', which can take the form of cleaning the shop, cutting the vegetables, doing the dishes and making pastry to sell. Women do many different things for the family business and contribute in diverse ways even though the owner of the shop is the male head of the family – usually fathers and husbands. Running an ethnic business requires an interaction, even if a minimal one, with the outside world, and men feel that they are more suitable for the job, as women have more home-bound duties and their contribution is considered to be 'help'.

The expansion of the Turkish ethnic economy, on the one hand, confined women in the domestic sphere, and, on the other hand, forced them to take up roles in ethnic shops corresponding with their domestic roles as wives, mothers, sisters or daughters. Some of these women worked as unpaid family workers in family-owned businesses but some became low-paid wage workers to provide additional income for their families and children. Moreover, those men married to second generation immigrant women utilize their wives' knowledge of the British system and language ability to run their businesses. In addition to all these roles, migrant women are perceived to have a major role in the construction and reproduction of national ideologies and identities. Therefore, the role of women in the Turkish ethnic economy is important not only as a source of unpaid or cheap labour but also as a signifier or bearer of Turkish culture. In fact, women's roles as mothers and wives ensure the continuation of Turkish culture in a new country.

2.3   Social integration of female migrants

The debate around the issue of migrants' social integration is mostly underlined by the efforts of immigrants to be assimilated, or by basic social policy goals that facilitate the integration of ethnic minorities into mainstream society. Despite the fact that social inclusion and integration have rested upon the adoption of ethnic groups into host societies, multicultural policies recognize ethnic identities and accord rights to the membership of ethnic groups. Multiculturalism, as a short-lived policy discourse, is replaced with the securitization of migration policies due to social and political anxiety around cultural diversity, terrorism, race riots, ethnic gangs and ghettoes. A consequence of this paradigmatic shift was that ethnic women who could not adapt to the fundamentals of Western culture such as language and lifestyle were labelled as the source of social exclusion and lack of integration by their communities. Ethnic women's role in raising the second generation feeds into generating further exclusion and marginalization of ethnic groups. For this reason, policymakers advocate an urgent need for pre-entry tests to ensure social integration through a better knowledge of language and life in Western countries. Therefore, this approach treats ethnic minority women as the scapegoat for non-integration and sees them as the presenters of non-Western values.

Before any further discussion of the discourses of female migrants' social integration, it is important to examine how the literature on integration, inclusion and multiculturalism constructs the general debate on migrants' social integration. In the following sections, the concepts of social integration, social inclusion and multiculturalism are introduced and then the changing discourses of social integration of female immigrants are examined. In the final part, there will be an analysis of the relationship between women's work in the ethnic economy and social integration, with special reference to Turkish women in London's ethnic economy.

2.3.1   Social integration

In the context of migration, the concept of integration has been used to refer to many different meanings at many different national or societal levels. It generally refers to the process by which migrants become part of their host societies. As a normative term, 'integration' reflects a different end goal, for example an optimal relationship between migrants and the native population. Thus, while some authors emphasize migrants' one-way adaptation to the host society, others emphasize the two-way process in which the host society also adapts, for instance by addressing barriers to integration such as discrimination. This distinction is significant in identifying responsibility for 'failure' in the integration process, as well as priorities for policy intervention (Spencer 2006).

Esser (2000:272–275, cited in EFMS INTPOL Team 2006) proposes four basic forms of social integration: culturation, placement, interaction and identification. Culturation is the transmission and acquisition of knowledge, cultural standards and competencies by an individual for successfully interacting in society. Placement refers to an individual's acquisition and occupation of relevant positions in society, like in the educational system, in the economic system, in the professions or as a citizen. Placement is connected with the acquisition of certain rights that belong to particular positions and with the opportunity to establish relevant social relations and to win cultural, social and economic capital. Culturation is a precondition for placement. Interaction is a case of social action characterized by mutual orientations of actors and the formation of relations and networks. Examples of social integration via interaction would be the establishment of friendships, of love or marriage relations, or generally of membership in primary groups. Identification as a dimension of social integration indicates the identification of an actor with a social system by which he sees himself as a member of a collective body. Identification has cognitive and emotional sides and results in a 'we' feeling towards a group or collective. There is, in fact, no monolithic culture or social order to assimilate to, as democratic societies contain many different lifestyles, values and institutional processes, which are constantly changing. This means that there can be no fixed end point for integration, and no set trajectory for integration processes. In many societies, however, social and political pressures to assimilate persist. In practice, it is argued that this can have the opposite effect to that intended, i.e. a reinforcement of social divisions. The forced concealment of differences can lead in practice to their accentuation (Esser 2000, cited in EFMS INTPOL Team 2006).

In many European countries, assimilation is used for migrants' integration, which usually means migrants' assimilation to a pre-existing, unified social order, with a homogeneous culture and set of values. They are expected to undergo a unilateral process of change, particularly in the public sphere, so that they can fit into a given order (Rudiger and Spencer 2003). Penninx and Martiniello (2004) define integration not as an end but as a process that spreads into the spheres of economic, social, cultural and political life. In the domain of migrants' integration, assimilation remains a powerful analytical and policy tool. In the political realm, Otto Schily, the German minister for interior affairs and 'father' of both a new citizenship and immigration law, was quoted in 2003 as saying 'The best form of integration is assimilation' (EFMS INTPOL Team 2006). Brubaker (2001) helps to understand how migrants become similar in some respects in the cultural and socio-economic spheres. Thus, the question is not so much 'how much assimilation' but assimilation in what respect, over what time period and in reference to what population. In the EFMS's report, it is stated that assimilation means the shrinking of socially relevant differences between groups. Assimilation does not imply then – to define it in a negative way – that the suppression of ethnic cultures is different from minority reproduction with clear ethnic boundaries, and this is different from residential and social segregation, ethnic stratification and marginality (EFMS INTPOL Team 2006).

2.3.2 Social inclusion

As social integration is usually conceptualized as a one-way assimilation of migrants, social inclusion is a policy goal for governments throughout the EU, directed at eliminating the exclusion of all disadvantaged groups to enable everyone to have access to use, participate in and benefit from a sense of belonging to a given area of society. Social inclusion is devoted to remedying the social exclusion that affects individuals or communities and whose full participation in the economic, social and political life of the society in which they live is prevented (Rudiger and Spencer 2003:5). There are different steps that must be taken to facilitate the social inclusion of migrants. Rudiger and Spencer (2003) use an example of migrant women's access to health services and continue that

> 'female migrant could be excluded from receiving preventive health screening because the health service provides information only in the main national language and because she cannot request a female doctor to carry out the screening. Some integration policies might be prepared to conceive of technical aides, such as promotional leaflets in different languages, to foster inclusion, but may not be ready for a change in personnel, as this would affect the structural make-up of the health service. In this case, it could be said that the drive to preserve the existing structure is greater than the impetus to integrate migrants'.

> (Spencer: 2003:5)

Cohesion may be achieved in a pluralist society through the interaction of different communities that build a bond through the recognition of both difference and interdependence. The concept of integration suggests an emphasis on unity and stability that appears to entail a normative vision of social cohesion. Multi-dimensional notions of identity, multiple senses of belonging and attachment often add self-confidence and thus stability to social networks. Far from hampering the process of integration, they can add a layer of respect and recognition to social interaction, thus deepening the cohesion of communities. Social cohesion emphasizes unity and stability (Zetter et al. 2006), is generally defined as an end state rather than a process and is spatially oriented. Ireland argues, however, that cohesion should not be confused with consensus. The key is to find a means of dealing with conflicts of interest which allow the airing of alternative views and the development of a resolution that is acceptable to all parties (Ireland 2004:234).

The integration of migrants may take different forms in different societies, and migrants can be integrated in some sectors of society while they are excluded in others. For example, migrants can be integrated in the labour market but excluded from participation in civil society and political processes. In other cases, migrants can be citizens but they can be excluded and can lack access to education and employment opportunities. This is the case for Turkish migrants in the UK, as most were naturalized after a long wait with the status of refugees, but their exclusion from mainstream society is evident. In this regard, avoiding the conceptualization of integration in a single mode is important, and integration can also involve completely different modes of interaction with the receiving society (Rudiger and Spencer 2003).

> For example, some migrants might establish social networks through work relationships and find a partner among the majority population. Many others, however, rely on family and kinship networks, or neighbours of the same racial or ethnic background, to create stability and develop roots in the receiving society. Both modes may be considered integration successes, and policies that stifle interaction in any form are likely to be counterproductive.
>
> (Rudiger and Spencer 2003:6)

2.3.3 Multiculturalism

In contrast to assimilation, multiculturalism acknowledges cultural difference between ethnic groups as a continuing feature. In this regard, difference is valued and accommodated. Empirical studies find variations in multicultural approaches across Europe with greater or lesser acknowledgement of ethnic identities in the public and private spheres (Ireland 2004:222), whether or not under the official label of multiculturalism. Multicultural policies do not necessarily accord rights to ethnic groups but do recognize ethnic identities and accord rights to members of ethnic groups. While some authors argue that such policies reinforce cultural boundaries, others argue that this need not be the case.

> Multicultural integration policies support neither the crossing of boundaries from one culture to another, as do assimilation policies, nor the preservation of those boundaries, as does segregation, but aim to foster their permeability. By facilitating participation of all groups in all social, economic and political spheres, such policies foster the continual development and cross-fertilisation of cultures and identities and can therefore help overcome divisions and segregation.
>
> (Rudiger and Spencer 2003:7)

The multicultural model is based on the idea that the nation state contains a degree of plurality that allows migrants to retain their cultural identity, provided they adhere to the political norms. This does not negate the existence of a dominant culture. Multiculturalism generally means the public acceptance of immigrant and minority groups as distinct communities which are distinguishable from the majority population with regard to language, culture and social behaviour, and which have their own associations and social infrastructure (Kofman et al. 2000). Multiculturalism implies that members of such groups should be granted equal rights in all spheres of society, without being expected to give up their diversity, although usually with an expectation of conformity to certain key values. It is this combination of recognition of cultural difference and measures to ensure social equality which is the essential feature of multiculturalism. Some authors argue that when certain ground rules are in place a multicultural society can be successful, stable and cohesive (Parekh 2004). Multiculturalism may also include the demand for economic and social equality between migrants and the wider society, thus leading to the establishment of anti-discrimination policies accompanied by sanctions. Multiculturalism is not always an entirely positive development, because, in practice, it may encourage and fix essentialist and static views of migrant identities (Kofman et al. 2000).

Parekh (2004) argues for a dialectic approach to multiculturalism by amalgamating the approaches of recognition and redistribution. Parekh (2004) pointed to multiculturalism as the politics of recognition and redistribution, and says that

'the politics of redistribution calls for the politics of recognition. The converse is equally true. Communities and their cultures tend to be devalued for a variety of reasons, their economic inequality and powerlessness being one of the most important of them. When individuals and communities are poor or oppressed, they tend to be politically and economically invisible and voiceless, and count for little'.

(2004:208)

Parekh (2004:201–202) further argued, recognition 'assumes culture is more important than the economy'; that since identities are subject to change, any recognition of identities by the state 'would necessarily formalise and freeze them', thereby arresting their future development. For this reason, it is argued 'the state cannot and should not recognise or have anything to do with identity' of any kind. Further, in offering advice to the oppressed, Parekh writes that since the pre-occupation is with 'difference' it 'undermines the solidarity of the oppressed and the marginalised' and 'makes it impossible for them to unite and act together' (Parekh 2004:208).

In recent years, critics of multiculturalism have claimed that it hinders integration and keeps immigrants separate from host populations by encouraging cultural difference. This has led to a shift away from multiculturalism in favour of integration policies. Feminists have levelled critiques against the patriarchal nature of multicultural policies that support male leadership and the persistence of traditional values (Martin 1991, Yuval-Davis 1997). They have also questioned who is empowered to interpret and impose cultural norms. The state and other institutions may accept cultural norms that communities have transplanted from their home society, such as the conduct of women in private and public, without any real consideration of the changes in the economic and social environment in which a custom is practised. This has been the case with polygamous marriages in France. There may be little reflection about the interplay of social forces between particular cultures and the wider society (Kofman et al. 2000). Multiculturalism may represent a more liberal tolerance of what goes on in the private sphere of different migrant groups, but this can leave intact gender inequalities and repressive practices towards women. The case of domestic violence exemplifies the tolerance of practices in the private sphere, on the grounds of non-intervention in the customs of others. Social workers may therefore fail to intervene in cases of domestic violence (Kofman et al. 2000).

2.3.4 Discourses on female migrants' integration

The EU's official framework on the integration process of non-EU nationals offers a dynamic understanding of integration, in which the integration is defined as two-way process of mutual accommodation by all immigrants and residents of Member States. In this regard, the Commission brings both the immigrants' own efforts for integration into the fore and the social policies of host societies that enable participation of immigrants. Therefore, social integration may be understood as access to resources, participation and belonging. The capacity to cope with problems and barriers, to achieve participation and access, and to realize belonging is broadly affected by conditions set by social and integration policies (Kontos 2009). The EU's analysis outlines common basic principles on which social integration must be built. These are integration with the basic values of the EU, to employment, the host society's language, history and institutions, education, migrants' access to public and private goods and services in a non-discriminatory way, frequent interaction between immigrants and EU citizens, the practice of diverse cultures and religions, and political participation. One should also be aware of the fact that women's integration into labour market activities is often low and the EU advised the Member States to take active measures to ensure better integration of women (EC 2005).

In the theoretical discussion, the debate of integration is mostly gender blind (Kofman et al. 2013). It began being discussed from the mid-1990s in relation to the failures of multiculturalism. Blamed for failures of economic and social integration, as evidenced by significant variations between ethnocultural groups in the take-up of educational opportunities, differential employment rates, differential crime rates and continuing high levels of residential segregation, multiculturalism was more closely linked to fears of Islamist inspired assassinations and terror attacks (Kofman et al. 2013). The outcome of these concerns was that governments have become more proactive in identifying and addressing problems of forced marriage, 'honour' killing or culturally sanctioned abuses of children; and tackling violence against women in minority cultural groups has become a more visible part of the political agenda in many countries in Europe (Kofman et al. 2013). In regard to the role of gender in the multiculturalism debate, Phillips and Saharso (2008) noted that gender relations and inequality have largely gone unnoticed in academic commentary in relation to the crisis of multiculturalism. Twenty years ago, such issues were rarely mentioned in critiques of multicultural policies except by feminist analyses of multiculturalism's threats and risks to women, and its utilization by male-dominated organizations (see Bottomley et al. 1991, Sahgal and Yuval-Davis 1992). Feminist scholars raised issues concerning the control of community organizations by male leaders, the promotion of conservative practices and the idea of women as biological, cultural and social reproducers of the ethnic community.

Kofman et al. (2013) argue that women migrants have been brought to the fore of the integration debate in recent years as representatives of 'explicit enunciations of sexual differences and the divide between migrants and non-migrants' (2013:3). The authors distinguish three different discourses built around the cultural differences between minority and majority populations that provide an ideological departure for governments' policies on migration and integration. In the first discourse, the main argument is based on the failure of migrants, due to their marginalization and the formation of an ethnic underclass. This vicious circle is reproduced by poorly educated mothers who have a major role in the success or failure of the next generation. Therefore, admission policies are to be designed to curb the entrance of poorly educated female migrants through marriage. In the second discourse, gender and sexuality are seen as the main areas of integration. Muslim women are seen as a main threat to Western 'liberal' and 'open' societies since their demands and practices are deemed to be incompatible with liberal ways of life.

> In response to such concerns, family migration and practices become the terrain for the control of cultural differences at the various stages from admission, to permanent residence and citizenship. In particular, breaking the transmission of traditional practices requires surveillance and intervention into transnational marriages, especially those that are forced, and in some cases even those which are arranged.
>
> (Kofman et al. 2013:4)

In the third discourse, it is claimed that pre-entry and civic integration tests are beneficial for the welfare of migrant women.

> Governments cannot make gender equality a marker of modern liberal European society and claim they are concerned about migrant women's welfare without also taking some action. This is especially true if there is a strong minorities' or women's grass roots movement, or a strong focal person asking for public action.
>
> (Kofman et al. 2013:5)

When the focus has been on the lack of integration, policymakers are more concerned with the urgent need for pre-entry tests to ensure better economic integration, through a better knowledge of language and life in host societies. This has been seen to be the result of unsuccessful integration of migrant communities and social exclusion. Women migrants who join their husbands through family reunification, who do not usually speak the language of their host society and hence pose economic strains on existing social services are blamed as the cause of non-integration of their communities. This book has questioned this proposal by introducing the case of Turkish immigrant women's social integration through their work in the Turkish ethnic economy. Before focusing on the case of Turkish women, it is important to outline the literature concerned with immigrant women's social integration in ethnic economies.

2.3.5   Turkish migrant women's integration

The findings of the literature clearly demonstrate that ethnic work offers little leverage for migrant women to gain power in their families and communities, with a slim chance for social integration into mainstream society. However, it is unfair to paint the circumstances in a completely negative light, as migrant women can find genuine ways of improving their social integration even with little prospect of changing traditional gender roles and relations in their ethnic communities. However, this book aims to introduce Turkish women's views on integration and how their integration is being shaped by their work in the ethnic economy. Women's integration into the host society shows a zigzag progression in London's Turkish community. The Turkish ethnic economy is the only way in which the Turkish community constructs its contribution to the British society and women's work in the ethnic economy is therefore the most visible way of social contribution and integration. Women not only contribute to the ethnic economy through their labour, but also have a major role to play in the construction and reproduction of national ideologies and identities.

First generation Turkish women show a stereotypical image similar to that described in the political discourse, which pictures migrant women as the source of social exclusion and non-integration of migrant communities. Most of the women cannot speak English and their lives are limited to their community circle. Women rarely step out of their ethnic ghetto. Turkish women define themselves as 'half citizens' who are contributors, but not full participants. Many migrants believe that their status as refugees in the country precludes a positive outside view about them and they are socially stigmatized for their welfare dependency without recognition for their contributions to the British society. This leads to feelings of exclusion and results in the women being isolated within the Turkish community. Women's understanding of integration is determined by their contribution to British society, which involves having a 'decent' job and actively participating in the labour market, an aspect that Turkish women severely lacked.

However, what is not true for first generation Turkish women in their stereotypical portrayal is their efforts to raise a well integrated second generation. In fact, women value their motherhood and future prospects of their children as the only way for their social integration into British society. Women conceptualize their role in the upbringing of their children as an important contribution to the British society. Women value their contribution through their role of bearing and rearing children, in which they wish their children to have a solid connection with their ethnic and religious cultural heritage as well as with the British way of life and values. Therefore, it is possible to argue that the political discourse claiming that the first generation migrant women's method of child rearing is feeding into social exclusion and non-integration of the migrant community is weak in explaining the Turkish women's hard work for their children to be well integrated into their host society. Hence, labelling first generation women as the source of non-integration is a false perception of how migrant women contribute to the well-being of their families and communities. Women not only contribute to their society through their major role in their children's well-being, but also through their role in the success of the expansion of the Turkish ethnic economy in London. Without any acknowledgment of these roles, any political approach blaming migrant women for social exclusion within their communities falls short in the understanding of the realities of female migrants' lives.

The contribution to the ethnic economy is one of the major means of social integration, but women also developed a sense of integration and belonging through their role as mothers and in raising children. Women conceptualize their role in the upbringing of their children as an important way that they can integrate. Meanwhile, women are pulled and pushed in different directions by the various demands put on them from different sources, such as their own families, their community and their host society. In one sense, women are obliged to be community members, good mothers and wives, with a strong emphasis on their communal roles rather than individuality. In another sense, women are pulled into the unknown in their relation with the state and state apparatus. This tension is not easy to manage, and may be a difficult task to overcome for first generation women.

3
The Ethnic Economy and the Turkish Ethnic Economy in London

When Turks started to arrive in Europe as guest workers, they were employed mostly in Fordist factories of the time. These migrants became industrial workers for the first time in their lives, and this marked a transformation of agricultural workers into urban labourers. Wives followed guest workers in supplying labour as informal workers in precarious jobs such as domestic work or other low-paid service employment. Then, following the crisis of 1973, neo-liberal policies marked a change in this employment pattern, and most of the guest workers became unemployed. This impasse was partially overcome through the generation of self-employment in the Turkish ethnic economy for the unemployed and the children of guest workers in the early 1990s.

Initially, the Turkish ethnic economy aimed to serve the ethnic food needs of migrants but later it spread more widely to Germany, serving the native population and in time becoming a European-wide phenomenon. Turks emerged as ethnic entrepreneurs in almost all Western European countries as Germany maintained its central role as the supplier of Turkish ethnic food because it was the central location of factories producing Turkish food such as *döner*-kebab and yogurt. Having *döner*-kebab manufacturers helped to standardize the ways in which kebab was served and people no longer needed to be skilled kebab cooks to own a kebab shop. Through wholesale productions in Germany, large-scale factories were owned and run by Turkish people, resulting in the easy engagement of Turkish migrants in the production and sale of *döner* takeaways all over Europe, which generated a considerable amount of employment for Turkish migrants in Europe.

Chapter 3 begins with an evaluation of concepts and theories of the ethnic economy, and questions its importance for migrants' integration. It then places emphasis on the Turkish ethnic economy in

Europe. The growing importance of the Turkish ethnic economy in Europe has become the focus of academic research, mainly centring on its capacity to generate self-employment and its contribution to the European economy. Growing commercialization has generated a web of networks in Europe for the distribution and sale of the Turkish *döner* takeaways. In addition, the structure of the Turkish ethnic economy in London is introduced through the findings of the ethnographic study. The operation of ethnic businesses in London is heavily based on family labour and ethnic networks of support, through which the growing ethnic economy offers enormous employment opportunities to people in the Turkish community. The central factor supporting this expansion has been the labour of women in families, and the young generation brought up in London provided the language skills and knowledge of the British system. The nature of the Turkish ethnic economy depends upon the utilization of ethnic networks/labour and the integration of the second generation into family businesses.

3.1   The ethnic economy in Europe: Is it social integration of sojourners?

Immigrant entrepreneurship has not only been a central issue in migration studies, but was also favoured by recent government policies as a way of integrating migrants into mainstream societies and generating employment for ethnic groups. Ethnic entrepreneurship has a long history in the United States where foreign born people have been over-represented in small-businesses since 1880 (Volery 2007). This has been explained as a reaction to lack of employment opportunities for ethnic minorities in the labour market. Europe, however, had a different historical trajectory of ethnic entrepreneurship since many countries had not had a migrant population until after World War II when a large labour force was needed for ever-growing industrial companies. Initially, the immigrants came as a temporary workforce, fulfilling jobs which required no skills and which could easily be replaced by a succession of sojourners (Waldinger et al. 1990a). As the immigrants started to settle down over time, the preconditions for ethnic businesses slowly started to evolve. In most cases, it was the ethnic community that created the demand for specific ethnic goods and services in the first place, which could only be fulfilled by co-ethnics with the same knowledge of tastes and buying preferences. The growth of entrepreneurial activities performed by immigrants and their descendants, whose business dynamism has shaped their social, cultural and economic incorporation in Western receiving societies, has been the focus of many studies in recent decades (Volery 2007).

The growth of ethnic economies has been observed in metropolitan areas such as Miami, New York, Amsterdam, Berlin, London, Birmingham and Paris. The number of small-scale entrepreneurs has greatly increased with the share of immigrants in the population, first in the United States and Britain, and later in other advanced countries in Europe (Rath 2000). It was shown, for example, in the United Kingdom, that Pakistani, Chinese and Irish ethnic groups have significantly higher rates of self-employment than other groups. One in five in the Pakistani group was classified as self-employed, as were one in six in the Chinese and Irish groups. Among the white British group, this was just one in ten (Panayiotopoulos 2010). The same research by Panayiotopoulos shows the distribution by industry and a tendency towards crowding out in particular sectors and sub-sectors. In his data, most of the Bangladeshi and Chinese men worked in distribution, and the hotel and restaurant industries, while Pakistani men were the group most likely to work in the transportation and communication industries. In regard to women, two in five Chinese women and one in three Bangladeshi women worked in the hotel and restaurant industries, compared with one in five of all women in employment (Panayiotopouls 2010).

The literature on ethnic entrepreneurship provides different definitions of ethnic economy and why a business becomes 'ethnic', and of how the concept of ethnicity is related to entrepreneurship (Pecoud 2010). The term 'entrepreneur' refers to a person who is simultaneously the owner and manager of a firm. These two roles may sometimes be performed by different individuals (Rath 2000). For Waldinger et al. (1990a) ' ... "ethnic business" may be no more than a set of connections and regular patterns of interactions among people sharing common national background or migration experiences' (1990:33). 'The term "ethnic economy" is used to describe enterprises from the same ethnic group, without assuming that they only have employees drawn from their own community' (Strüder 2003:187). In a more exhaustive definition,

Ethnic entrepreneurs are often referred to as simultaneously owners and managers (or operators) of their own businesses, whose group membership is tied to a common cultural heritage or origin, and is known to out-group members as having such traits; more importantly, they are intrinsically intertwined in particular social structures in which individual behaviour, social relations, and economic transactions are constrained.

(Zhou 2004:1040)

The underlying common traits of these definitions are the small-scale and self-employment nature of ethnic economy, with a heavy reliance on co-ethnic labour. In addition, the same ethnic group is doing a similar economic activity, as this book will show, such as Turks in the *döner*-kebab business. The literature also draws attention to the availability and concentration of their co-ethnic customers, and the pool of potential employees in a community may help to determine the viability of ethnic enterprises (Spenner and Bean 1999:1026). All of these definitions and analyses point to ethnic resource in the development of a specific ethnic economy. 'Ethnic resources are social features of a group which co-ethnic business owners utilise in business or from which their business passively benefits. Ethnic resources include values, knowledge, skills, information, attitudes, leadership, solidarity, an orientation to sojourning, and institutions' (Light and Bonacich 1988:18–19).

A number of characteristics underlined in the literature are common in many of the ethnic enterprises. Panayiotopoulos (2010:37) cautions us against the danger of identifying certain characteristics as ethnic when they are only a characteristic of small enterprise culture. He classifies the main characteristics of ethnic minority enterprises as follows:

1. The entrepreneur combines ownership and management functions
2. No clear division of labour exists between management and direct production
3. Levels of productivity are low
4. Both production and administration are conducted along traditional, personalized and paternalistic lines
5. Close personal relations exist both among those active in the enterprise and between the entrepreneur and other enterprises
6. There is a strong dependence on family labour
7. The enterprise finds it difficult to access formal and financial credit markets
8. There is a strong dependence on informal systems of labour recruitment, management and production. Such enterprises frequently act as contractors and sub-contractors in extensive and difficult-to-monitor production networks (Panayiotopouls 2010:37–38).

The most common form of ethnic enterprises are travel agencies, garment shops, specialized grocery shops, tearooms and fast-food stands, and they rapidly pop up and diversify with the expansion and growth of an ethnic community. An important prerequisite for the emergence of ethnic businesses within a community is a sufficient number of potential consumers of ethnic products; but also, community members should have access to sufficient funds for new investments and skills in operating a business (Waldinger et al. 1990b). Razin (2002) argues that the opportunities offered by the environment of a host society have a strong influence on the propensity of immigrants to turn to self-employment as a way of labour market integration and upward economic mobility. These external factors influence different ethnic and immigrant groups in different ways (Razin 2002). People pushed into ethnic business with no other chance of becoming employed are also pulled into it through the rewards and independence that it offers, as well as the upward mobility (Borooah and Hart 1999).

Entrepreneurship is seen as a response to migrants' disadvantageous positions in their host societies, and as a way of adapting to some of the social and economic trends that affect them directly, including discrimination, lack of qualifications, industrial restructuring, unemployment, welfare retrenchment and labour market deregulation. Through ethnic business, migrants are expected to turn their disadvantages into advantages. However, it is mostly the case that markets occupied by ethnic entrepreneurs are typically characterized by low barriers of entry in terms of required capital and educational qualifications, small-scale production, high labour intensity and low added value, while cut-throat competition reigns. This leads to the emergence of a large number of start-ups and, in turn, a high rate of failure. In order to stay ahead and remain competitive under such conditions, the temptation to employ informal practices with respect to taxes, labour regulations, minimum wages and employing children and immigrant workers without documents is quite high (Rath and Kloosterman 2000). After all these considerations about ethnic economy, it is time to see how the Turkish ethnic economy is structured, and to evaluate its main characteristics together with its development in Europe.

3.2   The Turkish ethnic economy in Europe

The '*döner* kebab revolution', as termed by Panayiotopoulos (2010), was the start of the Turkish ethnic economy in Europe. Its birth place was Germany and the main location was Berlin where the Turkish population overcrowded. *Döner*-kebab takeaway shops have been the single most significant source of enterprise formation for Turkish immigrants in Germany and throughout Europe. Hillmann's study conducted in the 1990s showed that some 3,600 firms were listed in the Turkish *Yellow Pages* for 1998, and estimates that by the end of the 1990s, 6,000 enterprises were owned by immigrants from Turkey. The bulk of the enterprises were located in working-class neighbourhoods of Berlin, such as Kreuzberg, Tiergarten, Wedding and Neukolm (Hillmann 1999). *Döner*-kebab was a hybrid food invented by the Turkish migrants in Berlin. It represented the commodification of 'traditional' ethnic food; another example being the 'Italian' pizza (Panayiotopoulos 2010).

The Turkish community in Europe is made up of a significantly younger population compared with the EU population in general. Even though self-employment began as an alternative employment path for many first generation redundant guest workers, it also generated significant opportunities for the second generation youth. Having a grown-up second generation has made the expansion of the ethnic economy possible through their language abilities and knowledge of the legal/business/finance systems of their host countries. Assisted by their parents who wanted to secure the future livelihoods of their children, the younger generation had a positive impact on the expansion of Turkish small-scale business in Europe. An increasing number of entrepreneurs came from the ranks of the second generation, and the emerging literature on the Turkish entrepreneurship points to rapid expansion across the generational spectrum (Panayiotopoulos 2010).

The location of enterprises is often a reflection of the pattern of contemporary Turkish immigration and community formation. A strong feature is the concentration in Europe's gateway cities. Working-class neighbourhoods in Berlin, Hamburg, Amsterdam, Vienna, Rotterdam and London become centres for immigrant enterprise, as well as areas of London such as Green Lanes, Tottenham, Stoke Newington and Hackney. The food sector, for example ethnic restaurants, takeaway shops, and grocery and vegetable stalls, became part of the neighbourhood shopping of many non-ethnic residents. Most of these shops were small enterprises, relying on family labour (four-fifths of employment) in the restaurant, services and retail sectors (Panayiotopoulos 2010:130–131).

Research conducted in 2003 shows that Turkish entrepreneurs represent a significant and growing economic force in Europe. During 2002, an estimated 82,300 firms employed 411,000 people. The research showed that between 1996 and 2002, more than 25,000 enterprises

Table 3.1   Turkish enterprises in the EU (EU-15): Economic indicators

	1997	2002	2007	2008	2010	2012
Total number of enterprises	62,000	82,300	102,000	108,000	114,000	119,000
Average investment by enterprise (€)	97,000	112,000	107,000	107,000	120,000	120,000
Gross total investment (billion €)	6	9.2	10.9	11.6	–	14.2
Total turnover by enterprise (€)	415,000	425,000	445,000	–	–	455,000
Total annual turnover (billion €)	25.7	35	45.4	–	–	54.1
Average number of workers per enterprise	4.1	5	4.6	–	–	4.8
Total number of employees	254,000	411,000	469,000	–	–	471,200

Source: TAVAK (2013).

were added to the total, representing a 41.8% increase. During the same period, employment increased by 225,000, an increase of 82.6%. Nearly 70% of all Turkish enterprises in the EU were in Germany, of which four-fifths were found in only three sectors: retail, restaurant and takeaways, and the service sector. Over one-third (39.7%) of the entrepreneurs had been living in Germany for 11–30 years (Araştırmalar and Vakfı 2003, cited in Panayiotopoulos 2010) (Table 3.1).

A more recent survey shows the continued rising trends and the expansion of the small-scale entrepreneurship and employment capacity of the Turkish ethnic economy in Europe. By including the Turkish enterprises in the new EU member states, the research shows that the total number of enterprises owned by Turkish people in the EU has reached 150,000. This indicates a 52% total growth between 1997 and 2012. Considering an 8.7% growth in the last 20 years, it is estimated that the number of Turkish entrepreneurs will reach 200,000 by 2025. A large proportion of Turkish entrepreneurs live in Germany, which has the largest Turkish population in Europe. This is followed by France, Austria and the Netherlands. Between 1996 and 2010, the total investment of Turkish entrepreneurs increased from 6 billion to 12.4 billion Euros. The total turnover was 25.7 billion Euros in 1997, which went up to 45.4 billion Euros in 2008. The rising trend has also generated a great employment opportunity for many people from Turkey, and those working in the Turkish ethnic economy rose from 254,000 in 1997 to 520,000 in 2012 (TAVAK 2013).

A study on Turkish entrepreneurs in Hamburg by Tolciu et al. (2010) finds that a relatively balanced proportion of first (52%) and second generation entrepreneurs (48%) are represented. The latter group is predominately made up of highly skilled migrants active in knowledge-intensive sectors such as the legal, tax consulting or health sectors. Most entrepreneurs are men (81% male, 19% female), representing the fact that Turkish women are substantially less involved in entrepreneurial activities than Turkish men. In regard to the age structure, at 37 years, Turkish people are the youngest business owners in Germany, whereas native entrepreneurs are on average 46 years old. The educational attainment shows a high level of university graduates (37%) in Hamburg, whereas only 8% of all self-employed persons with a Turkish background have a university or equivalent degree in Germany (Tolciu et al. 2010).

The same research also shows that Turkish migrant owners still tend to open their firms predominantly in traditional sectors, such as retail/trade and gastronomy, and comparatively seldomly in knowledge-intensive sectors and crafts. The majority of the interviewed Turkish entrepreneurs founded their business in the service sector (54%), followed by the retail/trade sector (36%) and craft sector (10%). The enterprises consist mainly of small firms (90% have fewer than 10 employees). This characteristic is typical of Turkish entrepreneurs in Germany. About 91% of the Turkish entrepreneurs in Germany have small enterprises with fewer than 10 employees, and only the remaining 9% minority have businesses with ten or more employees (Tolciu et al. 2010).

Further research in another European city, Brussels, studied 100 Turkish firms and found that most of the entrepreneurs were young, below 35 years of age, and that one-fifth were university graduates. Only one-third of them had any training specific to their work. Nearly 45% were in the retail sector (groceries) and had mainly Turkish customers. Over one-third of them used start-up capital of $15,000 or less, and only one in five used the commercial banking sector to do so. In terms of labour input, they are described as 'small-scale family enterprises', yet of the total of 412 persons employed, only 23% were actually family workers, and 65% were of Turkish origin. A significant proportion of employment generated (35%) thus consisted of the employment of other immigrant groups (Bayar 1996:6–7).

The overall outcome of these different research results is the expansion of the Turkish ethnic economy in almost all European countries with a significant employment generation capacity and high financial contributions to the countries in which they operate. What comes out of this picture is the transnational character of the Turkish ethnic economy in Europe and this has been the result of the commercialization of ethnic food production. According to Pécoud (2002:4), the internationalism of 'Turkish economy' has been the result of the emergence of the new form of transnational business practice that is initiated and facilitated by cheap labour in Turkey, and the growth of international trade. Panayiotopoulos (2010) eloquently explains the internationalization of the Turkish ethnic economy by focusing on how *döner*-kebab production has been commercialized through manufacturing and wholesale chains located in Europe. For him, the replacement of other forms of traditional kebabs with *döner* using a large lump of meat helped to reduce the labour-intensive nature of preparing kebab and it became possible to run kebab houses with two or three workers. This process was supported by the emergence of manufacturing companies specialized in the wholesale market. More significantly, we have seen the emergence of manufacturers and wholesalers of processed meat used in the *döner*-kebab trade. It is this, more than any other factor, which has made it possible for many entrepreneurs to start up. The application of economies of scale in the industrial processing of meat has eliminated the labour costs involved in the preparation of the *döner* by the individual takeaway shops and also lowered prices paid for the meat by the retailers of ready-made *döner* to the wholesalers. The application of economies of scale has also led to the resurgence of the shish-kebab, as thousands of immigrant workers are employed in factories cutting and skewering the meat, which is delivered to retailers according to demand (Panayiotopoulos 2010). An important consequence of the development of meat and food processing points to qualitative differences between Turkish entrepreneurs: that is, between the mass of *döner*-kebab producers and the smaller number of suppliers of these products. The suppliers are involved in value-adding manufacturing processing, while takeaway shops rely primarily on the price mark-up, self-exploitation and use of family labour. The development of Turkish wholesalers and the emergence of a significant layer of large capitalist enterprises and commodity chains which operate across borders, points to significant variation among enterprises and provides evidence that many of the enterprises have significantly moved out of the 'fringes' (Panayiotopoulos 2010).

   In recent years, there have been signs that the Turkish ethnic economy has taken a slight turn towards more diversification, and a true integration into the mainstream societies in which they exist. For example, Pécoud (2004) shows that Turks now participate in diverse sectors of the Germany economy, including highly successful and competitive industries like software and new technologies. This group of Turkish businessmen is becoming 'an elite'. Similarly, Mushaben (2006) has stated that many Turkish enterprises have moved beyond ethnic niches, and some of them possess an intercultural competence that contributes to the national economy. However, one must be well aware that this diversification is still limited to a small number of cases, and the primary economic engagement is in catering and the sale of ethnic food. Thus, it is important to go back to the initial question of the relationship between ethnic economic activity and migrant integration. The integration of sojourners through ethnic business in the Turkish case has exclusively remained limited to those taking advantage of the high value-added end of manufacturing and the supply chain. The masses engaged in the labour-intensive, small-scale retail business earn just enough to make ends meet and ensure survival. In some cases, they manage to survive by topping their earnings up with welfare benefits even though there is a race to the bottom in cutting costs by employing family members or undocumented migrant labour with very low pay rates.

3.3   The Turkish ethnic economy in Britain

In the UK, until the early 2000s, Turks mainly engaged in garment making, and after the downturn of the garment industry, many began to look for other economic opportunities. Their engagement in the garment production industry was mainly informal and almost all worked in the workshops that were owned mostly by Turkish people. This sector was the ethnic economy of Turks by then. When the business died out, it left some migrants with a large sum of cash accumulated through years of hard work, especially women's work in the textiles industry. By that time, those who had arrived since the early 1980s cut loose the hope of going back to Turkey, as they had settled well and had grown-up children in education or in other activities. Some of these families began to search for different economic activities, and this process overlapped with the increasing flow of Kurds coming into the UK as well as more diversified migrants such as students, au pairs and other professionals. This expanded the demand for ethnic food and other related supplies.

The growth of the ethnic economy began little by little with the emergence of *döner*-kebab houses and corner-shops selling ethnic foods mostly imported from Germany. In the beginning it mostly served the Turkish clientele but it expanded over time following the favourable reception of the *döner* by a wider customer base in the UK. The expansion is enabled through the entrance of new entrepreneurs and also through geographical dispersion. It became possible to find Turkish-run shops all over the UK, as more and more people wanted to take advantage of growing economic opportunities of the ethnic economy. Having a strong Turkish niche market in Germany has supported the fast expansion in the UK, since it was easier to bring products from Germany rather than importing them from Turkey, due to regulations such as the EU rule on milk and milk products such as yogurt and cheese. Together with geographical expansion, the Turkish ethnic economy has also diversified, now ranging from coffee shops, bars, restaurants, to bakeries, corners shops and dry cleaners.

It is not clearly known how large the Turkish ethnic economy is in the UK. A Turkish magazine reporting on the catering business in the community makes it clear that the number of restaurants owned by Turkish speaking people reached 15,000 in 2001, whereas the number was not more than 200 in 1975. The London Chamber Office (2003) reports on the concentration of Turkish businesses in the Hackney area where around 10% of all businesses are owned by the Turkish/Turkish-Cypriot minority. The London Borough of Hackney estimates that there are approximately 340 Turkish speaking businesses in this borough. Typical businesses are restaurants, cafes, kebab shops, fish and chip shops, supermarkets, off-licences, minicab firms and import/export companies (London Chamber 2003). In more recent, exclusive information on the *döner*-kebab business, it is stated that kebab businesses currently have an annual contribution of over £2.2 billion to the British economy. With over 2,000 tonnes of *döner* meat and over 700 tonnes of chicken produced a week and turnover in excess of at least £750m, the industry has a substantial impact on the UK economy, providing UK farmers with expanded markets for their lamb and meeting the demands of an industry that continues to grow and prosper (Kebab Manufacturers 2013[1]). This has also led to the expansion of suppliers in the UK. It is estimated that there are around 200 producers in Britain and thousands of shops. Wholesale dealers who offer meat already on a spit – weighing around 22–175 pounds – have also ballooned, to be able to meet the increasing demand. It is evident from the information that the *döner*-kebab is a full-scale industry, with associated producers, dealers and retailers.

The growth of Turkish entrepreneurship in the UK mirrors the wider growth of the Turkish ethnic economy in Europe, and resembles it with its focus on ethnic food sale through *döner*-kebab houses. However, scholarly studies have paid very little attention to this and to its particularities. The available information, although scarce, indicates its vibrant character and that Turkish ethnic business is the most rapidly growing ethnic business in the UK (Altinay and Altinay 2008). This has been related to the fact that the Turkish ethnic group has one of the highest proportions of self-employment. According to Altinay and Altinay (2008) 35% of Turkish-born residents own their own business, compared with just 13% of all UK nationals. This evidence supports the importance of self-employment among Turkish migrants. Entering into self-employment had other advantages for Turkish migrants, providing an easy visa waiver for those establishing their own business in the EU due to the regulation of the Ankara Agreement between Turkey and the EU. Those arriving in the UK for different reasons can then apply for a visa extension through the Ankara Agreement and when they get indefinite leave to remain they settle in the UK. Therefore, self-employment for Turkish migrants is a window of opportunity to settle in the country. However, this is not to say that the rising numbers of self-employed is the sole result of visa regulations, but that the Turkish ethnic economy is the only source of work and earning a living for Turkish migrants.

The main characteristic of the Turkish ethnic economy is its small-scale, family-based nature. Therefore, families pool their resources to run a shop and workers are often family members. It is customary to see a father and sons, brothers or relatives running a shop together. Basu and Altinay (2003) point to participation by the entrepreneurs' immediate and extended family, with wives often playing an important informal and invisible role, as critical in the enterprise functions. In the following chapters there will be more information on the role of women's labour. However, more importantly, whenever a business needs extra paid labour it is met from the community as it is always cheaper to hire a Turkish immigrant. The Turkish ethnic economy is also a good source of employment for undocumented Turkish migrants and for asylum seekers whose applications are still pending. Another source of labour is that of Turkish students, who arrive to study in the UK and are a fresh labour demand for the economy, as well as customers for its products and services.

3.4   London's Turkish ethnic economy

The Turkish ethnic economy in London is best observed in Green Lanes, which is a long street passing through Haringey. It is full of Turkish shops on each side of the road. Not only the usual *döner*-kebab shops but also the most elaborate examples of Turkish food culture can easily be found on Green Lanes. This manifests itself in the form of patisseries, bakeries, pastry-makers, heated nut selling shops and exquisite kebab shops. Even though North London is the area most dominated by the Turkish presence, Green Lanes is the prime location as the Turkish town of London. However, it is misleading to imply that this location serves only Turkish customers, it also interacts well with the rest of the city and attracts many British customers too. The Turkish ethnic economy is an important part of British culture, and is well embedded into the multicultural scene of London.

My fieldwork in London included 25 small-scale businesses operated by people from Turkey. These shops were *döner*-kebab houses (five), off-licence corner-shops (five), restaurants (five), coffee shops and tea houses (five), and the remaining five were composed of a Turkish food market, two ladies and men's hairdressers, an accountant and a solicitor. The first 20 firms served both Turkish and British customers. *Döner*-kebab houses and restaurants are typical examples of ethnic economy where both ethnic and native customers are served. In the UK, the Turkish food is widely accepted nationwide, but especially in London, where one can find very elaborate examples of Turkish cuisine. In addition, in recent years there has been a trend towards Turkish migrants buying small corner-shops and coffee/tea houses to serve mainstream customers all over England. The activities of the last group of entrepreneurs (five) were specifically focused on the ethnic community and their services for Turkish people living in the UK. Professionals such as the accountant and solicitor are second generation migrants, educated in the UK, who decided to serve Turkish people, especially the first generation migrants who had little language and institutional knowledge but who needed professional help to maintain their relations with the local and national authorities.

In regard to the location of Turkish businesses in London, most are clustered around the North London area. Although most of the firms were located here, where the highest concentration of the Turkish population is, there were a few located in different parts of London, such as Central London. The Turkish ethnic business in London has moved away from concentrating only on *döner*-kebab houses, and has diversified in other areas of catering and services. It is possible to find a small sandwich shop operated by Turkish people in Central London. However, it is still true that as the Turkish community in London is concentrated mainly in the Hackney and Haringey areas, followed by Islington, Stoke Newington, Turnpike Lane, Newington Green, Peckham and Lewisham, 20 firms in this study were located in Haringey, Stoke Newington, Hackney and Newington Green. Note that the locational spread of the ethnic economy is not restricted to London, and there are many people from Turkey running kebab houses, coffee/tea shops and other small-scale businesses all over Britain. It was reported to me during the interviews that people search for high streets in Britain where there is no kebab house, so that they can go and fill that gap. This was also mentioned by many women informants, who stated that their husbands were working in other cities and they talked about the difficulty of organizing life without the presence of their husbands. I would like to evaluate this as significant evidence of the widespread nature of the Turkish ethnic economy. The following section evaluates the significant characteristics emerging from the fieldwork on London's ethnic entrepreneurships.

3.4.1 Family-based establishments

Ethnic ties and solidarity among migrants ensure that assistance and cooperation exist among group members, and that non-members are effectively excluded from membership privileges. Ethnic resources of social capital are primarily organized according to group boundaries in immigrants' social relations (Cornell 1996). The micro unit of ethnic solidarity is the family, which has also been the core of the ethnic business activity in London. Family values emerged as a key theme that permeated most migrants' narratives. Most informants highlighted the significant role that their families played in their lives, including unrelenting assistance in the conceptualization, start-up and operation of commercial ventures. Families provided finance, labour and moral support in times of hardship, and emphasized the familial boundaries of social solidarity among co-nationals. In most cases, extended family proved instrumental in the creation and development of businesses. Thus, my data corroborate scholars' contentions that familial resources remain the cornerstones of ethnic economies (Phizacklea 1983, Espiritu 1999, Verdaguer 2009).

Almost all the establishments examined in this study were family-based, and most were dependent upon the sole use of family labour. Brothers work together to run a coffee shop or a father works with his grown-up children or wife in a sandwich shop. The labour-intensive nature of ethnic shops requires as much labour input from their own family as possible and it is an essential character of these shops in which family and ethnic networks are necessary to sustain a successful business. Not only is family labour essential for manual chores, but the language skills of the second generation and their knowledge of the systemic requirements of running a small-scale business are also essential.

In some cases, mediation between the owner and the system was established by a grown-up son or a wife fluent in English who migrated to London at an early age.

Fathers and sons, brothers, brothers-in-law and close family members are the most common forms of business partnerships in London. Two generations from a nuclear family working together were observed, and the division of labour is based on generational differences between fathers and sons. In fact, fathers usually acted as the head of the business while sons focused on paperwork and external relations of the shop. A father explained this in the following statement:

> It is good to have your kids. Without my son it would have been possible to open these shops. I run this kebab shop and my son is responsible from the pool-saloon in the Central London. Moreover, he does all our paper work, orders and payments. One can only trust their own people.

This father also had his wife and daughter working in his kebab shop, as well as two other part-time hired labourers. This is a good example of how a family pooled their labour together to succeed in the world of ethnic business.

The husbands of two sisters ran a *döner*-kebab house. Their business initiative was established after their marriages, when they became relatives through their wives. Pooling their savings and labour together enabled them to embark upon their entrepreneurship. Their partnership also included their wives' skills and labour. Ali was the husband of the younger sister, and spoke about the shop and his experience of running it:

> ...you cannot trust other people in this country. Turks are not like Turks you know them back in Turkey. Everyone is different. We have a good arrangement here. My-brother-in-law and I work together and run this shop. We share everything, cost and income... Our wives are also a part of our business and help us to deal with paperwork and other external relation where our English is not enough to solve the problem. They help greatly with many dealings with authorities.

The role of family labour was so central in the ethnic business that some closed down their shops as a result of a sudden change in family circumstances. A shop owner was planning to scale down his business due to his wife's sickness. Since he owned two shops, he wanted to sell his sandwich shop, which required too much labour and organization without his wife's contribution, and he thought it was too hard to go on. The Turkish ethnic economy in London is based on family-based establishments that pool families' resources of labour and skills together. Partnerships formed between family members and relatives are the most common business establishments. In addition, there are different generations employed in the businesses and the prime example is fathers and sons working together. First generation migrant families usually take advantage of their children's language skills and their knowledge of the British system. What is observed is that the business establishments are usually run by fathers and sons, and are mostly male-dominated environments. However, women are seen as 'helpers' or 'contributors', since their primary role is motherhood, with the burden of household chores.

3.4.2 Financial resources

Due to the common assumption of migrants not having financial resources and being out of employment, start-up capital and gaining access to financial means for the business are significant issues in the literature on ethnic economies (Verdaguer 2009). Among London's Turkish entrepreneurs, people initially used their savings made during the garment years to establish their own family businesses and it was an advantage to have run a garment shop for today's self-employed entrepreneurs. This facilitated the social capital and a communal network to pool financial and labour resources together. They additionally tapped into various sources of ethnic credit, including loans from family and friends, merchandise credit, personal savings and pooling of other resources from their ethnic and family networks. Further, they frequently relied on the direct support of family members who, by maintaining a second job on the side, provided the bare necessities that allowed informants and their businesses to survive in those first difficult years.

A former garment sweatshop owner explained his history of opening a corner off-licence shop in North London. During the high times of the garment industry, he was running his own workshop, filled with workers from his large network of relatives and family members. He was a kind of big brother (*abi*) for most of his close relatives living in London, as he facilitated their immigration to the UK. However, when the garment business began to go down, he went bankrupt. This left him penniless. Later, he decided to open up an off-licence shop in London and told me that 'I knocked every door I knew in London and collected money from people whom I know. I collected almost 75 grand a night! If I didn't have good relations with people when I was running the garment shop, no one would support me in my new venture.' His communal networks were strengthened by the role he played when his extended relatives wanted to immigrate to the UK. Moreover, he was a well known personality within his ethnic community. The trust and solidarity networks he nurtured throughout his life in London turned out to be a source of financial security in his new business venture.

Hüseyin's story was another interesting case of using the financial resources of a close, tight family. Before he opened up his *döner*-kebab shop in Southampton, he was living in London. In the late 1980s, Hüseyin and his wife arrived in London and worked in garment shops for more than five years, and saved up some money. After the collapse of the industry, they spent a few years unemployed, and waited for a suitable business opportunity. Then, the expansion of the Turkish ethnic economy provided a window of opportunity for them, and they decided to run their shop. They pooled their savings and added them to the savings of his brother-in-law to open a *döner*-kebab shop in Southampton where there were no other competitors. Hüseyin and his brother-in-law became business partners. These two families not only pooled their financial resources together, but put their labour together to run the shop.

Migrant entrepreneurs did not mention whether they used any commercial loans but stated how they got the lease of their shops from the local councils. Their heavy reliance on ethnic sources of credit underlines their lack of access to commercial loans. This is due to a large reliance of Turkish migrants on welfare benefits in maintaining their lives in the UK, and to the fact that their work in the garment industry was mostly informal and cash-in-hand work. They were not able to integrate these earnings into the formal banking system and their credit ratings are low. Therefore, their inability to obtain commercial credit both exacerbates their reliance on ethnic credit and fosters their participation in informal loan schemes which have been developed within the circles of migrants and are based on trust and solidarity. Some community figures acted like a bank by collecting the savings of migrants and crediting it to others in need of credit.

3.4.3 Migrants' motivations

The literature of ethnic economies has distinguished between two types of disadvantage affecting new immigrants upon their arrival to the host country (Light and Gold 2000). The first is related to resources possessed by immigrants prior to their arrival such as human capital and class-based resources (education, health, etc.).

Access to a good education, to a healthy diet, to a reliable healthcare system, to networking opportunities, and to a positive productive than others. As such, resource disadvantaged entrepreneurs are handicapped from the very beginning, and start their quest for economic incorporation from a lower starting point. Any discrimination they encounter throughout their journey is in addition to that prior discrimination they suffered early on in their lives.

(Verdaguer 2009:82–83)

The second is the labour market discrimination they face in their host countries, because of discrimination or blocked mobility in the labour market. These types of disadvantage are not mutually exclusive, given that immigrants can be subject to both simultaneously, or to none. It is assumed that the intertwined disadvantages result in migrants' engagement in self-employment in ethnic economies (Verdaguer 2009). Therefore, the migrants' major motivations are to overcome their labour market disadvantages through their economic activity as ethnic entrepreneurs.

My interview data confirm this theoretical argument, since the Turkish population in London was made up of resource disadvantaged entrepreneurs and experienced labour market discrimination. First generation migrants are usually from the low-income groups of the Turkish population, and have mainly rural backgrounds. Thus, migrants have low class-based resources and this translates into poor educational attainments as well as a poor capacity to master English. When immigrants do not have a good command of English language, have accents or when their educational credentials are not recognized by their host countries or employers, they suffer from labour market discrimination (Verdaguer 2009). The result has been that Turkish migrants remained out of the mainstream labour market and only engaged in informal economic activities with cash-in-hand incomes, such as garment work. This has combined with the migrants' concerns for not losing their access to the benefit system, as jobs in the secondary labour market with low pay and harsh working conditions are the only other option they have. In this regard, structural factors as well as migrants' low human capital emerged as another main determinant in fuelling migrants' determination to become self-employed. Here is a testimony from a shop owner:

We Turks only did garment work before and did not do any other work in London. It is very difficult for us to find good jobs in this country since we don't know English well... If I work for a supermarket I can only get five pounds an hour which will only pay my rent. How can I look after my family with this income?... This is why you can find so many Turks having their own shops so that I can at least make a living out of it.

It is often expressed in the interviews that Turkish people could only engage in the ethnic economy and take up the jobs offered by the ethnic economy. They were all aware of their limited economic opportunities and the low economic returns they could gain through their work in other jobs in the mainstream labour market. Therefore, this research confirms the fact that migrant entrepreneurs are more likely to become self-employed due to the lack of other opportunities available. Even with extremely limited mainstream job opportunities, Turkish migrants were quick to take up the self-employment opportunities generated by the Turkish ethnic economy. A growing demand for *döner*-kebabs was supported by the example of Germany, where many migrants became self-employed. A lucrative business opportunity for those who were ready to take up the rising tide of the Turkish ethnic economy was a good source of employment for many others.

It may be argued that the main motivation for self-employment is to serve mainly their own ethnic clientele (Tolciu et al. 2010). As expressed in the early pages of this chapter, the Turkish ethnic economy is not only for the Turkish clientele, but serves a much wider customer base and has an international character. However, there is a group which exclusively serves Turkish people, such as lawyers and accountants. This group of self-employed people is generally composed of well-educated second generation migrants who preferred to have their own businesses to serve their own community. Indeed, these people had a competitive advantage in serving Turkish clients as they could speak Turkish and were more likely to attract Turkish migrants than any other British professionals. Therefore, it is common to see the ads of lawyers and accountants whenever one attends a meeting or gathering arranged by Turkish community organizations. The lawyers advertise for accident claims, citizenship and welfare benefit claims, and the accountants target big kebab houses and restaurants to add to their client lists.

An odd characteristic of the Turkish ethnic economy in London is the fact that the first generation migrants generally served a wide range of clients, and managed to diffuse into British culture through their traditional food and entrepreneurial activities, which have diversified in many respects. However, second generation professionals target

Turkish clientele in their self-employment activities. For this group, it is much easier to establish themselves as professionals within the Turkish community due to their ability to speak the language and their knowledge of Turkish culture and people. These findings are in opposition to those stated in the literature with regard to migrants' self-employment motivations.

3.4.4   Intergenerational connections

The term second generation encompasses a very heterogeneous population, consisting of individuals that develop and engage in various forms with the ethnic economy. In London's Turkish community, I use the term mainly to refer to the children of the first generation migrants, even though they were not born in the UK but were raised and educated there. The second generation individuals' engagement in the ethnic economy is vital as because of the limited language ability of the first generation Turkish migrants, it would have been very difficult to integrate into the world of self-employment without support from the second generation members of their families. Some parents also embark upon running a shop because they feel that self-employment will secure the future of their children, or they will support their children's establishment financially.

A father whose two sons run a coffee shop in Dolston explained how he and his wife facilitated the business venture of their sons.

> My wife and I worked in the textile for a long time and did not really know the ways we could help our kids to succeed in school. So they dropped out of school as soon as they could and it is very difficult for them to find good jobs without a proper education ... But now we have this shop so we don't worry about their future any more.

Although this father stated that the business belonged to his sons he was very involved in the shop and worked there every day. He still wanted to make sure of its success and smooth operation. In this case, the sons were bosses and the father was a worker. However, this did not change the family-based character of the business.

In other cases, families formed a union with their children to run their businesses. A man who owned a corner-shop explains about his family business:

> My son is everything for the shop. I just do the manual work but he deals with every other things and paperwork. He was born and

raised in London, he speak good English. He is also familiar with the laws and regulations and knows his rights and duties in the UK but I cannot even speak proper English.

The response of his son was interesting:

My father would not be able to start his business in London without me. Many years ago, when he moved to London he had us to look after and he only worked in garment sweatshops with many others just like him and with my mum...He would not dare to set up his own business as he speaks little English. For me it is a different story, I grew up into this system that made it much easier for me.

It is evident that language abilities contribute to the general success of ethnic shops, and language is not only be seen in a linguistic way but also in a cultural way, knowing how one needs to behave within the British system, including rights, regulations and other systemic information. In this way, having the second generation brought up in Britain makes the running of their entrepreneurships easier as a result of their language and intercultural skills.

Another group of second generation individuals is those professionals serving Turkish clients. For them, being Turkish serves as a competitive advantage over entrepreneurs without Turkish origin such as in the cases of Turkish lawyers and accountants and, thus, is a rational entrepreneurial behaviour. Therefore, these second generation professionals rely on their linguistic and cultural assets to have access to a network of Turkish customers. In summary, the second generation is a bridge between the Turkish community and the wider mainstream society, using their so-called Western socialization and education experiences. They either help their families to go one step further in joining the ranks of ethnic entrepreneurs, or they become professionals mostly serving Turkish customers to help solve their juristic and other administrative problems. Thus, the second generation are evidently mediators of their communities and smooth out community integration.

3.4.5   Labour: Family, co-ethnic and self-exploitation

The small-scale nature of business in London's Turkish ethnic economy results in self-exploitation of the labour of business owners and their families. This is the only way to survive and succeed in the highly competitive business environment. They work extremely long hours, sometimes averaging 15 hours per day, and never have a weekly holiday or summer breaks. They have to run the shop around the clock, as they stay open very long hours. For example, one informant vividly described his routine of work in his shop:

> I come to shop early every morning. Before the opening I have to prepare the stuff, vegetables, do the orders and if I need to run errands I do it. When the shop opens I work to meet the orders and serve customers. The shop stays open till quite late. Even when I close the shop, I have to do the cleaning and etc. My life is here in this small shop, day and night... sometimes I feel like I stop living and just run this shop. I miss seeing my children's face as when I go home, they are asleep and I leave early before they are up!

One of the expected outcomes of self-employment is the sense of isolation. It is often expressed by the informants that they generally attributed their sense of isolation to long working hours and confinement to their shops. As I discuss in the following chapters, women married to *döner*-kebab shop owners also expressed their concerns about the long hours of work that their husbands do and the resulting loneliness it imposes on women in dealings with family matters and children. In addition, many participants stressed that their necessary self-exploitation prevented them from meeting friends, acquaintances and even family. The sense of isolation and marginalization may be even harsher for those working away from London since their families and friends are left behind in London when they take up a business opportunity in another city. Some men go solo in their business venture, leaving their wives and children behind and occasionally visit them when they have time.

Extra hired labour is needed in most of the establishments, especially in restaurants. In this case, ethnic entrepreneurs preferred to hire co-ethnics from their own referral networks. In fact, many informants explained that they prefer to hire from the circles of their own family, kin or from those people who have the same place of origin as them, *hemşehri*. A shop owner expresses his preference for hiring from his own community in the following statement:

> I like hiring our own *hemşehri*(s) because we know each other. As *hemşehir*s we understand each other. It is really difficult to trust strangers and people you don't know. For example I always hire people from my own family. For my shop, I had my sister's daughter

cook for the other staff and she also made pastry for customers. This is the best way to hire as I know that I can trust her.

In the recruitment process, word of mouth is the most used method and the vacancies are rarely advertised in ethnic media or in shop windows. In fact, many of the entrepreneurs liked to use co-ethnic referral networks because they could better trust these individuals, feeling more comfortable with their own. Ahmet, a restaurant owner, told me about his experience of hiring workers:

> Once I hired someone who told me that he was a student here, and I did not know about him at all. One day he came to the restaurant and told me that he needed to work. I always need extra labour in the restaurant and I hired him. After a few weeks of good work he asked a large sum of money because her mum was sick back in Turkey and needed money for her treatment. I gave him the money and the next day he disappeared. This was a good lesson for me not to hire people I did not know. This is why it is always best to hire from your own people as you can only trust them ... In our business you got to have trustworthy people around you because from time to time you leave your business and your money to those who work for you.

The operation of small-scale ethnic businesses is heavily based on family labour and networks of support. The size of the community and the extent of the ethnic economy are often dependent upon the constant flux of new migrants, which is an important source of growing numbers of customers. As more and more people try to take advantage of the growing ethnic business there is an increasing demand for ethnic labour which is usually topped up by the cheap labour supply of newly arriving migrants. The Turkish ethnic economy has a large labour pool from which it can draw its fresh labour supply and this labour works mostly on informal terms. The source of labour first comes from asylum seekers waiting for their applications to come through who not allowed to work, thus they take some cash-in-hand work in the ethnic economy. Second, London is an international centre for foreign students to learn English and it attracts thousands of students from all over the world. Thus, Turkish students offer their labour for service in the ethnic economy and they are a source of cheap and docile labour. Third, undocumented Turkish immigrants also earn a living through their work in the ethnic economy. Besides self-exploitation and family labour, ethnic shops in London mostly rely on these forms of cheap and reliable labour for their operation and these three sources of labour are also the customers of the goods and services that are produced in the Turkish ethnic economy. One may add women's labour to this list, but the degree of Turkish women's contribution to the Turkish ethnic economy will be discussed fully in Chapter 6.

Together with the slow-down of incoming immigrants in recent years, a new trend of hiring students from other Turkic countries such as Azerbaijan and Uzbekistan has been emerging. One can find these students working in Turkish restaurants such as Sofra and Tas in central London. This is a good indicator of how ethnic labour markets extend from the inner circle of labour outwards, but still try to somehow find an ethnic relation between employer and employee. In the world of the ethnic economy, the term 'ethnic' translates into cheap, reliable and docile labour that is ready to work for long hours for very small returns and mostly under informal terms. This economic cooperation of migrants living in the margins of British society promises success only in terms of the extreme exploitation of labour and communal sacrifice for very small returns and marginal incomes.

3.5 Conclusion

The Turkish ethnic economy is a European wide phenomenon, and has been attracting scholarly attention for its capacity to create employment and economic contribution in European countries where Turkish migrants reside. The growth of the ethnic economy was a response by the Turkish population in Germany to the neo-liberal industrial restructuring that left many industrial workers unemployed. Initially, the ethnic economy aimed to serve the Turkish customers but the invention of the *döner*-kebab has helped it to quickly become a popular food source all over Europe. As a result, Turks emerged as self-employed entrepreneurs in almost all Western European countries. The central role of Germany was maintained as the supplier of wholesale Turkish ethnic food and its distribution all over Europe. Having *döner*-kebab manufacturers helped to standardize the ways in which kebabs were served and people no longer needed to be a skilled kebab cook to own a kebab shop. Through wholesale productions in Germany, large-scale factories are owned and run by Turkish people, resulting in the easy employment of Turkish migrants in the production and sale of *döner* takeaways all over Europe, which generated a considerable amount of employment for Turkish migrants in Europe.

In the UK, the Turkish ethnic economy of London has been expanding since the early 2000s, and it became the main economic activity of Turkish migrants after the closure of garment workshops in London.

Despite the limited data available it is estimated that the *döner*-kebab business has an annual contribution of over £2.2 billion to the British economy. This indicates a large business with a large clientele base. Turkish people are the main entrepreneurs in the *döner*-kebab business but their ethnic entrepreneurship is not only limited to *döner*-kebab and has diversified in recent years to include corner off-licence shops, coffee shops and restaurants. Based on small-scale shops, family labour and resources, the Turkish ethnic economy in London is a typical case of ethnic economy. Families used their own savings accumulated in hey days of garment production to open their shops and utilized mainly family labour to run these shops. Many people opted to form a partnership with a family member or a relative to open their shops due to harsh working conditions and long hours of work required. Thus, the partners and other family members can share the burden of running a shop for almost 20 hours a day. Fathers working with their sons or brothers working together are the most common forms of business partnerships established in the community. The second generation's contribution through their input of language skills and their knowledge of the British system is a significant effect in the expansion of the ethnic economy. Since the ethnic solidarity and trust are the building blocks of the Turkish ethnic economy, when there is a need for extra labour, it is mostly recruited from the intimate circles of the ethnic community. In the regard of ethnic economy, the word of 'ethnic' means to be cheap, reliable and docile labour that work long hours, under the rates of minimum wage and in informal terms. Therefore, the economic cooperation of migrants living in the margins of British society promises success only in extreme exploitation of labour and communal sacrifice for very small returns and marginal incomes.

The overall picture of the Turkish ethnic economy in London is one with a vibrant character and growing nature. The success and expansion of the economy has generated a sense of accomplishment in the Turkish community. They feel proud of being able to transform the area in which they live, and realize that through their economic endeavours being acknowledged by the whole British society. Thus, as a result of their economic contribution they are a respectable part the London community and positively contribute to the society in which they live. In Chapter 4, an evaluation of the Turkish community in London, its migration trajectory, communal networks and the role of community organization in migrants' lives will be presented.

4
Migratory Trends and the 'Turkish' Community in London

Ali Haydar was from Dersim, a city with a large emigrating population in Turkey. Many opt to migrate as a response to the ethnic and religious discrimination they face. Now, it is possible to find people from Dersim in many different parts of the world. His sister, for example, lived in Canada, and Ali has been in the UK for more than ten years. He had a kebab shop in a quiet street in London. Like many Kurdish Alevis, he decided to leave Dersim when he was 23 years old. He entered the UK through a student visa, but then applied for refugee status. In the early days after his arrival he stayed with his relatives living in London and worked as a waiter in Turkish restaurants. After some years, he decided to open his own kebab house with a Kurdish partner from Northern Iraq, who had also entered the UK through Istanbul.

One hears many stories similar to Ali's, regarding people from Turkey in London. Many people escaping social exclusion and discrimination that lead to poverty and poor living prospects for themselves and for their children end up in London, which is one of the largest metropolitan cities in the world. However, the Turkish migration to Europe started with the guest worker programme after World War II. Early movements aimed at meeting labour shortages in Europe were replaced by family unification and increasing asylum applications of Turkish people from the 1980s onwards. Although the Turkish migration to Europe has changed shape and diversified greatly over time, it still generates a substantial movement of people across countries. This migratory trend has generated its own transnational space in countries where Turkish migrants are outnumbered, such as Germany, the UK and France. Migrants establish their own networks and social organizations, which provide political, cultural, religious or social ties with their country of origin, and the excluded identities of Turkey, such as the Alevis and the Kurdish, gain visibility.

Chapter 4 introduces the Turkish community of London and their migration patterns by outlining the details of their settlement and their lives in London. The literature examining the communities from Turkey in the UK mostly portrays them as an invisible or silent community, and most literature is devoted to the heterogeneous nature of ethnic and religious backgrounds of people from Turkey, but this book shows their visibility and economic contribution to the larger British society, by moving away from diverse identities and religious backgrounds, and focusing on the migrants' common experiences and survival strategies. This analysis contextualizes the ways in which the changing economic activities of the Turkish community over the course of their migration and the labour requirement of those activities influence the ways in which the Turkish community interacts with the wider society, as well as women's role in this interaction.

4.1   The Turkish migration to Europe: From guest workers to refugees

In Turkey, emigration to Europe has taken different forms and meanings for many people for more than half a century. This has meant remittances for economic development, or people moving away from the political oppositions in the 1980s or from the Kurdish ethnic minority in the 1990s. It also meant a shift in the pattern of Turkish migration to Europe from the guest worker regime to family unifications and then the migration of asylum seekers from excluded groups and minorities. Emigration was the dominant force in the Turkish migration system after World War II, and the country was a classic emigration country. Sema Erder shows that for a long time Turkey defined its migration regime as a country with no foreigners (2007) since the main driving force of its migration was based on the ideology of nation building that was to attract those of Turkic origins left out of borders after the collapse of Ottoman Empire to migrate back in Turkey. The country only accepted immigrants of Turkish origin, called *muhacir*(s), and granted them settlement and, eventually, citizenship rights. In this context, only *muhacir* came into the country and those who migrated abroad were seen as *gurbetci*[1] (Erder 2007). This regime was constructed around the nation building strategy of the Turkish Republic, and remained the main discourse in Turkish migration policy making until the early 2000s when Turkey began its EU accession negotiations (İçduygu 2010a).

Emigration to Germany had been a hallmark of the country's migration regime. In particular, after World War II, emigration was a significant part of Turkey's migration strategy. In view of Turkey's rapid population growth in the 1950s, and slow industrial employment generation capacity, immigration was a way of reducing demographic and labour market pressures (Paine 1974, İçduygu and Sert 2009, Bilgili 2012). Turkey's country specific situation overlapped with the labour shortages experienced by the flourishing economies of many European countries such as Germany, the Netherlands and France. In this context, Turkey started sending its citizens abroad as labour migrants, in the same way that Morocco and Southern European countries had. Before any official labour agreements were signed between Western European countries and Turkey, workers were recruited, for the most part, by firms on the basis of job availability (Bilgili 2012). The first official labour agreement with Turkey was signed by Germany in 1961, and other agreements followed shortly after, with Austria, Belgium and the Netherlands in 1964, France in 1965, and Sweden and Australia in 1967. Other agreements were signed with the United Kingdom in 1961, Switzerland in 1971, Denmark in 1973 and Norway in 1981 (Hecker 2006, İçduygu 2008).

The outflow of workers continued incessantly, and reached its peak in the 1970s. Between 1961 and 1973, one million Turkish workers travelled to Western European nations. The number of Turkish workers in Western Europe reached 1.3 million in 1973, of which three-quarters were located in Germany. In 1973, when Turkey's labour force was 15 million, including 10 million employed in agriculture, one-sixth of Turks with non-farm jobs were located in Western Europe. There were over 1.5 million Turkish workers on waiting lists to go abroad in 1973 (Martin 2012). According to Martin (2012), during the peak years of Turkish labour migration between 1968 and 1973, the Turkish Employment Service (TES) handled the exit of about 525,000 workers, 80% of whom went to Germany. Other Turks travelled on their own to Western Europe, found jobs and received work permits. The main characteristic of most guest workers was that they were from the Western, more modernized parts of Turkey, especially in the early phase of the Turkey–EU migration process, and the TES listed the workers as skilled. However, most of them ended up filling unskilled industrial jobs in Western Europe. About 80% of Turkish migrants were men between the ages of 20 and 40 (Martin 2012).

The guest worker programme was designed to be temporary for the host country and for the migrants themselves. The famous quote 'we asked for workers, but human beings came' summarized the situation of the guest workers in Europe. Moreover, many of these migrants had invited their families to join them in the destination countries; making family ties a more prominent cause for legal migration into Europe than active labour recruitment during the period following the 1970s. At the time of the guest worker programmes, Turkey introduced various measures to channel remittances in such a way that migrants' earnings could positively affect the country's economic development. With the inflow of hard currency, Turkey was able to import the inputs and technology that were crucial for industrialization and international trade (Penninx 1982). Hence, Turkish citizens living abroad, especially those living within the EU, were expected to provide economic support through financial remittances and investments back in Turkey. In the early years of labour migration, the country was successful in channelling remittances as the numbers show. Migrant remittances stood at $93 million in 1967 and reached $1.4 billion in 1978 (İçduygu 2006). Yet in the long-term, these programmes failed to achieve their objectives due to mismanagement and corruption (Abadan-Unat 2006, Akgündüz 2008, İçduygu and Kirişçi 2009). On top of this, the oil crisis in 1974 stopped labour recruitment, and the economic downturn that followed made it even more difficult to channel remittances back to Turkey.

The oil crisis that started in 1973 put an end to Europe's open-door policy regarding migrant workers, who were welcomed when the economy needed them but were expected to leave when times were hard. For example, with the start of the oil crisis in 1973, the German government halted the recruitment of low-skilled foreign workers. The migratory flow to Europe took a different path after the 1970s and the major trend become family unifications and migration through marriages. Although family unification was initially discouraged, it later became the main reason for migration to Europe from Turkey. When jobless guest workers began to unify with their families, rather than return in the mid-1970s, the German government discouraged family unification, including making spouses wait several years before they could get work permits and designating German cities with more than 6% of foreigners 'overburdened' and made off-limits to new foreigners seeking residence permits (Kofman et al. 2000). As will be shown in the following chapter, women following their husbands, but with no work permits, became part of the the the informal job sector, working for small returns to support their families left behind at home.

In the 1980s and 1990s the main migratory trend to Europe was the movement of asylum seekers. What seems to have contributed to this increase initially was the military intervention in civilian politics in Turkey in 1980, and then, an increase in violence surrounding efforts to suppress a separatist movement by Turkey's large Kurdish minority. On-going migratory flows were also supported by economic crisis and increasing income inequalities which were analysed as push factors that encouraged emigration in the 1980s and 1990s in Turkey. It was not, however, only the economic situation that created extreme push factors in the country. The political instability that emerged in the 1980s and 1990s, and the economic and political liberalization that took place in the 1990s, were among the main drivers of migration trends to Europe. According to United Nations High Commissioner for Refugees (UNHCR) statistics, between 1980 and 2010 almost one million Turkish citizens applied for asylum in various European countries (İçduygu 2010b). Although asylum applications were spread over different countries, there was a concentration in Western European countries such as Germany, Britain and France, due to the fact that the applicants preferred to travel to countries where earlier migrants had generated a strong web of networks and a transnational community. Since the worst of the conflict between the armed forces and separatist rebels wound down in the second half of the 1990s, and was followed by the gradual introduction of political reforms, asylum applications have fallen since then (İçduygu 2010b).

What has been observed in the last two decades is the diversification of migratory flows from Turkey to Europe. İçduygu and Kirişçi (2009) argue that globalization contributed to various types of mobilities and is responsible for new migration trends: among them, in particular, declining flows of new labour migration, asylum seekers and irregular migrants, and the increasing movement of highly skilled professionals and students (İçduygu and Kirişçi 2009). More recently, it is estimated that there is an annual arrival of 15,000–20,000 new Turkish citizens to Europe, who intend to stay long-term (İçduygu 2010b). More than one-third of these are highly skilled professionals and students. There are almost no new labour migrants, except those who arrive through family reunification, asylum seeking and irregular flows. There are approximately 3.5 million people of Turkish origin living in Europe, of whom about 800,000 have taken up the citizenship of their host countries (İçduygu and Kiriþçi 2009). Turkish data suggest that there were 3.8 million Turkish citizens living abroad in 2009, including 1.7 million in Germany, down from a peak of 2.2 million in the late 1990s (many Turks are also citizens of the countries in which they reside). Germany had about three-quarters of the Turkish citizens that were living abroad in the early 1980s; today, less than half of the Turks living abroad are located in Germany. Turkey had 1.3 million foreign-born residents in

2000, including almost one million Turkish citizens who were born outside Turkey (Martin 2012).

The current issues surrounding Turkish migration to Europe mostly relate to integration and future migration. In regard to the Turkish immigrant presence in Europe, there are many who fear the arrival of more migrants from Turkey if Turkey were to become a member of the EU. However, the latest trends show the opposite, as some members of second/third generation Turks are finding the Turkish labour market more attractive for job opportunities. More and more people are returning to Turkey since the economic crisis of 2008 began in Europe. According to Baysan (2011:5), almost 35,000 people per year return to Turkey from Germany. A further major issue related to Turkish migrants in Europe is that of integration. The integration problems of Turks, which were associated with employment in the early 1970s, are today concerned with economic inactivity as exemplified by low labour force participation rates and high unemployment rates (Martin 2012). Therefore, the growth of the Turkish ethnic economy all over Europe needs to be contextualized in relation to the visibility and contribution of Turkish communities in Europe. It has changed the outlook of the community from a welfare dependent group to a more productive, active and visible migrant community. This book aims to highlight this point further in the following chapters. The remaining part of this chapter examines the migratory flow of people from Turkey into the UK.

4.2   Counting in or out: 'Turks' in Britain

The literature examining 'Turks' in the UK mostly portrays them as an invisible or silent community and most research is devoted to the heterogeneous nature of ethnic and religious backgrounds of people from Turkey. The main disadvantage of this analysis is its power in shifting the focus away from homogeneous characters and common experiences of the community. Through an emphasis on their economic activity, this book aims to build a picture of the Turkish community in Britain that focuses on their visibility and economic contribution to the larger British society, rather than by dividing them along the lines of their ethnicity and religious beliefs. However, this does not mean a lack of acknowledgment of the fact that there are different ethnic and religious backgrounds that are also divided by political and ideological aspects, such as leftists, radical Muslims, nationalists, etc. Even while acknowledging this fact, throughout the book I will be using 'Turk' or 'Turkish' to refer to the different groups from Turkey. Using the adjective 'Turkish' is for practical reasons and does not refer to an ethnic group. Therefore, Turkish, in this context, means people or citizens of Turkey. During the interviews conducted in this research, people were quite open about their identities and ethnic backgrounds. In most cases, they described themselves as Turkish or Kurdish, but in other cases as Alevies or Sunnis. In these diversified identities, the only common character is their homeland and birth country.

It is true that the Turkish community in the UK is relatively small, compared with the much larger ethnic minority groups originating from the Caribbean and Indian subcontinent, which has certainly contributed to what is seen as their 'invisibility' within multicultural Britain. Mehmet Ali (1985), for instance, has often referred to Turkish speaking communities in the UK as a 'silenced minority'. Another factor contributing to their 'invisibility' is their self-sufficiency as a group, due to their employment in the ethnic labour market. These strong kinship and social networks, however, disguise many of the social problems faced by large sections of the Turkish speaking population, a significant number of whom live in some of the most deprived areas in London. The population is disproportionately engaged in low-wage employment, while much of the Turkish speaking youth population leaves education with few qualifications. Another concern is the poor level of English among many first generation immigrants (Enneli et al. 2005).

According to the 2011 Census, the Turkey-born population living in England and Wales numbered 91,115. This is an increase of 72.3% from 52,892 in 2011. This does not include the second generation of UK-born Turks and Turkish Kurds. Altogether, 101,633 people identify themselves as Turkish, another 19,057 as Turkish-Cypriot and 48,935 as Kurdish (form Turkey, Iraq, Iran and Syria), although the proportion of Kurds originating from Turkey is probably the largest group in this category. Further to this, 99,423 people said their main language is Turkish (these include Turkish-born, UK-born to Turkish-born parents and Cypriot-born Turks) and 48,239 said that it is Kurdish (of these a certain proportion would be Turkish-born or born to Turkish-born Kurdish parents). Of the Turkey-born, 59,596 (65.4%) reside in London, and 37% were concentrated in only three boroughs – Enfield, Haringey and Hackney. Kurdish speaking people are far more dispersed across the UK than the Turkish speaking population. Of the Turkish speaking population, 73% reside in London, in contrast to only 31% of the Kurdish speaking population (D'Angelo et al. 2013).

Statistics are invariably too imprecise in migration studies. This is also true for Turkish migrants in the UK and, for example, the Turkish

Consulate website provides an estimate of 150,000 Turkish nationals living in the UK, noting that they mostly reside in London (Islington, Hackney, Haringey, Stoke Newington, Turnpike Lane, Newington Green in the North, as well as Peckham and Lewisham in the South), Birmingham, Manchester, Liverpool and Leeds (Consulate General for the Republic of Turkey in London 2006). The Consulate's estimate, which is higher than the official figure, is rather dubious, although it most likely includes the children of all those settled in the UK who were born in Turkey, as well as a number of 'illegal immigrants' as stated by the Consulate website. Erdemir and Vasta (2007) compiled data from the Home Office Statistical Bulletins and between 1984 and 2005 alone, the numbers granted citizenship amounted to 47,008. The Home Office records also show that between 1986 and 2005, there were 36,569 Turkish nationals applying for asylum in the UK (Erdemir and Vasta 2007).

A 2009 report by the Greater London Authority (GLA) shows that London is home to a large proportion of the Turkish, Kurdish and Turkish-Cypriot communities. Between 1991 and 2001, the number of people born in Turkey living in Britain doubled and two-thirds of this increase was in London. Within London, there are particular concentrations of communities in Enfield, Haringey, Hackney, Islington and Waltham Forest. The age structure of the communities reflects their likely time of arrival in the UK. Turkish-Cypriots have been in the UK the longest, and have an age structure very similar to the overall population. The Turkish population is younger and the Kurdish population, who mostly arrived more recently, are younger still. Adults born in Turkey and Cyprus were less likely than the general population to hold higher-level qualifications, and far more likely to have no recognized qualifications. Those born in Iran, Iraq and Syria, on the other hand, are much more likely to hold higher-level qualifications (GLA 2009).

A 2007 study from the Institute for Public Policy Research (IPPR) on Britain's immigrants estimated that for Turkish-born people the unemployment rate was about 7% compared with 4% for the whole population, and the proportion of Income Support claimants was 21%, which is more than five times the national average of 4%. The proportion of the population living in social housing was 4% for Turkish immigrants while the rate was 9% for the whole of Britain. For those Turkish-born who were employed, the IPPR estimated an average annual income of £14,750, compared with a national average of £21,250. The average hourly earnings of Turkish-born people was £8.20, compared with a rate of £11.10 for the UK average (IPPR 2007). Another research study by D'Angelo et al. (2013), with 112 participants from the Turkish-Kurdish community in London, showed that 60 participants were in employment (either full-time, part-time or self-employed), while the others were students (8), housewives (18) or unemployed (21). Twenty-eight people declared they had never had a job in the UK and 12 had a partner or spouse in this situation. This is a strong indicator of the low rate of employment in the community, which corresponds with a high level of welfare dependency. In the same research, it was found that most respondents received some kind of welfare benefits. In particular, 62 households received housing benefits, 52 council tax benefits, 32 child tax credits, 24 working tax credits and 19 income support (many respondents reported receiving several of the benefits) (D'Angelo et al. 2013). In an overall evaluation, the Turkish community has an extensive reliance on welfare benefits and has low levels of recorded employment.

In regard to the main economic activity of the community, the IPPR (2007) report shows that the Turkish community has the highest number of self-employed people. The self-employment rate among the economically active working age population is 35% for the Turkish-born, followed by a rate of 33% in the Pakistani population. The rate for the UK-born population is only 13%. This is a significant indicator of the growing importance of the Turkish ethnic economy in generating self-employment for Turkish immigrants. In fact, it shows that Turks stand out as the immigrant group with the highest self-employment rate and frequency of running their own business. The most common employment and business activities are in the retail and catering areas, including restaurants, takeaway foods, cafés, supermarkets, minicab offices, off-licences, jewellery, fashion and import-export. The GLA report gives more specific information in regard to the community's economy activities. The GLA report (2009) also shows that over 25% of Londoners born in Turkey and 19% of those born in Cyprus were involved in the wholesale and retail trade, compared with 14% of the general population. Twenty-two per cent of those born in Turkey and 12% of those born in Cyprus were employed in hotels and restaurants, compared with 5% of the general population. Nearly 48% of Kurdish employees worked fewer than 30 hours per week, as did 34% of Turkish employees and nearly 26% of Turkish-Cypriot employees. The London average was 16%. Unemployment was more than twice as high for Turkish and Kurdish people than the London average. Rates of limiting long-term illness were also higher for Turkish and Kurdish people than for the population of London as a whole. Those who came to the UK as asylum seekers were especially likely to have sustained physical and psychological injuries from war or torture. Kurdish and Turkish people were more likely to live in property rented from the council or a housing association than the London population as a whole, while Turkish-Cypriots were more likely to be owner-occupiers (GLA 2009).

4.3   Turkish-Cypriots, mainland Turks and Kurds from Turkey

The migration of Turks to the UK displays distinct historical patterns and trajectories, as they arrived at different times and for a range of reasons. Three immigrant groups make up the Turkish community: Turkish-Cypriots, mainland Turks and Kurds from Turkey. These three groups can also be divided into sub-groups according to their ethnic, cultural, social and political backgrounds. Communities are also different with regard to their processes of migration, as the three groups migrated to the UK within different time periods and under different circumstances. Before presenting the London fieldwork findings of Turkish and Kurdish groups, it is necessary to lay out the migratory trajectory of the Turkish community in Britain.

The Turkish-Cypriots were the first to immigrate. Although the first arrivals began in the 1930s, the main influx took place in the 1950s and 1960s. Since Cyprus was a British colony from 1878 until 1960, this made the UK a prime destination for many Cypriots. Arrivals peaked in 1960–1961, two years that coincided with the withdrawal of British troops and the loss of well paid jobs associated with the British colonial presence. The political situation in Cyprus was also an important factor affecting migration patterns until the 1970s. According to Enneli et al. (2005), an estimated 120,000 Cypriot Turks across three generations live in the UK. Cypriot Turks are the wealthiest group among Turks and Kurds because they were the first group to migrate to the UK and because their ability to speak the English language provided them with advantages in establishing businesses. Turkish-Cypriots arrived mainly with their families, intending to settle in the UK, and emphasized their affinity with the 'British way of life' as a pragmatic attempt to be accepted (Robins and Aksoy 2001:690). They were assisted by earlier Greek-Cypriot migrants in finding housing and employment. They were predominantly employed in the textile industry, and in hotels and restaurants in London (Thomson 2006). After opening up their own businesses, Cypriot Turks started to employ Turkish migrants. They created social networks in London. Mainland Turks and Cypriot Turks who live and work in the same areas of London are involved in similar social and cultural activities. Within the Turkish community, Cypriot Turks were the first to migrate to Britain and they have had an important role in setting up businesses for themselves and for mainland Turks and Kurds from Turkey (Şimşek 2012). Over time, the Turkish-Cypriots became more self-sufficient as a group by establishing their own businesses (such as textile factories, retail and wholesale shops), while a significant number of Turkish-Cypriot women worked from home as dressmakers – a skill they had learned back in Cyprus (Thomson 2006).

Mainland Turks began to arrive from the early 1970s onwards, first single men, then later in the decade they were joined by their wives and children. The migration increased following the military coup in Turkey on 12 March 1971. As a result of this situation, the first political migration from Turkey to the United Kingdom began with educated young people who established an organizational structure and socio-political networks with regard to their political stand in the United Kingdom (Şimşek 2012). Another significant political event in Turkey that accelerated migration to the UK occurred in 1978, when Sunni-Muslims attacked Alevi people in Kahramanmaraş. As a result of this massacre, more than 100 Alevi people were killed, and many villages and houses were destroyed. In the late 1970s and early 1980s, a large number of Alevi people from Kahramanmaraş migrated to the United Kingdom. It was the starting point of the Alevi migration from Turkey to the United Kingdom which established transnational networks among Alevi people in Turkey, the United Kingdom and Germany (Şimşek 2012). The military coup in Turkey in 1980 brought a subsequent wave of Turkish immigrants to the UK, many via Germany in 1984 (Thomson 2006). The 1980s coup pushed many intellectuals, educated people, trade union activists and professionals into migrating to Europe, some seeking political asylum in Britain (Mehmet Ali 2001:7–8). People who migrated after the 1980s came from the rural areas of Turkey, and differed from the educated migrants who came to England in the 1970s from the larger cities of Turkey. The military coup in Turkey further motivated not only politically active people, but also those who were disillusioned with economic and political instability to seek alternative places of work and residence. The process of migration has led to economic stagnation and political instability.

The first arrivals of Turkish migrants worked with Cypriots and lived in the same areas. The reason for living in the same areas might be related to being closer to other members of communities, their relatives and their workplaces, as well as not being able to speak English. When choosing locations, knowing someone was important for newly arriving migrants, and so the number of Turkish migrants increased within certain locations. Many Turkish people live in London.

> My shop is in the Turkish area. I can't work at the centre of London, because I can't speak English. It will be difficult to communicate with people whose mother tongue is not Turkish. I have to work in the Turkish area with Turkish people. I don't have any other choice.
>
> (cited in Şimsek 2012:75)

The third wave of immigrants from Turkey was the Kurds who arrived as political refugees from south-eastern Turkey. These migrants were internally displaced by the conflict between the Kurdistan Workers' Party (PKK) and government forces, and fled to the UK and other European countries. The Turkish Kurds, estimated to be 50,000 in number (most of whom again live in London), arrived spontaneously from the late 1980s in unexpectedly high numbers (Thomson 2006). Although it was strongly believed that those arriving were economic migrants rather than political refugees, as Thomson states 'The response of the UK government of the time ... was to impose visa requirements on all Turkish nationals coming to the UK' (2006:20). A high number of arrivals from Turkey meant that the UK authorities were unprepared, and the refugees could only rely on voluntary organizations and churches to take care of their housing and welfare (Wahlbeck 1999). Thomson's research shows that Kurdish groups already had existing networks of support to help them settle in the UK but the main difficulty they faced was the unfavourable economic conditions that hindered this group's access to stable jobs and earning a steady income.

> This was partly due to the less favourable economic conditions they faced in the early 1990s, by which time the UK's textile industry had declined significantly – a sector which had, over previous decades, provided employment for many in the Turkish-speaking communities. It is also due, especially amongst Kurdish women, to their lack of education or training, and poor English-language skills. Unlike Turkish-Cypriot women, neither do they have a tradition of dressmaking, nor do they have the opportunity to learn skills such as using a sewing machine though training at work as much of the work is carried out at home and paid on piece rates.
>
> (Thomson 2006:20)

4.4   Hidden injuries: Ethnic and religious identities

Transnational social spaces are created through cultural, social and economic exchanges, involving the country of origin and at least one other country. Faist has a broader definition for transnational social space, defined as 'combinations of social and symbolic ties, positions in networks and organisations that can be found in at least two geographically and internationally distinct places' (Faist 1998:216). In his definition, the idea of transnational social space represents a constant movement of not only people but also goods, thoughts and information in two or more nation states which brings them into a single social space. Faist (2000) discusses three analytically distinct types of immigrant transnationalism: kinship groups, circuits and communities. These groups represent different types of transnationalism, which arise from different patterns of integration and types of activities that migrants practice. For instance, kinship groups represent the sharing of familial tasks, and transnational circuits signify trading networks, i.e. Indian trading networks and transnational community are constituted on the basis of collective representation (Faist 2000).

In regard to the identity construction of migrant groups, transnational exchanges reproduce the culture of the country of origin and also lead to the development of new identities. For the communities in London from Turkey, transnational social space is also a place where they can embrace their ethnic and religious identities which are stigmatized and oppressed in Turkey. This, in turn, helps to improve ethnic and religious identities back in the country of origin, and this has been observed more in the recognition of Kurdish and Alevi identities in Turkey. Turkish immigrants in London can be placed into different groups in terms of their socio-economic and cultural differences. There are Sunni Turkish immigrants, Turkish-Cypriots, Alevi Turks and Kurds, and Kurdish immigrants. I class all these groups as 'injured' communities because the main reason behind their migration was deep societal ethnic and religious problems, and stigmatization. For example, Alevis fled to the UK because there was a massacre against them in the south-east city of Kahramanmaraş in Turkey. Now there are many people with Alevi religious background from the small town of Kahramanmaraş living in London. There are also those who left Turkey due to the military conflict between the Kurdish PKK and the Turkish army which resulted in the migration of almost two million people in the region, starting in the early 1990s. Some of these people became refugees in the UK.

There is evidently a large diversity in the ethnic and religious backgrounds of people from Turkey, and a lot of research on Turkish/Kurdish people in Britain focuses on these identities and representation of the groups (Küçükcan 2004). The migration process means that people hold on to their ethnic and religious identities because getting access to information and institutional guidance is mainly facilitated through community organizations which base their existence on these political, ethnic and religious identities. Therefore, there is a strong correlation between the day-to-day survival of migrants and their ideological/ethnic/religious belonging. One older man expressed his experience of carving his identity when he arrived in London in the early 1990s:

> I am an Alevi but I came to London for economic reasons. When I arrived I applied for an asylum and my friends told me to highlight my religious identity as an Alevi and also social discrimination we faced back in Turkey... It was not all wrong what I said... After some years I began to come to *Cemevi* and I am such a devoted member now. I kind of rediscovered my faith here.

The London fieldwork in this research shows that the differentiator is religious affiliation, whether people are Alevis or Sunnis. Thus, being a member of any religious sect is more often regarded as an identity than an ethnic background. Women also used similar connotations to define their religious and ethnic origin. For some women, being Turkish can mean being from Turkey or being a Kurd, as they did not always make a distinction between the two. However, they usually meant being a Turkish citizen rather than a Turk. A woman also said that 'you know that we are Kurds, I mean that we are Turks' – even she was aware of her ethnic identity. In some cases, they only used their place of origin in Turkey to describe their identity, such as being from Maraş, Pazarcık or Kayseri. This somehow disguised the fact that they were Alevis or Kurds, communities which were stigmatized in Turkey for a long time, and allowed the injured communities of Turkey to talk about their identity without openly stating it. This enabled people to connect with each other over their common history and experience in Turkey. Therefore, the strongest identification factor is centred on the place of origin in Turkey and kin relations, as well as religious orientation.

The Alevi community is one of the largest groups from Turkey, mostly organized around their religious worship house, called *Cemevi*, in London. Being an Alevi is built on their exclusion and being seen as the 'other' in Turkey, so how the Turkish state and government approach Alevism is very important for Alevi migrants in London. The interviews often revealed their concerns about the attacks made in Turkey on their religious identity, on which their common cultural heritage is based. One woman expressed her feelings as follows:

> We never feel that it is our country. They always treated us badly and we are always discriminated. The AKP government clearly is a party of Sunni people and does not hide this at all. This is worrying for Alevi people and I think that it is going to go worse for the Alevis in Turkey.

Transnational social space is an arena for Turkey's discriminated people and oppressed identities to freely embrace their identities and religious beliefs. Alevis and Kurds are prime examples of these groups. In London, these groups generate their own transnational space through cultural, social and economic exchanges involving Turkey, together with similar other communities in Europe and the UK. Therefore, the migration process is essential in building and re-establishing those identities, and in generating claims for the recognition of these identities in Turkey and in Europe.

4.5   Migration to London: 'We are refugees'

The injured communities of Turkey usually find their way into Europe through the asylum system, and most have been smuggled in. Turkish migration has been associated with high rates of smuggling, for instance Bennetto (2005, cited in Düvell 2010) alleges that up to 100,000 Turks, that is around 40% of the total Turkish and Kurdish speaking population, have been smuggled to the UK. During the 1990s, irregular migration from Turkey, in the form of illegal entry and overstaying, was a regular occurrence (Jordan and Düvell 2002), but it seems to have continued in the 2000s (Erdemir and Vasta 2007). Migration trends have been clearly supported by societal events, and the increasing migration from Turkey to London in the 1980s and 1990s was the result of three overlapping socio-political events that occurred in Turkey. In the first instance, the Maraş massacre in December 1978[2] resulted in the emigration of the Alevi population from Turkey. In addition, the early 1980s, following the military coup in 1980, was a period of strong oppression of the leftist people in Turkey and a lot of people left the country to find refuge in European countries. In the 1990s, the Kurdish people were evacuated from their villages by the military forces as part of their fight with the PKK militants. This increased Kurdish migration to European cities and to London. All three of these trends stimulated refugee flow to London.

Most of the first generation migrants from Turkey arrived in the UK as refugees escaping life threatening situations in Turkey. As members of leftist groups, Alevis and Kurds are the prime groups that chose to seek refuge in a European country. For these groups, emigration became part of the local cultures and survival strategies, and became a way of life. Therefore, it has been a way to plan and strategize their futures. This is evident in one informant's testimony:

> In our village in Kayseri, everyone migrated to different European countries. We were an Alevi village. Some went to Germany, some in Holland, some in Sweden and Austria. Actually I was quite happy with my life in the village. But my wife kept asking when I would go! She kept complaining that I was the only man in the village who did not emigrate. Because remaining out of this was being out of the community. I had to build my life as others. Then I decided to go as well. After that, I got into a plane and flew to London. We were all refugees in that plane going to London.

Being a refugee is a survival strategy for many of the injured communities of Turkey. This is not to say that they are not real political refugees, since migrating for economic and political reasons is always act in a intertwined way in leading to the decision to migrate. Alevis in Turkey are already discriminated against in many different aspects of life, and the only way out is to migrate. Their socio, economic and political lives in Turkey are determined by their religious identity. An off-licence shop owner in Green Lanes told me how he applied to become a refugee in the UK:

> I arrived in 1989 as a student. Everyone around me told that I must apply for refugee status. This was for my own good...I had to build a life from scratch and being a refugee was the best for me as I got support from the British state for my basic needs. They provide you with housing and etc. I first applied to be a refugee and then eventually I got indefinite leave to remain in the UK...The only down side was that it took me until the year of 2000, when I could go back home.

Another account was from a woman who fled Turkey and arrived in London from Dersim, where there is a large population of Alevi Kurds. She said:

> I was a very bright student and determined to continue my studies but then started this conflict in the region. Every day, our village was under attack by either the Military or the PKK forces. Our everyday life was like a torture. The forces broke into our homes and treated us like criminals. In this situation, there was only option for me, and that was to run away. Leaving meant a lot for me; I had to leave my family and my studies, although I was such a hopeful and bright student. Coming to London cut my studies off and cost me good life prospects in Turkey.

It was not only men who played a leading role in the decisions regarding migration; women have also been active in the decision to migrate and in choosing the destination for settlement. The refugee community from Turkey that is in London is composed of women whose actions and decisions affected the Turkish migration patterns to London. One of my female informants reported how she and her husband settled in London:

> My husband and I first went to Germany because we had relatives there. During our stay in Germany, we got lots of information about England from our relatives and other family members. We heard that there were garments sweatshops in London where our relatives and *hemşehris* worked and they did earn a good living. Therefore, we decided to come to London in the end. By that time, we did not have to get a visa to come here.

Historically, the main migration trajectory followed by Turkish people was via a guest worker regime to Europe. However, this changed dramatically after the 1980s and migration began to be dominated by people from discriminated groups. Thus, asylum seeking in Europe has become the main form of migration and a part of day-to-day survival for those groups. In the case of the UK, their status as a refugee community in London has important implications in the way in which Turkish communities develop their integration into their host society. A further significant aspect of this migration trend is the role of women in the decision to migrate and settle, which is quite different from the guest worker system in which men were the main decision makers. In the following section, there will be an account of how migrants develop their social networks and communities in London.

4.6   Chain migration and social networks: Communities and families in London

Social networks are used to explain migrants' decisions regarding where to go and settle. These networks provide a foundation for the dissemination of information as well as for patronage or assistance. Interactions within social networks make migration easier by reducing the costs and risks of moving. The social network paves the way for establishing transnational migration networks (Faist 1997). It is established in the migration literature that given the multiplier effect of social networks, they may result in a migration chain. Informal networks help migrants to finance their travel, to find a job or get accommodation. Migration networks enable migrants to cross borders, legally or illegally (IOM 2003:14). Personal relations which connect migrants, former migrants and non-migrants with each other in places of origin and destination increase the probability of international labour migration in connection with circular migration and chain migration processes (Boyd 1989).

Migrant networks are an important determinant of migration plans and the choice of destination. Being embedded in social networks thus has a significant impact on migration decisions. These decisions are shaped in a number of way: firstly, in terms of whether migration takes place; secondly, in what form migration takes place, i.e. whether it is permanent or circular; thirdly, the choice of destination; and fourthly, migrants' experiences in their new environment. The demographic structure, i.e. size of family, age and sex, stage in the life cycle, and various aspects of the social structure of families such as kinship patterns, influence the availability, expectations, motives and incentives with regard to migration (Harbison 1981).

In regard to the Turkish community in London, one can argue that it could be classed as a chain migration. Although there are different groups with different ethnic and religious backgrounds, the common characteristic of the Turkish migration to London is its nature of chain migration. The dominant groups are from similar regions of Turkey, such as Kayseri and Maraş, and many have relatives and *hemşehri*(s)[3] living in a close community and vicinity in London. The migration pattern is that of chain migration, in the sense that if one arrives in London and settles in the city, that person became a chaperone to mediate his/her family members' arrival. A newcomer initially stays with relatives or *hemşehri*(s) (people with the same village origin from Turkey), who have previously migrated and adapted to London, until income and housing is secured.

In every interview, it was highlighted that people have their own communities, and live together with their families, relatives and *hemşehris*. It is even mentioned that all of the people from one village in Kahramanmaraş were in London, a total of more than 300 people. 'Our village is all in London' was the common phrase people used to describe their networks and community. A shop owner explained this arrival, and the chain migration he generated, after his settlement in London:

> When I came to London, it was 1989 and I was one of the early arrivals. In my family we are seven sisters and brothers, I am the eldest son. In my life I always looked after my family and protected my siblings. After I came to London and settled, I brought all my sisters and brothers here. Now we have a very large family here. All Maraş is in London.

A woman migrating to London in the late 1980s also mentioned how she brought her sister and brother. 'We had a sister and a brother. When I arrived here I saw that there is work people can do. I asked my brother and sister to come here. So now we are all here.' The migration pattern shows that elder sisters and brothers take the initiative to move abroad after receiving information and financial support, and other members of their families eventually join them.

Not being part of these networks can mean deprivation and loneliness for those who have no extended families and relatives in London. The story of a woman who came to London by marrying a man from Adana highlights this argument. Until her husband became ill things were fine, and she enjoyed her life and her nuclear family structure in London. However, after her husband passed away, and her children were old enough to leave home, she lived on her own with no support networks. Later, she decided to engage with and generate her own networks in the Alevi community of London, and she now has a network of support based on her religious identity. She is a devoted and regular member of the Alevi community in London, where she has gained a sense of belonging to a community.

Another strategy used by migrants that results in the strengthening of community networks in London is that of marriage (see Chapter 5). The first generation migrant parents prefer their children to marry someone from Turkey. Parents arrange their children's marriage with someone from their own group of relatives or from *hemşehri*s so that they know the person who is coming into the family. Alternatively, there are in-community marriages, especially where relatives and extended family members marry their children. It is a common practise in some regions of Turkey to have arranged relative marriages, and this is also practiced in the Turkish community in London. A woman told a story of marrying her son to the daughter of her sister:

> When we first came to London, my boys were quite young. Then of course they grow up and became adults. When the time came to marry them I searched suitable girls in my family for my boy and arranged a marriage for my older son to the daughter of my sister back in Turkey … So, we did not get a stranger in our family.

In London, Turkish migrants live in their own familial networks, in which migrants have access to safety nets, information and support. Migrants not only rely on these networks for support but also facilitate the expansion and continuation of them by bringing in new members from their place of origin as well as other family members. This has been carried out in different ways, both to encourage and facilitate the emigration of their family members or to allow their children to marry other family members and relatives in London. As social networks are extended and strengthened by each additional migrant, potential migrants are able to benefit from the social networks and ethnic communities already established in the destination country.

4.7   Social life and migrant organizations in London

Community organizations are important in the mediation of the migration process and the settlement of migrants in their destination countries. The general aims of community organizations are to strengthen ethnic ties among migrants, to connect them with the culture of the country of origin and the mainstream society in which the migrants live (Şimşek 2012). They also play a role in teaching the native language to the young generations (Mehmet Ali 2001, Thomson et al. 2008) and in defending the rights of migrants in the destination country.

The recent literature identifies two main roles for migrant community organizations. Firstly, community organizations help to provide a sense of ethnic identity and provide cultural resources (Mehmet Ali 2001, Takenaka 2009, Goulbourne et al. 2010). This is the role of community organizations in providing political, cultural, religious or social ties with the country of origin. For instance, community organizations with a political background will reinforce not only the collective identity, but also political incorporation (Mehmet Ali 2001, Portes et al. 2008). Secondly, community organizations act as bridges between the host society and the migrants in providing information between these two groups. Ethnic organizations are automatically associated with transnational practices, because community organizations are structured to allow the transmission of cultural values and the practices of the country of origin to migrants, as well as the institutional structure and regulations of the host society. They play the role of mediator between migrants and the host society (Şimşek 2012).

There is a range of Turkish-Cypriot, Kurdish and Turkish community organizations in London, differentiated by their ethnic backgrounds and political ideologies. Mehmet Ali (2001) explains that Turkish and Turkish-Cypriot migrants establish their organizations and schools to spread a sense of national identity, whereas Kurdish migrants establish their organizations to protect their ethnic and cultural rights. He suggests that Turkish-Cypriot, Kurdish and Turkish communities protect their own rights through community organizations, but in doing so, clearly create ideological separation among Turkish communities. Küçükcan (2004:252) also highlights this separation, and argues that it creates diversity among 'Turkish' organizations: 'the institutionalisation of identity politics assumes diverse meanings according to the cultural, religious and political orientations of Turkish organisations'. Turkish-Cypriot, Kurdish and Turkish communities are heterogeneous: there are ethnic, national and, at some levels, cultural differences between these communities which are reflected in their everyday lives. Turks and Kurds establish different organizations which work for the rights of their communities. The distinction between Turks and Kurds is also visible in the structuring of community organizations. While Kurdish organizations hold seminars about Kurdish issues in Turkey and maintain their ethnic identities through Kurdish language courses, Turkish and Turkish-Cypriot organizations are more likely to promote national culture through language and history courses, and the celebration of national days (Küçükcan 2004).

The most important examples of these organizations are Halkevi and Daymer, which are among the biggest organizations in London. Halkevi has 6,000 members and Daymer has 1,000–1,500 members out of the 300,000 migrants in London. Daymer and Halkevi organize meetings which aim to resolve Kurdish-Turkish conflicts (Şimşek 2012).

Community organizations provide different methods of establishing transnational connections for migrant communities. First of all, they bring migrants together and create a social environment where they can discuss the recent socio-political issues happening in the country of origin, their life in the UK and they can generally socialize. Secondly, some community organizations promote a particular political ideology for specific groups and migrants who support this idea. Although most of these organizations are orientated towards political activities, some – the Turkish and Turkish-Cypriot groups in particular – also combine cultural activities (Şimşek 2012).

Older migrants who moved to London in the mid-1980s mentioned the central role of Halkevi in their initial settlement and their applications for refugee status in the UK. In the early days of their arrival, the migrants initially lived in Halkevi for a couple weeks, which acted like a refugee centre for newcomers from Turkey. Their applications were administrated in the Halkevi building, and migrants were briefed about their rights and status in the UK. Therefore, Halkevi's role was central in the lives of migrants and their day-to-day survival. Later, this central role was expanded further, and took on the guise of 'big brother' or an autonomous central administrative body for Turkish people in the UK; it influenced even small actions and decisions such as opening a kebab house in a certain street in Britain (Şimşek 2012).

The other role that community organizations play is in regard to the help they give to migrants in their communications with institutions such as schools, housing associations and local municipal bodies. The first generation of Turkish migrants are mostly incompetent in English, and they need interpreters when dealing with authorities and institutions. As British institutional culture is based on correspondence by letter, Turkish people need people or organizations that are competent in written communication (see Chapter 7). It is evident that without the existence of community organizations, it would have been impossible for Turkish migrants to sustain their daily life in the UK. This is why many of these organizations have public days in which they help their members by reading their letters and writing responses.

There are different activities that some of these organizations undertake. Among these, the most important ones are curriculum support for school children, where children receive additional classes in maths and English. Considering the poor school records of migrant children, these courses are very beneficial for pupils. Many families are not able to support their children academically, as they have little knowledge of the English language and have poor educational levels themselves.

Therefore, courses offered by community organizations are beneficial for pupils and have the potential to encourage school success for at least some of the children (see Chapter 7). However, it is often stated that children drop out of school earlier than their counterparts, and spend fewer years at school. It is ironic to see so few migrant children reaching university education in London, when there are so many students travelling from Turkey every year to pursue higher education in British universities.

In addition to these activities, community organizations arrange cultural activities and courses that help to maintain the cultural identity of migrants. There are art and cultural festivals held every year by some of the organizations. The best-known is the annual Day-Mer festival, which attracts quite big crowds. During these activities, migrants also have the opportunity to perform folk dances and sing in chorus and theatre shows, and artists come from Turkey to attend the festivals. In recent years, the Alevi organization Cem Evi has also started an Alevi festival in London. This festival is devoted to strengthening the identity of the Alevi community in London, and has a range of seminars, theatre shows and other activities to engage people from different parts of London.

Migrants utilize the services of community organizations for different purposes, and the most important function of community organizations is in helping migrants to obtain information and guidance in their day-to-day life in an environment in which they have little knowledge of institutional structure and administration. In doing so, these organizations also strengthen ethnic, religious or national identity and belonging. It helps the migrants to keep in touch with each other, and with their local culture and identity. Therefore, it can be argued that community organizations play a significant role in the migration patterns and migrants' lives in their new host society. They also build a bridge between the migrants and mainstream society.

4.8 Conclusion

London's silent community from Turkey is not as large as other ethnic groups such as Indians and Caribbeans, and it is also not a homogeneous group, as it is divided by ethnic and religious differences. Three distinct groups are the subject of studies of Turkish communities – Turkish-Cypriots, mainland Turks and Kurds of Turkey. The migration of these groups was due to deep socio-economic upheavals, conflicts and violence imposed upon certain groups who received injuries because of their religious and ethnic identities. These injured communities of Turkey found refuge in London and began a new life. The migration process has opened up a place for Turkey's discriminated people and oppressed identities to freely embrace their identities and religious beliefs. Sunnis, Alevis and Kurds generated their own transnational space through cultural, social and economic exchanges involving Turkey and similar communities in Europe and the UK.

Most migrants in London define themselves either by their religious sect, such as Sunni or Alevi, or call themselves Turkish, which refers to their status as Turkish citizens rather than their ethnic origin. The most common signifier of identity was their place of origin in Turkey, such as being from Maraş, Adana or Kayseri. By using the place of birth people also explicitly refer to their ethnic and religious identities without openly stating them. A further important characteristic of Turkish migration to London is that most first generation migrants are refugees who sought asylum in the UK. This has generated a refugee community in London. Another significant aspect of this migration trend is the role of women in making the decision to migrate and settle, which is different from the guest worker system in which men were the main decision makers in migration.

The chain migration from Turkey has been a silent enforcer of migrant networks and organizations in London. The earlier arrivals facilitated the arrival of new migrants from their own families. This has been done either to encourage and facilitate the emigration of their family members or to allow the marriage of their children to other family members and relatives. As social networks are extended and strengthened by each additional migrant, potential migrants are able to benefit from social networks and ethnic communities that are already established in the country of destination. Therefore, there are many people from the same place of birth living in London, and close networks of families maintain traditional social and cultural practices in the new country.

The foundation of migrants' community organizations is based on these close migrant networks and communal relations. However, they also build bridges between the migrants and the host society. Migrants utilize the services of community organizations for different purposes but their most important function is in helping migrants obtain information and guidance for their day-to-day lives in an environment in which they have little knowledge of institutional structure and administration. In doing so, these organizations also strengthen ethnic, religious and national identities, and sense of belonging. They help the migrants to keep in touch with each other and with their local culture and identity. Therefore, it can be said that community organizations play a significant role in migration patterns and in migrants' lives in their new host society. They also build a bridge between the migrants and mainstream society.

5
Turkish Immigrant Women in London

The first group interview for this research took place in Cemevi[1] in Dolston, London, where women were meeting for a breakfast get-together. This was one of the usual gatherings of the devoted members of Cemevi. Alevis are the largest group of immigrants in London from Turkey and they use Cemevi not only for their religious practices, but also to meet their social and cultural needs. It is common during week-days and at weekends for women to bring their children to attend various courses and for women to get together to talk about their problems and needs. For example, a group of women (not exclusively Alevi women) holds its weekly meeting (*kadın günü*) in Cemevi. Although the migrant women are of various age groups, and from different cities in Turkey, their migration history has brought them together in London. Their migration process, refugee status and their role in the Turkish ethnic economy in Britain are similarities that the women share. Moreover, being a practising Alevi in a foreign country is another feature of the women in Cemevi. All of these factors highlight women's common experiences in London.

This chapter explores the lives and motivations of a sample of women working in the Turkish ethnic economy. The chapter opens with an introduction to the debate over the determining factors of women, gender and migration, and the historical trajectory of Turkish women's migration to Europe that started as a guest worker programme and evolved into family unification and, in recent years, asylum seeking. In providing the backdrop to the lives of these migrant women, the ethnographic section focused on a sample of women workers to explore the demographic characteristics and household structures of women who are engaged in the ethnic economy. The attempt to introduce women here is significant, as no studies have been conducted on this group, and they largely remain invisible to academic interest. The chapter takes up the issues of women's personal experiences of migration, and how they conceptualize their lives in the UK as migrants. This chapter is also an attempt to consider important sociological contentions concerning women, gender and migration in analysing the question of how migration reshapes gender relations and contributes to women's emancipation and empowerment in the context of Turkish immigrant women. It shows that women's positions in the Turkish community have mainly been shaped by the economic activities of the community. When women's labour is needed in the textile industry, they are pulled into the economic realm, and when there is less need for women as workers they are pushed back to the domestic sphere, thereby reducing their earning potential.

5.1 Women and migration: An overview

During the 1960s and early 1970s, women were seen as invisible in the migration process. Migration was mainly the movement of male migrants and was usually described by the phrases 'migrants and their families' and 'male migrants and their wives and children'. The main focus of the literature was male migration and women's situations were never questioned. The result has been the near-invisibility of women as migrants, their presumed passivity in the migration process and the assumption that their place was in the home (Boyd and Grieco 2003). In the 1970s and 1980s, women were integrated into migration research, not so much as active participants of migration but in connection with the question of how migration 'modernizes' women or emancipates them from their traditional roles and attitudes. This stereotypical picture of immigrant women has ironed out all of their differences. As Kofman states, 'Women's diverse backgrounds in the society of emigration were lost upon arrival in the country of immigration as they began their journey to modernity' (1999:270).

In the push-pull demographic model, migration was seen as the outcome of individual decisions. The responsibilities of women as wives and mothers were thought to influence the decisions of women. These gendered responsibilities were believed to explain why women were less likely than men to participate in migration decisions or in the labour force of the host country when they did join their husbands (Boyd and Grieco 2003). When family unification became the dominant mode of legal entry to many European states, women migrants were perceived as dependents. However, the reality showed a different picture of immigrant women. For example, while women were rare in official labour migration in countries such as Belgium and the Netherlands, there were many single and married working women in Germany during the peak years of the guest worker regime (Kofman 1999). Abadan-Unat also showed how women were recruited within the guest worker regime towards the end of the 1960s, due to preferential recruitment procedures of employers (Abadan-Unat 1980).

Following the slow down of the migration trend through family unification, there appears to have been a diversification in modes of entry, duration of residence and employment patterns of migrant women. The seminal work of Mirjana Morokvasic (1984:886) demonstrated the role of women in migration and showed that 'birds of passage are also women'. Following the rising trend in women's movements and the increasing influence of women's studies in social research, numerous studies over the past 30 years have demonstrated the various ways in which gender relations – notably patriarchal family structures – fundamentally condition the migration process and the decision making behind it (Pessar and Mahler 2003, Mahler and Pessar 2006, Silvey 2006). Castles and Miller (1993:8–9) rank the feminization of international migration as one of the major migratory tendencies of the past 20 years. Feminization of migration is marked by the increasing visibility of women's movements across borders and the role of women in the labour market of their host countries.

There is now more information regarding women's migration and the implications of gender relations on issues surrounding migration. The major focus has been on the diversification in female migration trends. Asylum seekers and refugees now constitute one of the largest groups, and in some countries they are almost as numerous as those entering as family migrants. At the same time, these categories are not fixed – asylum seekers gain rights to employment and settlement, family migrants participate in the labour market, and students can marry and/or obtain employment and settle in the country permanently (Kofman 1999). The expansion of service and care sectors in Western countries promoted the phenomenon of women moving across borders as solo/single migrants. Women migrants emerged as the main source of supply for domestic workers and carers for middle-class households in most countries. As Luts (2008) shows, it is now estimated that at least one in ten households in several European countries uses domestic 'help'. In these informal jobs, women take on a wide range of activities, such as cleaning, cooking and caring for small children and the elderly, and nursing the disabled and ill. Increasing use of female migrants in domestic services has been the result of more structural changes in Western Europe. As Luts states:

> This development is incomprehensible if one does not take into account the increased participation of 'native' women in professional occupations which did not lead to the redistribution of care work and family tasks, formerly performed by them, between spouses; neither did it cause states to enhance their efforts in the provision of care facilities; rather, it led to the outsourcing of care work to an external, often migrant worker.
>
> (Luts 2008)

The analysis of women and gender in migration research has evolved through four different stages. Helma Luts (2008) demonstrates these four stages in the following order. In the first stage, efforts were directed towards making women visible in the migration process by documenting women's migration patterns. In the second stage, there was a focus on the contribution of women to various migration movements, including the specific role of women in migration and their particular migration experiences. The third phase was developed around the 'perception as (ethnic, cultural or national) "others", thereby reifying the binary of sameness-otherness and thereby reconstructing migration as a deviant social phenomenon or the female migrant as deviant from her male peer' (Luts 2008:7). This debate involves the understanding that gender relations are always mediated by other socially constructed categories such as 'race'/ethnicity and class, and also the understanding that the analysis of 'race'/ethnicity, class or nationality cannot avoid looking at its gendered dimensions. In the fourth stage, from the mid 1990s onwards, gender was introduced in the social sciences to emphasize the difference between a person's 'biological' (sex) and the 'socially acquired and performed' (gender) identity, way of living and role in society (Luts 2008).

A great shift has taken place in migration studies in analysing the gendered impacts of migration and the role of women in migration processes. We now know more about how men and women often migrate for fundamentally different reasons and under different conditions. The effects of gendered perspectives on migration studies often questions whether migration itself reshapes gender relations and contributes to women's emancipation and empowerments. The conclusions show that migration can lead to a degree of empowerment for women, but this depends on the particular migration context they are embedded in.

In adding to the considerable progress in 'bringing gender into the core of migration studies' (Mahler and Pessar 2006), this research is an attempt to understand the relationships between migration, work and women's role in the Turkish community in London, focusing on a possible outcome of Turkish women's social integration into British society.

5.2   Turkish women's journey to Europe: An *Almancı's*[2] wife or a worker?

The general understanding is that Turkish women migrating to Europe are dependent migrants who follow their guest worker husbands. Turkish women in Europe are represented through a homogenized image – as uneducated and backward migrants, and as victims of patriarchal culture and values. However, this common perception was critically questioned by Nermin Abadan-Unat who showed that in the mid-1960s women were migrating to Germany as workers. Abadan-Unat (2006) emphasizes the fact that, after a brief economic recession in 1966, many employers preferred to hire women workers as they were considered to be less interested in trade unions, were submissive and were ready to work for lower wages. This led to the migration of many women from Turkey who had no previous work experience in modern industries. In 1978, 215,000 Turkish women migrated to Europe for work. Of these, 31,800 were located in Austria, 134,342 in Germany, 12,979 in Sweden and 5,175 in Belgium (Abadan-Unat 2006:163). In 1965, the number of Turkish women workers was around 17,000 as against 115,000 male workers; women made up 15% of Turkish workers. However, this increased to 159,000 in 1974, whereas the number of male workers was 457,000, and so women accounted for 25% of all Turkish workers. Abadan-Unat also shows that women's employment rate in the non-agricultural sector in Turkey was just 10% in 1975 (Abadan Unat 2006:164–165).

Family reunion was the main route for legal entry to Germany by many Turkish women from 1973 to 1979. During this period, the German government prevented dependents (women and older children) from entering the labour market and issued them with temporary residence permits. This was a precaution taken after labour recruitment was ended, and aimed to curtail the number of incoming migrants. However, this expected outcome did not materialize; as Kofman et al. (2000) notes, 'Despite the stoppage in recruitment in October 1973, the total number of immigrants did not drop drastically, and by 1976, the annual numbers entering were beginning to increase... It is estimated that about half of the immigration in the 1970s and 1980s was derived from family reunion' (2000:51). There is also evidence that women who migrated through family union were also active in the labour market and took on informal jobs. In Kadıoğlu's work, 'Migration Experiences of Turkish Women', a female respondent recounted her work experience as follows:

> When she arrived in Germany as a dependent spouse, she did not have a work permit and was willing to work at any job. She obtained a cleaning job in a school... After four years, she obtained a work permit and began work in a factory assembling electrical appliances.
> (Kadıoğlu 1997:550)

Following the 1980s and 1990s, the migration trajectory of people from Turkey to Europe began to take another shape, and the number of asylum seekers and refugees increased dramatically. The military intervention in 1980 generated a significant flock of asylum applicants from Turkey to Germany, numbering 57,000 in 1980. The brutal measures taken by the military to oppress the political opposition led many political activists to flee the country. Between 1985 and 1994, there were 175,048 asylum applications to Germany, and this continued to increase with the devastating result of the armed conflict between the Turkish military forces and PKK. Abadan-Unat (2006:293) shows that there were more than 100,000 applications between 1996 and 2001. She also states that with the increasing emphasis on identity and cultural representation, the communities politically and culturally stigmatized and discriminated in Turkey – not only leftist group members and Kurds but also extreme right groups and Islamists – left the country as asylum seekers (Abadan-Unat 2006). This was a sign of diversification of women's migration to Europe, and these developments divorced Turkish women's migration from its family-based nature and gave it a bit more individual flavour.

The late 1990s and 2000s were years of diversification, which increased further with the impact of irregular migration. Women used different strategies to enter Europe, by means of asylum seeking, marriage or illegal methods, such as human smugglers. Whichever strategy women used, they usually became a labour supply for lower paid jobs, whether in the service sector, such as cleaning or caring, or in the expanding Turkish ethnic economies of Western European countries. In her ethnographic study among Turkish cleaning workers in Germany,

Ünlütürk-Ulutaş (2013) shows that women's access to informal jobs has been supported by government policies, through the generation of mini-jobs, and having these jobs has given women the ability to manage their migration process. Women used their income to clear their debts or send remittances to those left behind in Turkey.

The Turkish women in Western Europe are always shown as classic examples of so-called 'oriental femininity' living in a system of values dictated by Islam and patriarchal relations. The ideal Muslim woman in a rural community is one who is subordinate to her husband or father. This image is the complete opposite of the image of European women who are urban, modern and emancipated. Although Turkish women's migration to Europe is mostly seen as part of a family union, and women are considered dependents, the reality indicates that women are never dependent members of their families but are active economic agents of their families and communities. They were either industrial workers in the guest worker era or informal service workers during the family unification process. The remaining part of this chapter aims to develop an insight into women migrant's lives in London, and shows that women are not only dependent migrants but also active participants of their communities.

5.3   The 'birds of passage' are women in London

The focus of the literature on female migration in recent years has shifted away from depicting women as passive, dependent migrants towards showing women as independent and solo migrants with an increasing feminization of international migratory flows. This has been seen in the rising demand for immigrant women's labour in domestic and care services. Attempting to analyse the profile of Turkish female migrants either as dependents or solo migrants is rather difficult, as Turkish migration to Britain does not fit well with the frame of family union migration or the pattern of individual female migrants. No scholarly attention prior to this research has been paid to Turkish immigrant women in Britain, so women's migration experiences and changes in their lives post-migration are not known. However, this does not mean that women are absent from Turkish migratory flows. As will be shown in the following pages, the presence of Turkish women is more significant and visible in the migration flow to Britain when it is compared with the subtle nature – women's family unification – of Turkish women's migration to Germany. The flow to Britain has somehow been a more gender balanced migration due to the regulation easing family unification and the nature of economic activity that Turkish migrants undertook in London. Since the early 1980s, Turkish migrants worked in the garment production industry in London, which influenced the trend of female migration as women were always considered to be better at garment making, which helped to push up the number of women employed in the production.

The claim that Turkish migration has taken on a more feminized nature is supported by the results of the 2001 census. The population living in London was almost equally composed of women and men. In the general UK population there is a slightly higher proportion of females than males as women tend to live longer. In 2001, the Turkish and Turkish-Cypriot populations were split almost evenly, while the Kurdish population had a higher proportion of males. This is characteristic of more recently arrived migrants, who are more likely to be male, and who may not yet have been able to bring their families to the UK or do not have the economic stability to start a family (GLA 2009) (Table 5.1).

For this study, 60 immigrant women living in London were interviewed, in order to examine their role in the Turkish ethnic economy. To meet this aim, first generation women migrants were interviewed. The first generation refers to those born outside the UK who migrated as adults[3] of their own will. Although it is difficult to present a homogenous migrant profile, it is still possible to present an image of first generation Turkish women, based on their class and educational background as well as their place of origin in Turkey. The women in the sample were of different ages, from 25 to 60 years.[4] Having different age categories in the sample enabled a focus on a longer time span of migration, starting from the early 1980s and ending in the mid-2000s. The number of years women spent in education varies depending on their age; younger women had the most years of schooling. Almost half of the sample (45%) had a five-year compulsory education and 34% had eight

Table 5.1 Proportion of population by gender, by ethnic group, London, 2001 Census

	Kurdish %	Turkish %	Turkish-Cypriot %	All London %
Female	45.7	49.8	49.8	51.6
Male	54.3	50.2	50.2	48.4

Source: Greater London Authority (2009:16).

years of schooling. The illiteracy rate (9%) was more common in the oldest cohort of women who were over 50 years old. The remaining 12% was composed of high-school graduates.[5] The educational attainment of immigrants is a good indicator of their social-economic background. All of the women were from low-income families. Indeed, being from a rural part of Turkey was a common characteristic, with only a few arriving from large cities such as Istanbul, Ankara and İzmir. Therefore, they all shared a common motivation for migrating, namely that they wanted to achieve better living and working conditions abroad.

Most women lived in a conjugal union[6] and had children. There were a number of cases where women were divorced and living alone with their children. Even though they complained about the changes in the structure of families and increasing rates of divorce, family union was a strong social institution among Turkish migrants. Relationships not only with close family, but also relatives, have been an important aspect of people's identity construction as well as their membership in the larger community. The first generation parents are keen for their children to marry their relatives living in London or those back in Turkey. The family is seen as a cocoon, protecting them from all ills outside, but it is also a shell in which it is hard for women to break free from traditional patriarchal relations, values and practices. In fact, work in the ethnic economy has acted as the glue which keeps the close familial and communal ties intact, and very little has changed post-migration. The expansion of the ethnic business mostly relies on pooling family resources and labour together. Therefore, it is even more significant to have a family and to be a family with strong connections to the community in London.

With the purpose of examining women's work in the ethnic economy, the migrant women in the sample had a relationship with the ethnic economy as workers, wives or mothers. The overwhelming majority of women (60%) were unpaid family workers and their position in the family business was very ambiguous. As will be detailed in Chapter 6, women's engagement as family workers might take different forms, depending on women's domestic roles and responsibilities. For some women, this involves only one day of work a week in her husband's corner-shop to clean the shop and unpack the delivery, while for others, it involves only the shop's paperwork. There are also women working full-time in their family businesses. Women with young children refrain from working long hours in shops; they only work part-time. The second largest category of women is that of wage-workers, accounting for 30% of all interviewed women. These women worked as pastry-makers, cooks or cashiers. The employment offered in the ethnic economy was all hourly pay, and unregistered jobs resembled the services women carry out for their families in the domestic sphere. The final group of women were unemployed, and remained out of economic activity. It was important to include this group in the sample, as most of the female population in London is unemployed and lives on welfare benefits.

What united the women in the sample is their sense of being refugees in the UK. Migrating to the UK as a refugee was a common experience for the women, even for those who followed their husbands and migrated through family unification. Women's identity as refugees builds the base for their social exclusion. This was vivid in one woman's testimony: 'The British government treated us very well and provided almost our every needs. We live in council houses and have pocket money coming in. This is because we are refugees. The same will not happen for our children.' In this regard, their welfare dependency resulting from their refugee status has led to their exclusion from their host society. Therefore, the process of migration was a life changing experience for all women, and women played an important role in their decision to move to Britain.

5.4   Decisions to move: The role of women

The prevailing ideologies of gender in Turkish society not only outline what it means to be a man or a woman, but also affect how social change may impact women's positions in their families and communities. One major area where a radical change emerged is women's decision making power in regard to migration. Women's testimonies in London show that they have been active participants in the decision making process, in addition to their husbands. This might not be a sign of a significant change in existing gender relations, but it signals the importance of women's role in the family decision making process. Regardless of women's biographic characteristics, the migration process was a major life changing event for all women. Their accounts vividly reveal the role of women in the decision regarding migration. A woman respondent echoed her and her husband's journey to London.

> My husband and I decided to go abroad and to look for opportunities somewhere else outside Turkey ... I can still call that it was around 1982 or 1983. First we went to Germany as we had other close family members there. We stayed there for a few months. While we were

there, we found out that England was better and also English did not want visa clearance from Turks. We also heard that there was textile work in which we could work and their money was dear. Then we got here.

Migrants' prior knowledge of the availability of work opportunities is crucial in terms of decisions about where to go and who should migrate. In this regard, gender composition seems to be the outcome of these opportunities, and is shaped by the availability of work. In this sense, the Turkish migration to the UK was never the same as the guest worker regime that was established in Germany, in which women were perceived as being passive and subordinate to their husbands. In London, the greater demand for women's labour made women more active participants in migration. A man who used to run a textile workshop confirmed the importance of female labour for garment production:

I first arrived to London on my own. My brother-in-law was already living here. So I stayed with him for a while. As soon as I arrived I started to work in a textile atelier. As you know women are much better in doing textiles. The ateliers were full of women. However, I had to wait a bit until I could bring in my family, till my file was finalised. When I had my wife with me, it was much better to work together. Then, we could earn twice as much or more. Without her contribution it could have been very difficult for us to live better in this country.

These two cases exemplify the role of women in earlier migrations who had moved to London and taken advantage of textile production. This generated a gender balanced outcome for women and men as women's labour was valued in the garment making industry. Even for those who arrived after the demise of textile production, women's initiation of the migration process is significant in their testimonies. This proves that the role of women in the decision making process of whether they should migrate or not has been central among Turkish immigrants in London. For example, Zehra who has been living in London since the early 2000s told the story of her journey:

My husband and I were newly married and living in Tunceli where we were literally being in the middle of two fires (she means the conflict between the Turkish military and PKK). One day, I told my husband that we must go. Then we had to wait and save up money to be smuggled to London... It was me who wanted to come here most.

Women's agency in the decision making process of whether to move to London has been central for many families. The Turkish community's reliance on women's labour in textile production has given women a leverage in which they can expand their power in their homes and community. This is not to ignore the fact that some women also moved to London as dependents, mostly through arranged marriages. As will be discussed further in this book, women's active role in the migration process may not mean a radical change in traditional patriarchal gender relations in which women take on the role of home-makers as mothers and wives.

5.5   A close up on immigrant women's profiles: Who are they?

There are two broad typologies of women in London, each coinciding with different generations whose economic activity also differed. The first generation is what can be referred to as the textile generation. This group of women migrated to London in the mid- or late-1980s, and were in their 40s and early 50s. Most entered the UK when there was no visa obligation for Turkish people and then became asylum seekers. Later they were granted residence permits and eventually had British citizenships. Having a rural background meant that women came to London from small villages, mostly from Sivas, Maras, Kayseri and Adana. It also meant that the education attainment of this group of women was quite low, and most had only compulsory primary school education, which used to be five years. Being from a rural background, in the relatively older age cohort and having only a few years of schooling are the main traits of women's social background in the first group of interviewed women.

Fatma was one of my key informants, and I spent quite a lot of time her with on several occasions. She was 50 years old and had been living in London for 25 years. She had migrated from the small Alevi village of Sivas, which is located in east Turkey. In 1985 she and her husband decided to migrate; they had four children. They first headed to the Netherlands and stayed there for a while before deciding to go to London. When they left their villages, they had to leave their children behind, which was a very hard decision for the mother. Her mother-in-law took care of them in their parents' absence. She explains the process of leaving her children back at home.

> My daughter was the oldest among them. She had to take care of her brothers and help her grandma. It took us four years to meet them again and we brought them here. It was very challenging experience for us, especially for me. As a mother you always feel guilty because you feel that you are not good enough for your children. My daughter and I are not getting along well at all. I think that this is because we could not bond well enough. I feel like from time to time, she does stuff just to annoy me and she wants to take a revenge of those days that I had to leave her... But I had no any other option at that time.

Fatma and her husband started work in a textile workshop as soon as they arrived in London. Then, they applied for refugee status and it took them 12 years to return to Turkey. This is a common experience for most Turkish migrants in London. Only those married to someone with a residence permit or those entering the country through legal means were exempt from this experience. If they had applied for asylum status to stay in the country, they were banned from going back to Turkey until their case was finalized. Usually this process took quite a long time, and people stayed in the country for years before they could return to Turkey. This was the same for Fatma and her family. During this time, their lives evolved in London and the children grew up.

After Fatma's family had settled in, her brother and sister came to London. Therefore, her family and support networks began to grow. Other members from her husband's family arrived, and her-sister-in-law looked after the children of close family members who all worked in textile sweatshops. Fatma and her sister worked in the textile industry, along with many others who also migrated to London in search of a better life for themselves and for their families. Fatma's older daughter and eldest son did not want to pursue their education and finished school as early as they could. However, her younger two sons managed to get into university and became graduates. Educational attainment is not very high among second generation Turkish migrants, and it is rare to see the young generation pursuing higher education.

With the demise of the textile sector in London, Fatma retired from working life but the family started a new venture by opening their own business. Her eldest son was living in Brighton and had his own coffee shop. Her younger sons ran a coffee shop in Dolston. The family was able to support these businesses using the financial gains they accumulated from their textile work.

Fatma has been a powerful figure in her family, a classic example of a patriarchal family in which women gain authority and decision making power over the younger generations as they age. Fatma is a strong authority figure in her family, as her husband and children consult with her on every decision they make. This is due to the power she gained through her economic contribution to her family as a result of her work in the textile industry. Even though it is not explicitly stated that the family's prosperity was due to her hard work in the textile industry, there was a silent consensus about this. Although not eager to show her power in her family, she had a handle on every bit of information about what was happening in the family and controlled the main decisions and actions. However, in her testimony, she undermines her role and shows only her soft power.

> I don't interfere with their business. For example, this shop is ours but my sons are in its charge. I don't get in their way. I came here every day and sit for a few hours and don't say anything!

The profile of Fatma is a classic example of women migrants of the textile generation. These women gained power and status in their families through their hard work, age and material contributions. As will be discussed in the following pages, the classic patriarchal belt theory claims that senior women have power over younger women and men as they gain power and status through age and by bearing children (Kandiyoti 1989). Gender relations shaped through this classical family structure are inevitably forced to change when families move to a new place. The result of migration can lead women to become economically more active and take on jobs they would not have been able to do prior to their migration. The women working in the textile industry in London are a good example of this, because the female labour force participation in Turkey is quite low and women rarely work in industrial jobs. Women's economic activity in London gave them some leverage to change traditional gender roles, in which they are only expected to be mothers and wives; moving to London has provided women with an opportunity to become industrial workers and prove their financial contribution to their families as much as their husbands did. In fact, in some cases, women earned more than men and shed doubt on the myth of the male bread winner.

The second group was composed of a younger generation of immigrant women. The arrival of this group was later than that of the textile generation, and they faced a different structural setting in London. In the past two decades, most immigrants had been running away from the effects of the Kurdish conflict in southeast Turkey, and the migrants were from cities in this region such as Adana, Mersin and Tunceli. These women had a much higher education level than the first group, and most were high-school graduates (12th year). Due to the nature of the sample, all women interviewed were adults with children, and were married or divorced. Thus, if we consider women in the first group as the first wave of Turkish migrants to the UK, this group was the second wave. Both groups were first generation migrants, but they had different experiences of life in London. For example, first wave migrants worked in the textile industry, which brought cash income and the benefits of working in an industrial job. Even as informal work with little pay, the textile industry offered a good source of income in a Western country where the wages earned were much more than what they could make in their home country.

The second wave of women faced a different economic environment, and did not have jobs in the textile industry when they arrived in London. Thus, the migrants had to reshape their survival strategy, and the only economic opportunity available was the Turkish ethnic economy. However, most of the migrants in the second group also lacked the economic and cultural resources for integration with the increasing numbers of people owning their own shops in London. The only paths for women were as wage-workers in the ethnic economy or staying out of economic activity altogether, since the ethnic economy is not as women friendly as the textile industry. It is a male-dominated environment, where women can only do certain jobs. The limited work opportunities resulted in the 'housewiveziation' of most women.

One of the women interviewed was Filiz, who arrived in London in 1997. She was 35 years old and a high-school graduate. Her husband arrived first and then she followed to London with her daughter. The family is from Kayseri, Elbistan, a place from which a lot of people have migrated to London since the mid-1980s. She was a housewife and had two more children after she arrived in London. Now she has a 14-year-old girl and boys who are 12 and 6. Her husband works in a coffee shop as a cook.

She feels that her life is monotonous. She wakes up and gets her children ready for school and then does household chores. At 3.30 p.m., the children return from school and have their meals. She also tries to keep herself busy with other activities. For example, she attends an English language course two days a week as well as the Women's Support Group meeting once a week. Other than these activities, she has relatives and neighbours, she maintains a social network and she socializes. Her sister is also in London and they keep each other company.

> I don't know what I can do any more. I feel like everybody has physiological problems here as people are all depressed...I have a very boring life. I do the same thing every day over and over again. After the closure of textile workshops there are no jobs for women. Of course there are jobs but they are for those who can speak English. But when you think that even those speak English cannot find work. Where can I work?

Declining work opportunities have resulted in an over emphasis on women's motherhood and wife roles. As will be explained further in Chapter 7, changing expectations of women is common in the Turkish community in London, and women represent the culture and tradition on which the ethnic economy rises. Therefore, the women in the second wave of migration are usually housewives and mothers, and this makes them distinctly different from the first group.

Another informant in this group was Ayla, who came to London when she was 19 years old through her marriage to a Turk who was raised in London. At the time of the interview, she was 29 years old and had two children, aged five and three. Her husband was working in a kebab shop. She had a simple life organized around her husband's family members and relatives. From time to time, she travelled to Turkey to visit her own family. She had never worked since her arrival, and thought that there were no jobs for migrant women in London.

Another informant was Dilek, who was a representative of the second wave of women migrants. She and her husband came to London seven years ago as refugees. Now they had a four-year-old boy. She says 'I am devoting all my time to my child. I take him parks, drop him to nursery and pick him up. I do meals and clean the house. My son is my only job.' Her husband worked in a kebab shop for a while and then became a mini-cab driver. He worked on and off to make some pocket money but then he injured his back and was unable to work. The couple usually lived on welfare benefits, and were waiting for the results of their asylum applications.

Dilek found her life in London depressing, and explained that her depressive mood is due to her legal status in the country. She illegally entered the country and since then she has not gone back to Turkey. She says:

> I feel depressed. There is no sun here and I miss my home very much. I don't want to live here. If I had money I would have gone back to Turkey. I miss being there very much. But I know that my life is here now. If I go and see my country once I may want to stay here more. I don't know!

A cursory glance at immigrant women's profiles shows that there are two different groups of first generation migrants. The characteristics of these groups are different not because their move to London took place in different time frames, but because their access to economic activities is different. During the era of textile work, women were the main workers, and they gained power and status through this. In the last two decades, we have seen a rising trend in Turkish ethnic economy as the main economic activity for the community. This, however, resulted in women returning to their traditional roles as mothers and wives, and dropping their income generating activities. The following sections discuss the implications of migration on gender roles, family life and marriages.

5.6 Migration, women and gender relations

In feminist analysis, gender is a very ambiguous concept, and has undergone various phases of conceptualization. These variations in the definition of gender have led to the production of ambiguities, inconsistencies and contradictions in feminist practice and the presentation of women's interests. The concept of gender has been used differently by different scholars. Gender was initially conceptualized as distinct from sex, in order to present differences between men and women that are not biological. Thus, gender was a concept used to identify cultural and social differences related to biological differences (Nicholson 1994). Gendered categories and attributes such as behaviours, roles, personality traits and attitudes embodied in the notions of masculinity and femininity are argued to be socially and culturally constructed categories. As socially constructed categories, they are not fixed, but can change and transform over time and space. Socially constructed gender differences are a reflection of the unequal relations that reproduce the social and cultural differences between men and women, through which the female/male distinction reproduces inequality in access to, and control over, resources at every institutional level (Moser 1993, Agarwal 1994, Hart 1995, Kandiyoti 1998). Scholars arguing for the heterogeneity of social categories such as men and women point to multiple, contested and contradictory meanings associated with male/female identities and distinctions. Moreover, these relationships and differences within the categories of male and female also take different on shapes within each specific socio-economic and historical context (Moore 1994). The conceptualization of gender as a relational category in analysing women's access to and control over available resources in relation to men is a useful tool, as it reflects the categories used by members of local communities themselves. This is more desirable than importing Western conceptual frameworks that are dismissive of local articulations and understandings (Kandiyoti 1998). This approach also allows a consideration of how patterns of subordination are reproduced at the level of household, economy and society.

Gender is also crucial in understanding the relationships within and outside the household, as well as how these relations are defined, reinforced, renegotiated and challenged (Agarwal 1994, Hart 1995, Kandiyoti 1998). Therefore, a gender approach helps us to see 'how multiple understanding of "male" and "female" are socially constructed and embodied in every day practices both within and beyond the household' (Hart 1995:41). Moreover, one could argue that gender operates in at least three distinct yet interconnected ways: (1) ideologically, especially in terms of gendered representations and valorizations of social processes and practices; (2) at the level of social relations; and (3) physically, through the social construction of male and female bodies (Marchand and Runyan 2000).

Attempts to challenge the existing male dominance institutionalized in the household, community, market and state are theoretically examined in relation to women's roles and bargaining positions in households and communities. The rules and practices through which familial relations are constructed, and the scope that they give women to challenge, negotiate and transform them, are variable, taking different forms over time and in different settings (Kabeer 1994). Therefore, it is crucial to consider the implications of migration on gender relations and women's positions in their households and communities. Gender affects and is affected by social, political, economic and religious forces. Migration represents a drastic life change, and gender roles and relations often shift in this process. At the same time, gender permeates many of the practices, identities and institutions involved in the processes of immigration and integration.

5.6.1   'Bargaining with patriarchy': Gender relations in Turkey

Before analysing the changing aspect of women's status in the Turkish community in London it is important to broadly outline the main conceptualizations of gender relations in Turkey. One of the major theoretical contributions of the understanding of gender relations in Turkey came from Kandiyoti, with her concept of 'bargaining with patriarchy' (1988). In her analysis, the classic patriarchal family appears to represent the actual structural arrangements of family life even though it may vary in form and shape. It embodies the forms of control and subordination associated with the patriarchal family system, in which women receive protection and security in exchange for submissiveness and propriety, and adopt interpersonal strategies that maximize their security through manipulation.

The allocation of roles and responsibilities in the household is made among family members on the basis of gender, age and seniority. In the extended family, senior men have authority over all members of the household, including younger men. The young bride is brought from her family, through marriage, to another male-headed household in which her husband's close female kin – mother, sister, brother's wife – exercise considerable power over her. Therefore, women can establish higher status in the household and gain their economic security by having sons. The hardship that younger women endure is eventually superseded by the control and authority they exert over their own daughters-in-law. During their lives, women have varying degrees of power and status. At a younger age, women are in a subordinate position to older women in their families. It is also argued that women have not just been submissive and passive victims of patriarchy; they have also acted strategically to obtain recognition within the existing ideological framework of gender relations. Women's power of manipulating their husband's and sons' affection in return for enduring lifetime security makes them active in the perpetuation of the patriarchal order (Kandiyoti 1988).

In this system, men, as fathers and husbands, bear the responsibility for the security, honour and reputation of their families, and women should be legally, economically and morally dependent on men. Women's code of behaviour, whose identity is constructed on their dependence and submissiveness, may bring their family honour or shame. Kandiyoti (1988) describes women's relation to this system of male domination as 'bargaining with patriarchy'. Women receive 'protection and security in exchange for submissiveness and propriety' (1988:280). However, socio-economic changes in Turkish society, coupled with urbanization, migration and the commodification of agriculture, have generated 'new areas of uncertainty and a renegotiation of relationships based on gender and age' (Kandiyoti 1995:307). The result of the social changes has been that men's unquestioned authority has become less secure and not for granted. Women's diverse responses to male authority have taken the forms of accommodating and subverting. My aim here is to show that the transformations of social conditions such as migration in which the authoritarian and protective patriarchy is embedded do not always mean a general change in the relationships between men and women or a radical reform of what it means to be a husband or a wife. The reproduction of familiar traditional practices continues in new social contexts. Whatever the form that women's responses to changing patriarchy take, whether accommodating its traditional protection or subverting it, they need to be contextualized within the framework of classical patriarchy, which women themselves internalize. In the next section, there will be an analysis of how Turkish women respond to the changes taking place following migration to London and whether radical transformations taking place in traditional gender relations will improve women's status and power in the Turkish community of London.

5.6.2   Gendered implications of migration

The literature on female migration generally focuses on two broad aspects of status that can change as a result of the migration process. The first is the position of migrant women within their families. For some women, migration may mean an increase in social mobility, economic independence and relative autonomy. Theoretically, migration may improve women's empowerment and social position if it leads to increased participation in employment, more control over earnings and greater participation in family decision making (Pessar 1984). New economic and social responsibilities may change the distribution of power within the family, leading to greater authority and participation in household decision making and control over the family's resources. These may also cause positive shifts in the relationship between immigrant women and their husbands and children. Alternatively, migration may leave gender asymmetries largely unchanged even though certain dimensions of gender inequalities are modified (Espiritu 2005). The second aspect of status change discussed in the literature on women and migration focuses on the impact of moving from one form of gender stratification system to another. In general terms, this means moving from one system of patriarchy to another.

Analysing the changes taking place in gender relations is challenging, and needs to be framed within analytical categories. Thus, it can be evaluated using the framework of Elson and Pearson (1981), who conceptualize the impact of social change and female employment on gender subordination in terms of tendencies to decompose and intensify existing forms of gender subordination and to recompose new forms of subordination. The decomposition of gender subordination may be seen in the status and power that immigration to London brings to women, both at home and in their community. It is also discussed in the literature that 'Work enhances women's self-esteem as wives and mothers, affords them income to actualize these roles more fully and provides them with a heightened leverage to participate equally with men in household decision making' (Pessar 1986:281). As shown in the case of Fatma, she became a powerful figure in her family and had great decision making power as a result of her work in the textile industry. Her case also coincides with ageing women's roles in the classic patriarchy model in which women exercise a considerable amount of power over younger members of their households. Emerging opportunities for informal work and economic pressures to generate extra income always have to be balanced with women's traditional roles, which ultimately affect the meaning and value attached to women's work. This change in gender relations has been accomplished by women themselves, but moving to a new society may also bring some additional rights and protection that women may use to change the asymmetric power relations between women and men. In this regard, there are more women opting out of their abusive marriages and exercising their rights in their new country. One woman reported that 'Women have rights in this country. They don't have to put up with a cheating or beating husband. Here we had many cases where husbands were put into prison because they beat up their wives. Everything is different here!' Women exercising their rights is not the result of women's economic contribution, but a result of a set of rights and protection offered to women by the British state's domestic violence laws and the long history of women's movements to end gender-based violence. Not all women report domestic violence, and some men resist this shift in power and continue beating their wives, often with the knowledge that their wives cannot go to the police because they are undocumented and so would jeopardize their entire family's position in the country.

The recomposition of gender subordination may be seen in the consolidation of women's roles as housewives or mothers. After the closure of textile workshops, women returned to their traditional roles and retired from labour market activities. The inactivity of women has been the result of the expansion of the male-dominated Turkish ethnic economy. Therefore, women lost their high income earning power in industrial production, and those in work only have low-paying service jobs in the ethnic economy. This meant a step backwards for women whose earning potential was reduced, and a rising proportion of female inactivity in the Turkish community. In fact, motherhood became the only occupation for women and they returned to the domestic sphere. Therefore, immigrant women refocused on their motherhood and wife roles, which rebuilt traditional gender roles under new social conditions.

As indicated earlier, chain migration can also be seen as a way to transfer the social relations that are dominant in a community to the new host society. It re-establishes the various aspects of social structure, such as kinship patterns and familial ties as well as gender relations. The close networks in the Turkish community in London meant the continuation of the classic patriarchal family structure in which the man is the head of the household and has power over women and younger men. In this regard, the intensification of gender subordination is observed in the public policing of women's behaviour. It is mostly observed in the public voices, which blame women for not being 'good' enough mothers and always looking to make money. Therefore, women are blamed for the second generation's unsuccessful school records and their involvement in criminal activities. Moreover, the motherhood practices of women are observed by the whole community and measured by their children's success in life. In fact, to prevent second generation children falling into the 'wrong hands' many girls are married at a young age and most of these marriages are arranged by parents. This confines women to a tight cage; not only are they expected to submit to the traditional gender roles but their value is measured by their children's behaviour. This has resulted in the intensification of gender subordination among Turkish female migrants in London.

The gendered implications of migration in the case of Turkish migrants show that the socio-economic changes have affected the practices dominating gender relations in the community and have resulted in conflicting outcomes for women. On the one hand, women gained power and status as a result of their economic income generating opportunities in the textile industry and through ageing. On the other hand, women are pulled back into the domestic sphere in times of ethnic economy, as the community highlights the need for women to be full-time mothers and wives. The most powerful gendered implication of migration for women is being in a country which protects them with an extensive women's rights framework, ranging from domestic violence to other forms of gender-based discrimination, if they ever want to exercise those rights.

5.6.3   Gender relations, family life and marriage

The continuation of strong familial and community relations leaves limited leverage for women to confront traditional gender relations, since women have weak connections with mainstream British society, and the employment opportunities that may well be a starting point for changing the asymmetric gender relations are often found in the Turkish ethnic economy. The community has a strong tendency to reproduce existing gender roles and relations that are perpetuated by preserving the traditional family structure based on marriages. The emphasis on establishing a traditional Turkish family is enforced by the Turkish chain migration to Britain, and the importance of the familial and community networks for the continuation of the ethnic economy. Thus, marriages are at the heart of the patriarchal family and the young generation is encouraged to marry and become part of the ever expanding community.

The customary practice of marriage is still dominant among the Turkish community in London and arranged marriages are practiced widely. This is even though most people complain about increasing divorce rates and the fractured nature of families. The community leaders blame the better rights women have in Britain to protect themselves against domestic violence for fostering the increasing number of divorces. Women blame men who do not look after their families and who go after other women. In this regard, both the Turkish community and women complain about the changes brought to the patriarchal family values would like to hold on the traditional gendered roles and relations and keep them intact. Therefore, it is important to provide a brief overview of what these traditional domestic roles are in Turkish society.

In Turkish society, marriage gives women a certain status, although in a controlled and restricted way. Delaney (1987:42) suggests that 'Unmarried women are socially invisible' in Turkey. The relationship between husband and wife is based primarily on duty and obligations, men are the main bread winners and are responsible for the economic well-being of the family, while women are confined to the domestic sphere by the ideologies of mothering, caring and nurturing (Dedeoglu 2012). Women tend to marry either one of their kin or someone from their village or region. The reason for the custom of marrying someone from the village of origin (*hemşehri*) or network of kin is that the families know each other. This gives families certain knowledge about the character and qualities of the prospective bride and groom. For example, mothers try to find a groom with secure employment or income who will support their daughters. Families with sons try to find obedient girls from 'good families' with good labour skills. Through marriage, a woman secures the protection of her husband in the form of personal security and financial support, and a man establishes his role of patriarch as head of the family. In respect to practical needs, a man marries to be cared for by a woman, because men are considered to be incapable of taking care of themselves. The idea that a man must have a woman to look after his daily needs is reinforced through childhood training. A boy is served by his mother and sister(s), and all of his housekeeping needs such as food, laundry, cleaning and ironing are provided by a woman. When men marry, this role passes to their wives. Men's involvement in housekeeping activities is socially discouraged and ridiculed. The enforcement of men's lack of interest in household chores is also a way of keeping men tied to the marriage contract (White 1994).

The wealth and labour exchanged between families are transferred through the cultural practices of *çeyiz* (trousseau) and *başlık* (bride price). The bride is expected to bring a considerable amount of *çeyiz* (trousseau) items, such as lace bedspreads, quilts, pillows, night clothes, slippers, and hand-woven cardigans and jumpers that represent the girl's handicraft (*elişi*) skills, when she marries. Bride price is a widespread customary practice, which involves the transfer of wealth to the father of the bride in the form of *başlık*. In some regions, this transfer is made in the form of cash, but in some it is in the form of gold bracelets that are presented as a wedding gift to the bride. Despite the consideration of the gold bracelets as a gift, families negotiate the number that the bride should be given. The difference between the customary practice of *başlık* and gold as a gift is that the bride has possession of these gold bracelets, whereas the possession of *başlık* is kept by the family of the bride as the price of bringing up a woman who is given away to the service of the groom's family. The exchange of gold bracelets and their number are always negotiated before the marriage and it is seen as the provision of financial protection for the daughter in case of breakdown of the marriage. In Turkish society, marriage is a medium of labour and wealth exchange between families. Families make alliances through marriage to bring an extra strand of security into the web of reciprocity that supports the system of related families. The alliances between families of similar social classes not only establish access to extra labour and economic resources, but also access to social relations and networks. Marriage, according to White (1994), is the single most powerful way of declaring membership of a community, and also a signal of the willingness to remain in the community.

5.7   Conclusion

This chapter has examined the details of Turkish women's migration to Britain, and how this has had an impact on traditional gender roles and relations in the post-migration process. In a comparison with the classic case of Turkish women's migration to Germany, the British case is a gender balanced migration and the popularity of women's labour in textile production in London encouraged more Turkish female migrants to come to Britain. Therefore, it is difficult to simply explain women's migration as a family unification process. The ethnographic section focused on a sample of women workers to explore the demographic characteristics and household structures of women who are engaged in the ethnic economy. This showed that migrant women are first generation migrants, who mostly have a low level of education and who are from working class families with rural backgrounds in Turkey. The women were in a conjugal relationship and lived in a family union, which is the strongest social institution of the Turkish community. Migration has been a common experience for all of the women in the sample. Their status as refugees has led to their sense of exclusion and isolation in Britain, and is a common experience for these women.

A detailed look at the women's characteristics focused on two generations of women. The characteristics of these groups are different not so much because their move to London took place in different time frames, but because their access to economic activities varies. Those who arrived earlier in the 1980s worked in the textile industry, which brought power and status for women in their families and community. Recent arrivals did not have the opportunity to work in the textile industry, so became unpaid family or low-wage workers in the Turkish ethnic economy. For some women, the expansion of catering based family shops resulted in the withdrawal of women from paid work activities. This led women to return to their traditional roles as mothers and wives, and drop their income-generating activities.

This chapter also dealt with a particularly controversial area of womens' studies, which explored the role of gender relations and gendered implications in the migration process. In the Turkish culture, where social organization is heavily based on the family unit, family and marriage are important sources of identity and security as well as economic support for women. Women mitigate 'patriarchal risk' through marriage and complying with traditional gender roles and relations. Publicly voicing themselves through the roles of motherhood and wifehood, women can only gain status and decision making power to the extent that they assume those roles. Thus, the confinement of women to their roles as mothers and wives is the only way for women to attain power in both private and public spheres. Only through the manipulation of these relations can women effectively negotiate with their husbands, their father and other members of their family and community. Within this context, this chapter showed how gender, work and women's domestic roles are entangled with each other, and that the changing economic activity of the Turkish community had a long lasting effect on women's positions in the community and has affected women's opportunities for paid work, as well as the way in which women establish their priority as 'the woman of the home'.

6
Women's Work in London's Turkish Ethnic Economy

While strolling through Green Lanes in Haringey one comes across many restaurants with Turkish names, such as Gökyüzü, Hala, Yayla, Antepliler, Diyarbakır and many others. A short glance reveals that there are not many women workers in these restaurants. The most visible ones are those working as waitresses. During the day, one can see women pastry-makers through the shop window where they appear to be sitting and making pastry. This is the most visible type of female labour in the Turkish ethnic economy but it is only the tip of the iceberg. There are many other categories of women involved in the ethnic business. However, their contribution remains invisible, and is classed as domestic work or reproductive activity. This chapter aims to highlight the invisible work carried out by women and to analyse it in relation to the textile work that women used to do in the 1980s and 1990s in London.

Female migrants in London experienced a major shift in their economic activity, which changed from work in the garment industry to either being unpaid family or low-paid workers in their ethnic enclave business. This shift occurred with the closure of textile workshops and the expansion of ethnic catering shops. This shift meant a move towards economic inactivity for a large number of women. The expansion of the Turkish ethnic economy, on the one hand, confined women to the domestic sphere, and on the other hand, forced women to take up roles in ethnic shops to balance with their domestic roles as wives, mothers, sisters and daughters. Some of these women worked as unpaid family workers in family-owned businesses, but some became low-paid wage-workers to provide additional income for their families and children. Moreover, men married to second generation immigrant women utilized their wives' knowledge of the British system and language ability to run their businesses.

In addition to all these roles, migrant women are perceived as having a major role in the construction and reproduction of ethnic identities and cultures. Therefore, the role of women in the Turkish ethnic economy is important not only as a source of unpaid or cheap labour but also as a signifier or bearer of Turkish culture. In fact, women's roles as mothers and wives ensure the continuation of Turkish culture in a new country. As the symbolic figuration of a nation, women construct and reproduce particular notions of their specific culture through their involvement in rearing children, and in social and religious practices. Through strong emphasis on women's motherhood roles in the community, women not only care for their children, but are also representatives of their ethnic, religious and cultural identities. Moreover, these identities seem to set the foundation for national culture on which the Turkish ethnic economy depends. In this regard, this chapter pays special attention to the experience of migrant women, the ordeals to which they are subjected and also their capacity to assume their destiny, to give it meaning and to represent it.

6.1   Women's work in ethnic economies

The main focus of the literature on ethnic economies has been on the relationship between certain migrant groups and the host society in which these groups live. This early literature had no specific reference to sex or gender (Hillmann 1999). The economic activities of ethnic groups are seen as the result of their inability to integrate into mainstream economic activities and the organization of work within the ethnic communities is described as paternalistic and close to pre-industrial capitalism (Hillmann 1999). What happened in the 1970s and 1980s was the increasing significance of ethnic economies in Europe and the USA where migrant entrepreneurship was seen as a 'potent economic force in big cities' (Light and Bonacich 1988:8) and ethnicity was seen as a ladder to economic success. Ethnic solidarity and reciprocal obligations are seen as the key elements of ethnic economies, in which an integration of co-ethnic manufacturers, workers and customers are a starting point. Access to ethnic social networks that provide easy reach to informal labour markets is identified as a facilitator of the success of ethnic economies (Hillmann 1999).

The literature concerned with the composition of the workforce in ethnic business has highlighted the extensive use of unpaid family labour. Light and Bonacich (1988) showed that 60% of all Korean firms in the United States relied on the use of nuclear family or extended family members in their businesses. Therefore, the success of self-employed men is highly criticized as disguising the contributions and efforts of other family members, especially those of women (Hillmann 1999). Zhou's study on the Chinese ethnic economy shows the gender specific outcomes as follows. The ethnic economy is mostly dependent upon women's labour, and their education level is higher than that of men, but women remained invisible as their earnings were lower than men's and their contribution to the Chinese ethnic economy had little impact on their professional advancement. Therefore, Zhou's study (1992) showed that the ethnic economy as a ladder of success for ethnic families was limited to men, while women were silent contributors to ethnic economies. Other studies emphasized the fact that women earn lower wages and have fewer opportunities for career advancements as well as limited emancipation (Bonacich 1988, Anthias 1992, Gilbertson 1995).

As ethnic economies are usually formed by family-based establishments and heavily rely on family labour, the role of women's work has been identified as essential in ethnic businesses. The use of female kinship labour has even been considered a necessary 'building block' for the development of ethnic minority enterprises in Britain (Anthias 1992). However, gender sensitive research shows that ethnic economies do not necessarily support the professional advancement of women as much as they do for men, and can keep them in a subordinate position, thus preventing their inclusion in the host society. It is proposed that female immigrant workers are 'generally captive by other relationships than that of a wage' (Panayiotopoulos 1996:455). The predominantly male-controlled and labour-intensive nature of many ethnic economies is marked by 'social structures which give easy access to female labour subordinated to patriarchal control mechanisms' (Phizacklea 1988:22). In this framework, women are seen as being under the control of the patriarchal and ethnic ties of their community.

Hillmann (1999) distinguishes three stages of integrating gender in the research on ethnic economies. The first stage is complete gender-blindness where women are considered to be absent from ethnic businesses. The second line of research focused on women's situations compared with men's where women earned lower wages and had minimal benefits in terms of human capital and upward mobility inside and outside their ethnic enclave. In the third line of research, highlighted especially in the studies of the 1990s, the main focus was on the subordination of women to patriarchal control as a mechanism for the survival of ethic business. Hillmann also shows that the professional activities of women in the ethnic economy did not change their status in their families, and they had the double burden of work and family-related care and domestics tasks (1999:270).

This book is closer to the third approach and has shown that women's participation in income earning activities, whether be it in the garment industry or the ethnic enclave economy, is shaped by the influence of patriarchal control that has intensified with the expansion of the Turkish ethnic economy and pushed women further into the domestic sphere as mothers and wives. When women's labour is needed in family-based businesses, their contributions are mostly seen as just helping out, and as an extension of their domestic roles. Women are included in the ethnic labour workforce through their domestic roles as mothers, wives and daughters. In the garment industry days, women's work was visible and widely accepted by the community as a valuable contribution to the well-being of immigrant families, but women's work was silenced when the ethnic economy did not need women's labour as much as the garment industry did. Therefore, women are pulled and pushed in different directions when the socio-economic structure shifts in the host country. In the following sections, there is a special focus on women's work in the garment production industry, as well as their ethnic economy work in London.

6.2 Women's work in the garment[1] workshops in London

Margaret Chin (2005), in her illuminating study of *Sewing Women: Immigrants and the New York City Garment Industry*, shows that for the most immigrants work is central to their survival and a migrants' decision to move is motivated mainly by the availability of work opportunities. In this regard, work is not just a means to earn money to survive but it plays a large role in societal status. She explains how immigrants prioritize labour market opportunities, and says:

> Many intermediary factors determine how and where immigrants get jobs. Immigration status and the long-term goals of the individuals (to become U.S. citizens or to return to their home country) affect the kinds of jobs that they strive for and are willing to take. Wages, work hours, and benefits are important considerations if an individual has family and children... Given a choice, immigrants favour jobs that complement their household roles as parents, providers, or supporters of relatives overseas. These bonds can be used to advance work prospects – that is, to gain access to jobs and higher wages. They can be positive when members reap benefits from ethnic ties. The ties

can also be constraining when they are used to limit access to jobs or other economic opportunities.

(Chin 2005:2)

In regard to the labour market behaviour of Turkish migrants, many worked in the textile industry until it completely stopped in the early 2000s. There were a number of forces that were channelling these immigrants into garment production. The clustering of ethnic labour in the garment industry was the main force bringing more Turks to London. There are a number of questions that this section aims to analyse, such as: the importance of structural factors, including route of emigration; neighbourhoods, or the way the industry is organized in channelling migrant labour into a specific industry; and to what degree does gender role dictate where an immigrant works? What I found is that immigration status, ethnicity and gender are intertwined and cannot be totally disaggregated. Examining immigration status and gender provides insight into the specific mechanisms and conditions that alternately turn ethnic ties into resources or barriers in the pursuit of employment.

The employment opportunities for Turkish immigrants in London had for decades been limited to a number of sectors, among which the garment industry was the leading sector. Since the early 1980s, textile work was the main employment sector for people and it continued until the early 2000s when the industry completely stopped production and moved overseas. Initially, London garment production was controlled by the Jewish community which operated many sweatshops in north London. Women from Bangladeshi and Turkish-Cypriot backgrounds worked in the sector, either in the sweatshops or in their homes as home-based workers (Kabeer 2000). As the sector expanded, 'Turkish Cypriots, Turks, and Kurdish refugees were all employed, and later became employers in this sector. They followed each other in filling the workshops and creating a case of "employment by rotation"' (Atay 2010).

Atay (2010) provides a historical account of the development of the textile production industry and the involvement of Turkish communities within it. For him, the first group to enter the industry were the Turkish-Cypriots who also replaced the Greek Cypriots. Atay (2010) also shows that the Jewish community was the early owner of the business and people used to work for them. When the Jewish community moved on to better and more prestigious branches of business, such as retail and shopping industries, the gap left by them in garment workshops was filled by the Greek Cypriots as both employees and employers, and later by the Turkish-Cypriots. From the late 1970s, Turkish immigrants entered the scene as labourers. Eventually, they too started to buy the workshops and become employers. Finally, the Kurds of Turkey joined the process, first as hired workers and then, in turn, as employers in the sector (Atay 2010).

Atay (2010) also provides information on the structure of the industry. As he states:

> ... observers have stated that in 1986 and 1987, 1500 out of 2000 textile workshops in London were either owned or controlled by Turkish-speaking immigrants. The average number of people who were employed in a mill was 30. This number can be added to the other 500 workshops owned by Greek Cypriots. So, for this period we can estimate that around 50.000 people from the Turkish-speaking community were working in this trade. It is reasonable to think that these numbers increased until the early 1990s. In this period, nearly 95 per cent of the community in London was either directly or indirectly linked with textile work for their livelihood. The textile industry stayed under the control of the Turkish-speaking community until it collapsed in the mid-1990s.
>
> (2010:128)

Towards the end of the 1990s, the industry began to slow down, and the subsequent collapse was caused by the relocation of the business to countries with low labour costs and textile retailers importing their products from overseas. For Atay (2010), another reason for the collapse was the unlawful business practices of the workshop owners. By the end of the 1990s, nearly 90% of the textile industry had moved abroad.

The significance of garment production has been expressed in the interviews conducted in London. Almost all respondents mentioned how immigrants from Turkey used to work in workshops. It seems that the rising trend of migration from Turkey was directly related to the availability of work opportunities in the garment industry. When the early arrivals found that there were work opportunities they contacted other family members to come and join them. This therefore generated a chain migration. The expanding industry required more labour input and led to immigrants inviting their relatives to join them. One of my informants explained his experience:

> A few months after I arrived to London, I got used to being here. I called my brothers to come to London. I told them there was work

here. What could they do over there? There was no work in Turkey but there was work here for everybody...We were also treated well. They gave us houses and pocket money. I also worked in a textile shop. At that time, everybody worked in textiles. Husbands and wives worked together. We earned good money.

From the testimonies of migrants, it seems that the authorities had also turned a blind eye to the economic activities of Turkish migrants and did not prevent new migrants coming in when the business continued to flourish in London. Towards the end of the 1990s, when the garment industry died out, strict controls were implemented on migrants coming from Turkey. A respondent explained this in her statement:

...they knew that we were working there. Even the day we took the plane to come to London, they knew that we would come here and work in the textile workshops. Because the business grew over the time, they needed labour, but the workers were only in Turkey. None of the English would have worked here so they needed us.

A common memory of the textile days for the migrants was described as being like a commune, in which people from Turkey lived in London. Whenever people talked about those days, they always mentioned that 'everybody worked in the textiles'. There was even mention of a couple who were school teachers who had run from Turkey after the 1980s military coup d'état and who then worked in the textile industry. The couple ran away from the imprisonment of the military government and found refuge in London, where they stayed for about five years working in a textile workshop together. When the political environment improved in Turkey, they went back and took up their teaching positions again. The distinctive character of this case meant that the community remembers them because they saw that even educated people undertook textile work in London. Moreover, the locational clustering of the industry meant that people interacted with each other, and shared similar experiences. This helped to develop a good sense of community and belonging. Thus, there was a vibrant and reactive community that developed in those 'good old' textile days.

People even remember the textile days as happy times of their lives in London. However, the working conditions and the structure of the industry were not all rosy. Firstly, the nature of the production required a network of migrants coming together to set up their business and meet the labour requirements. The labour-intensive nature of the work required a good network of people, whose connections went beyond the relationship of employer and employee, and dedicated workers whose labour could be integrated into production through familial and kin relations (Dedeoglu 2011). Therefore, in the context of London, the chain migration of people from Turkey whose family members had arrived in London earlier helped some migrants to own their own textile workshops. A former textile workshop owner explained this in the following statement:

> I started as a worker and worked in the textile more than five years. As my other family members arrived I began to consider having my own workshop. To be honest we are very crowded here, there are many people living in London from our village back in Turkey. So I had a lot of support from them. You cannot manage on your own since the textile work is very difficult and you need a lot of help from people dedicated to your cause. I had my brother and my-wife's family members. We are a big family here.

Secondly, harsh working conditions and long working hours were usually associated with textile production. This was true for London's textile production. Many migrants remembered how they used to work in a building with other migrants from Turkey for long hours, day after day for years. They had little contact outside of their close community. One of the female respondents recalled those days in the following statement:

> We were in the workshop from early morning till the late in the night. Everyone worked hard and tried to do as much as we could. Because we were mostly paid on the basis of each piece we did. So, working long hours meant that you earned more. There was nothing in our lives, just work and home.

Thirdly, women were the main workers in the industry. Migrant women's work in the textile industry in Western countries is well documented and is connected with women's migration status in their host countries (Chin 2005, Bastina 2007). In her analysis of Bolivian women in Argentina, Bastina shows that undocumented women who have fewer work opportunities when they migrate have to take up jobs in the garment industry. Working in a garment workshop meant staying in dim workshops for long hours with no health and safety conditions. Their work day might have lasted up 12–17 hours a day for almost six days a week (Bastina 2007). Turkish women's experience was no different from the Bolivian workers in Argentina. However, there is a difference in that Turkish women migrated to London with their families rather than as solo independent migrants.

Women in London were actively involved in textile production, and their contribution was visible and highly demanded by the industry. Most of the women interviewed mentioned the extensive use of women's labour in the industry as women were seen to be naturally more suitable for garment making. Most men learned their sewing skills from their wives. Thus, women's earning potential was higher. One woman commented:

> … people usually worked as couples so that they could earn more. My husband and I also worked together. In the beginning he did not know what he needed to do as he never did garment work before. I thought him what to do. As time went by, he eventually became a garment worker.

Since it was thought that women were more suitable for the work, women's earning potential was higher than men's. This affected the pattern of Turkish women's migration to London and made it different from that of the guest worker system in Germany where women were seen as dependent family migrants. One of my informants stated:

> I started working as soon as we arrived. I was an over-lock sewing machine operator. I did 250 pieces a day and got paid 70 pounds. We earned quite good amount of money during that time. I was working together with my husband. It was always good to work together so you got more at the end of the day. That's why wife and husband always worked together. I worked for 13 or 14 years like this and during that time I had my children grown up.

Although no one would dispute the benefits of the jobs and money that the textile industry provided for the community and for migrant families, it also increased women's status in the community as workers and earners. For most of these women, working in the textile industry was their first industrial job, as they had a rural background and had never worked in their lives, other than in their small family-owned land in their villages. This did not mean that women left their traditional roles and family obligations; they remained responsible for domestic roles and childcare. Women's domestic roles and identities had an impact on their working pattern, and some women preferred working from home while caring for their children. In other cases, women generated their own care networks and caring schemes.

> I had my sister here so I left my children to her. I had three children and each was around same age, just a year or two apart. We worked quite long hours and without those relatives and family members caring for our kids we could not stay in the workshops for those long hours. My sister made a living out of child caring as every woman was working in the textile they needed to get day-time-care for their children.

Although women had the option to arrange their place of work around their domestic responsibilities, textile work involved long hours and tedious work. This meant that women worked long hours with people from their own communities or in an isolated home environment with minimal contact with the outside world. However, the distinct character of women's work during this period was its visibility to their families and community as it had high financial returns and brought economic rewards. However, it did little to overhaul traditional gender relations because the work itself took place within the ethnic circle and women remained confined in their traditional roles with little prospect of changing them. In fact, this type of work compounded the psychology of being a migrant, and the desire to save up as much as they could so that they had enough savings to secure a life after their return to Turkey. Long work hours, cash-in-hand income and flourishing businesses kept the Turkish population going for some years as workers and employers. For women this work meant more visibility of labour for their family and community but also isolated them within their small community circles with no contact with the outside world.

6.3   Women workers of the Turkish ethnic economy in London

Women's work in ethnic economies is usually conceptualized within the framework of their contribution to family-based ethnic business as an unpaid family or lower paid worker. It is also accepted that few economic opportunities exist for immigrant women outside the ethnic enclave (Hillmann 1999). This is also true for first generation Turkish migrant women in London. Turkish women's work in the ethnic economy helped the success of the ever expanding ethnic business and their work became a part of the Europe wide Turkish ethnic economy and entrepreneurship. London's Turkish ethnic economy is also part of this European phenomenon and women contribute to it in many diverse ways, but usually as unpaid family workers. This chapter offers an inside view into migrants' experiences, and shows how inequalities through social change are reproduced, as well as focusing on their economic and social consequences.

The significance of women's work in the ethnic economy was the change it generated in women's economic positions. With the expansion of the ethnic economy, women's economic activity had dramatically changed and remarkably diminished following the closure of textile workshops. The most significant outcome was the change that women experienced in their economic activity and how the Turkish community's demand on women's labour altered since the high days of textile production in London. Now, there is greater emphasis placed on women and their role as mothers by the community, as women's work in the textile sector was seen as the reason for many young people of the second leaving their family and community. They were also drawn into gang culture, and became involved in a web of criminal activities. Community leaders were mostly concerned with the fact that many young men were imprisoned in the UK and that there was an extraordinary frequency of suicides among the second generation of Turkish migrants. This issue will be dealt with in Chapter 7 and its further implications for changing the emphasis of the main roles of women in the community.

With the dominance of ethnic economic activity in London, Turkish women are not as actively involved in ethnic businesses as they used to be in textile production. Women have not completely withdrawn from the labour market but, rather, their contribution has become invisible and under-recognized. This was due to the nature of the business; the Turkish ethnic economy is a male-dominated environment that involves serving strange and unrelated men. Working for the catering industry means that shops remain open until late serving customers from various backgrounds, mostly men. In the Muslim Turkish culture, women's contact with unrelated men is forbidden, and is only allowed when it is imperative. Therefore, male business owners do not allow their wives or mothers to work at the counter in their shop after 11 p.m., even though their businesses rely on extensive use of family labour and kin-networks.

Due to the widespread nature of family-run shops in the forms of *döner*-kebab houses, off-licences and coffee shops, women's labour is mostly utilized as 'help'. This 'help' takes the form of cleaning the shop, cutting the vegetables, doing the dishes and making pastry to sell. Although women work hard for family businesses and contribute in diverse ways, the owner of a shop is always a man, either father or husband. Running an ethnic business is a public sphere activity requires a constant interaction with outside world and it is believed that men are more suitable for this job, as women have more home-bound duties and their contribution is considered as 'help'.

Families running a shop usually expressed the fact that it was very difficult to run a shop without a large family. Different family members offer different contributions to the family business. Family members provide a reliable and low-cost workforce through which families not only utilize their labour but also their English language skills and other administrative knowledge that is necessary to conduct a business. In this regard, grown up children are the best option for families aspiring to own their business and aiming to pool their resources as their English language skills are a must for the business. In some cases, it is reported that children are prevented from pursuing higher education so that they can help with the family business. However, women usually become casual workers or helpers and the running of the business is left in the hands of male members of the family. The male-dominated nature of the ethnic business in London is the reason for women's marginal role and their withdrawal from economic activities. The rest of this chapter focuses on different roles women play in London's Turkish ethnic economy.

6.3.1 Unpaid family workers: Mothers, wives and daughters

Early studies examining the role of women in family-operated small-businesses draw attention to the fact that women, even with pro-fessional backgrounds, eventually found themselves helping out in family-owned grocery stores, restaurants and gift shops (Brettell 2007). The impact of self-employment on gender roles is explored in regard to how women's roles change in the family. Espiritu (1999) observes that for immigrant women in small-businesses, their work is an extension of their domestic responsibilities. Often they find themselves cooking at the store. Indeed, she argues that the Asian immigrant small-business sector is built on the back of Asian and other immigrant women. One of her points is that depending on where they are in the labour market, there are different outcomes for Asian immigrant women. Overall, however, Espiritu's conclusion is that in this form of family-based self-employment women experience extreme isolation and family dependence (Espiritu 1999).

In London's Turkish ethnic economy, female family members exchange their labour for their loyalty to their families and their membership in their community. Offering their unpaid labour is a way of confirming their domestic roles as mothers and wives. In this regard, what Sharma (1986) calls 'household service work', in which domestic tasks extend beyond meeting the physical needs of household members to providing and maintaining ties with kin, neighbours and friends, who are a source of information and aid, is a useful framework for explaining women's work and contributions to the ethnic economy. By combining their household work with ethnic business activities, unpaid family workers play a vital role in connecting the areas of production and reproduction. Yet these women consider themselves to be just housewives.

Women's roles in ethnic businesses differed depending on their domestic roles and positions in families. For example, mothers were less involved in businesses than wives. The mothers were from the older generation whose contributions came from the financial means they accumulated in the textile days. For this generation of the family, the ethnic business is usually supported to secure the future of their grown up children and is left to their management. Even in this situation, women make important labour contributions to maintain their shops. In the Dalston area of London, there was a coffee shop owned by a family and run by two brothers with the help of their father and mother. The mother of the brothers was in her early 50s, and, in principle, she said that she did not intervene with the business of her sons. Even though she said that she did not get in their sons' way she visited the coffee shop every day, and stayed there for a few hours. She helped with the dishes, and sometimes she made Turkish pastries to be sold.

> My husband and I worked so hard in the past. I did work for 15 years in textile workshops and raised four children. I wanted my sons to have a good future since we could not manage to keep them in the school. These days the best thing is to own your own shop and everyone does it. We invested the most of the money we made in those days to this shop ... I come here so often and help them out. I do different things. I used to make pastry but I am old now and I twisted my wrist and it is difficult for me to do it now. But I do the dishes and clean up the place from time to time. My husband is here everyday to watch over the boys ... We are a family and my duty is to support my children.

The survival of ethnic businesses is mainly dependent upon the utilization of unpaid family members, as this is the only source of reliable, flexible and cheap labour. As more and more people open up their own shops there is a thin margin of profits on which the family-based shops rely. Thus, the only way to survive is to exploit your own family members' labour. In this regard, female labour is a vital input for London's ethnic establishments and is utilized in many diverse ways. A woman who is the wife of a restaurant owner talked about her work in the shop:

> I worked as a cook in our shop. There are tons of things a woman can do in a restaurant and I do almost everything. If I don't work there he pays someone 500 pounds a week for the same thing I do. However, no one sees them as contribution to the business. When I complain that I fell tired they ask me what I did.

A woman whose husband runs a kebab house in London also spoke about her work in their shop and complained her husband and others not valuing her work.

> I work in the shop from 9 am to 2 pm until my kids come back from school. After work I rush to school to pick them up. I do everything in the shop and I also make pastry. Pastries sell very well. If I don't make them they need to hire a woman to make them... But at the end of the day, my husband never appreciates my work here. He feels that this is his shop and I am only a help.

It is also possible to observe the invisible work carried out by women in off-licence shops, in which men are usually seen serving customers. Mothers and wives are the invisible workforce in these shops and their contributions range from cleaning the shop and shelving products to cooking meals for the shop workers. Leyla was a mother of two, and her husband owned an off-licence shop near to their home in north London. She explained her work in the shop as follows:

> My husband works with his brother in the shop. They are always busy and there is a lot to do. Especially when there is delivery that day is quite hectic and they call me to help them. I help them to get goods replaced in the shelves. I clean the shop from time to time and I cook for them everyday as they work longer than 12 hours a day.

Family enterprises are organized through a labour hierarchy. Positions within the family translate into working identities for men and women, and family members usually participate in the family business by offering services that directly or indirectly contribute to the success of the business. In return, some are unpaid workers, while others receive payments for their contributions. For the Turkish immigrant women in small-businesses, their work is an extension of their domestic responsibilities, and they often do the cooking and cleaning. The Turkish immigrant small-business sector is built on the back of Turkish women's unpaid labour. It seems true to say that this form of work results in women's extreme isolation and family dependency. Thus, women's contributions within their domestic roles and identities usually remain unpaid, invisible and unrecognized by the family and community.

6.3.2   Paid women workers: Employment in the ethnic circle

In the studies examining women's positions in the ethnic economy, it is argued that ethnic economy is a site of empowerment for immigrant women if they are the sole owners and operators of their businesses and the primary bread winners (Dallalfar 1994). Dallalfar (1994) describes Iranian women in Los Angeles and how female business owners used their gender, class and ethnic resources to start up businesses, and introduce products and services into the ethnic economy. However, this situation is different. Gilbertson (1995) concludes that immigrant women who are employed in small-businesses within enclave economies do not achieve the same level of success as their male counterparts. Indeed, they are often highly exploited.

Not all women workers in the ethnic economy are family members or relatives. Although most family members are involved in family-based work, in some cases it becomes necessary to hire extra help. The help usually comes from close family circuits. This is also true for women's labour and ethnic establishments obtain their required female labour from their own social networks. This also shows a hierarchical relationship between families who have the resources to own their shops and those who do not have access to similar levels of financial resources so have to be employed by those who have. This divide is most apparent for those who migrated in the mid-1990s or later, who could not accumulate enough financial means to open their own shops. Thus they became a source of cheap labour for other families who had enough capital to run their own shops.

For women, working in a family-owned ethnic establishment perpetuates the existing gender and social relations based on kinship. The intimate connections with kin and friends working at the same place are maintained outside the home. In every interview, many informants emphatically expressed the fact that a family or friend connection had helped them to get their current jobs, suggesting that women's entry into the labour market is constrained to the places where they have acquaintances. Moreover, women always felt obligated to those who had given them job opportunities, and kept those relational ties going. The sense of obligation and respect compelling them to work hard and show dedication to their employers creates a work ethic and commitment to the workplace, as if it were their own home. As a result, women sometimes find it difficult to change jobs, even when they have better opportunities elsewhere. White (1994:47) calls these social relations based on reciprocity and trustworthiness the 'power of debt', which allows people to feel obligated to one another in return for a favour, such as offering a job or lending money.

For some Turkish migrant women, wage work offered by the ethnic enclave is the single most important job opportunity for Turkish women, and is accessed through the connections and networks of family and relatives. Hazal worked in her uncle's off-licence shop and prepared meals for the shop workers.

> Where else could I have worked? This is my only opportunity as I cannot speak English. Working in the shop helps me to make some pocket money and I spend it for my children. So I have a better life. Actually I am grateful that my uncle's son offered this job.

The most common job women do is working as a pastry – *gözleme* – maker, as observed in almost all Turkish restaurants in London that have one or two women making pastries during lunch and dinner time. Making pastry also represents Turkish culture, and bears reference to their home culture. In a traditional sense, mothers prepare hot pastries and breads for their children and family members. A similar trend of pastry-making 'mothers' has become popular in big cities in Turkey such as Istanbul, Ankara and Izmir in which many domestic migrants were located during the last 40 years of urbanization in Turkey. Therefore, pastry-maker women generate an image of nostalgia and home culture in London too.

Pastry-maker women were older and had a rural background, as this skill was much more related to village life in Turkey. One of these women, Ayse, was working in a coffee shop in London and had two grown up children. Her husband was too sick to work, and did not work for a long time. Her work was the main income source for the family, topping up the welfare benefits the family received from the state. She said:

> Actually it is not very easy to find women who can make pastry the young generation do not know it. I learned it from my mother and making bread was our daily work back in our village. People like it here, and we offer pastry with different stuffing ... I never thought that I would do such a job one day. Life is interesting.

Ayse said that women's traditional skills helped them to make a living in a modern world, even in London. As will be discussed further in this chapter, women's economic activities based on their domestic roles are not as lucrative as the work of some women in days of the textile industry.

In the group of women employed in waged work in the Turkish ethnic economy, there are a few who work in off-licence shops at cash tills. These women are better at using the English language so they can handle the contact with English customers. Ayla was one of these few women and worked in her relative's shop. She had two school-aged children. She arrived at the shop at six in the morning, and worked until her children came back from school at 3 p.m. Her work day was arranged according to her children's school schedule.

> As I have been living in London for a long time and arrive here at quite young age my English is much better than others. You need a bit of English to work in this job ... After I separated from my husband I needed to work to earn some pocket money. The shop owner is from our own family and they trust me. It is very difficult to trust a stranger in this kind job as money is involved. So we trust each other.

The ethnic economy does not generate a wide spectrum of jobs for female immigrants. Women either work as a pastry-maker or cleaner, or cook for other staff members. Women's wage work in the ethnic economy is structured around their obligations in their family circles and they have access to these jobs through their relatives and family members; hence they reinforce their identity as mothers and wives as well as assure their group membership. Another important aspect of this work for women is not seen as making a living but as earning pocket money or additional income for the family budget. Thus, work is temporary for women, and it never challenges their traditional patriarchal roles in their families and communities.

6.3.3   The role of 'second' generation women in the ethnic economy

Another group of women whose contribution is also important for the Turkish ethnic economy in London is that of second generation women. This group's work could be analysed under the unpaid family workers category but their input to the business goes beyond mere manual labour and includes their skills and knowledge. In fact, their contribution is in the form of administrative labour and putting their social capital to work for the maintenance and success of their family-based establishments. These women migrated to London at a young age and were schooled in the UK. However, their life patterns are dominated by Turkish culture and social practices; they remained close to the first generation migrants rather than integrating into mainstream society. The first indicator of this is their education histories, which ended at the earliest stage and none of these women pursued further education, they finished school as soon as they could. Başak was one of these women who migrated to London when she was ten years old and she spoke about her education as follows.

> I was ten years old when my parents came to London. In the beginning it was very hard as I did not know any English. But after a while I got used to system and was schooled until I was 16. As my parents both worked in the textile and I had two little sisters I decided to leave school and look after them. I kind of regret this decision now because we have every opportunity to go to school.

As a result of leaving school early, second generation women remained confined in traditional patriarchal family values, which has impacted upon the options available for these women. This was most obvious in their marriages to first generation migrants or people who resided in Turkey before their marriage. Başak married a man who migrated in the early 1990s and they met through their close family circle as they both shared the same place of origin – *memleket* – in Turkey. It is easier for parents to arrange marriages if people are *hemşehri*(s). She spoke about meeting and dating her husband:

> We saw each other in a couple of occasions. It is easier, you know, to meet if you had the same social setting and the same acquaints.

> We are both from Sivas and had shared a common circle of relatives.
> He came here as a student and then sought asylum. My parents knew
> his family back in Turkey. It then became easier for us to date and get
> each other to know better. After dating a few months we got engaged
> and then married.

Marriage to second generation women turned out to be a stepping stone
for first generation men in their ethnic business endeavours, as they
relied heavily on their wives' English language ability and skills in dealing with the administrative details of the business. Women bring a solid
source of help in every aspect for the family and the business since
men are not accustomed to the British business system at all. Zeynep's
husband owned a *döner*-kebab takeaway in London and she said that
'whenever there is a letter from authorities or a phone call to make he
asks me to deal with it. I actually do not work in the shop, but you
know, every other day there is something he needs me to do.' Zeynep is
not involved in the day-to-day running of the shop or matters that her
husband can handle within the Turkish business circle such as order-
ing wholesale products like *döner*s, chips and drinks. Because all the
suppliers are Turkish providers, there is no difficulty for him in this
regard. However, her skills are essential in the administrative activities
of the shop.

In the world of the Turkish migrants of London, these women are
seen as educated and independent. Başak's husband runs an off-licence
shop in London and she expressed her contribution in the following
statement:

> Basak does every kind of paper work for the shop. We are a family
> and there is no such thing you and me!. Her contribution is enor-
> mous. She manages to finalise everything she undertakes. I would not
> been able to do this job without her contribution...We are Alevies
> we value women differently [as opposed to Sunnis he means]. They
> don't walk three steps behind men and we walk together. Actually, in
> our society women walk ahead of us!

During the time of the interviews, Başak and her husband were car-
rying out construction work to open a bistro next to the off-licence
shop. Başak was going to be the owner and she was busy with the deco-
ration and hiring staff for the bistro. Her husband also used her role in
their business to indicate women's strong and powerful position in Alevi
families. However, the other side of the coin is that Başak was solely

responsible for caring for their children while her husband worked full-time in their shop and she only worked part-time while her children were at school. This is not to undervalue Başak's contribution, but to indicate that women have a powerful position, due to their skills and contribution. Moreover, due to their cultural and religious values this does not free women from their domestic roles. Therefore, working in an ethnic economy creates a double burden for women.

The contributions of this group of women to the ethnic economy are in the form of helping their husbands with the administrative paperwork, and as interpreters to solve any problems their businesses may have. They rarely offer manual labour to the family business. They remain housewives and are burdened with their domestic duties such as caring and cleaning. Even though they work in the business this work does not relieve them from their domestic responsibilities. In London's Turkish society, if women do not have a professional occupation, the most important role they have is that of motherhood and wifehood, as society values makes these roles much more visible and values them over other roles they have, through their contribution to family businesses.

6.4 Working conditions: Earnings and working hours

The emergence of the Turkish ethnic economy in London has radically changed women's economic engagement. This change has resulted in some women's withdrawal from income generation and other women's engagement as unpaid or low paid ethnic workers. Little demand for female labour has been the result of the male-dominated nature of ethnic economy. Thus, working in the ethnic economy is not seen as suitable for women and is seen as a man's business. When a job is described as being suitable mostly for male workers, women's labour is channelled into the business through subtle and invisible ways. In comparison with women's involvement in textile production, there are only a small number of women in the ethnic catering sector. This is in opposition to the generally accepted explanation that the decline of industrial jobs leading to the dominance of service sector employment would increase women's presence in employment. Within the Turkish community in London, what is observed is women's declining economic activity with the expansion of working opportunities in the ethnic economy.

The most apparent outcome of the shift has been the reduced wages women receive in return for their work. Women now work in the ethnic economy for much lower returns in comparison with the earnings they made in the textile industry. One of my informants, Emine, worked as a pastry-maker. She worked six days a week between 9 a.m. and 3 p.m. She earned £150 a week. Women working in other kinds of jobs in the ethnic economy earned a similar amount. Thus, women's six hours work a day earns them between £150–160 and they sometimes work six days a week. The national minimum wage rate was £6.08 in 2011 for workers over 21 years old. If a woman makes £150 for five days work a week working from 9 a.m. to 3 p.m. she makes £5 an hour which is below the national minimum wage rate. If these women work six days a week, then their hourly rate falls further. This is evidence of women providing cheap labour for the Turkish ethnic economy even when they are paid for their work. The consideration of unpaid family workers and how much their work is involved in businesses are ample examples of the heavy reliance on female labour.

Women's earnings were much higher in the days of the textile industry. One of my informants told me that she made £70 a day by sewing 250 pieces. If she worked five days a week she could make £300 a week, which is double the amount of a female worker in the ethnic economy. Note that this reported rate was the income earned ten years ago when textile production was at its height. This makes the earning difference between a woman working in the textile industry and in the service sector even higher, assuming that textile workers worked more hours a day than a woman working in a coffee shop. In the past women used to have a higher earning potential and the local labour market offered unskilled women higher economic returns.

What is evident in this comparison is that when women engage in any kind of work that resembles their domestic responsibility such as cooking, cleaning and caring, their work is usually underpaid and undervalued. It is possible to consider women's work as ethnic in the textile industry but it is also a good indicator of deterioration of wage incomes in the UK or in Europe in general, which would be seen as a part of neoliberal economic policies curbing wages against rising profits and rent incomes. This example is also a good case to show that the industrial work paid much higher, even to those migrants who worked in the last chain of textile production, than those jobs available in family-owned businesses of the Turkish migrant community. Therefore, the Turkish ethnic economy largely relies on the exploitation of unpaid family labour and women's labour to survive in London.

The tight margin in which the migrants try to make a living in the ethnic economy is best shown by the long working hours. Working long hours is the nature of the business and extends to more than 12 hours a day. This is especially true for owners and male workers. However, in many cases, it is declared that since most people live upstairs from their shop or *döner*-kebab takeaways, there is a mix between domestic life and business, and the line between these two is easily blurred. A woman expressed their life in the following statement:

> Women's labour in family-businesses is enormous. Imagine that you live in the same building where your work is. So, women are always there. Men have to stay at work to keep the business going so women run around to mind the paperwork and seek help and advice for administrative support. Thus, in our lives, everything is all about work. You get to work early in the morning to do the preparations and the shop stays open until the mid-night. When you finish at the end of the day you only think about getting some sleep until the next day's hassle starts again ... You go and talk to any woman whose husband works for a shop she will complain about his long time absence and she will tell you that her husband works all the time.

'Working from 9 a.m. to 12 p.m. is a usual practice in kebab shops. I believe that the Turkish community thought good things to the British society but never learnt anything back from them.' Another woman explained that the Turkish ethnic economy generated a vibrant social environment in Britain by introducing shops that stay open until late and commented on the fact that in this way Turks made a difference to the society in which they lived. However, she thinks that this has gone too far as men spend all of their time at work and stay open until late to serve more customers.

> They [shop owners] think that if they stayed on business long hours they would learn more. But they never think that even they stay open for shorter hours they would probably serve the same number of customers, and earned the same amount. In this case, when they keep their shops open for such a long time they need to hire a worker to keep the shop open. This is not as profitable as they might think.

It is evident that women's work in ethnic shops is poorly rewarded, and has been financially downgraded since the days of the textile industry in London. It has been shown that women earned less per hour than the national minimum wage in the ethnic economy. Considering women's contribution through their unpaid labour it is possible to argue that the Turkish ethnic economy flourishes based upon women's unpaid or low paid work. This is topped up with the long hours of work involved in the business. Men's long hours of work have increased women's responsibilities in the domestic sphere and generated a feeling of loneliness for women. In fact, women's contributions to the Turkish ethnic economy have a double facet. On the one hand, women contribute as unpaid family or underpaid workers and work long hours for little financial return. Conversely, they try to fill the gap that men leave in the domestic sphere and allow men to put in long hours in their business. Without these contributions, it is impossible to keep family-owned shops going as the success of ethnic business is dependent upon the fullest exploitation of labour provided by owners and family members.

6.5   Women's role in social reproduction

The notion of social reproduction is a useful one in expanding the meaning of economics, by looking beyond the market to include households and women's unpaid work. It enables them to move beyond the simple divide between public and private sphere and to evaluate how women's role in the private sphere contributes to the development of men's economic activities in the public sphere. In London, when men devote all of their time to their business, women have to take up more roles in maintaining the upbringing of their children and keeping social ties alive for the family. The most common role for women is social reproduction, through which the success of the Turkish ethnic economy is secured.

Women expressed the consequences of their husbands' long hours of work; that is 'men are absent in this society there are only women'. This was a reaction to long hours of work undertaken by men in the ethnic business or to men's absence when they work in other cities. A Kurdish woman's experience of having a husband working in another city is an interesting one to note. Dilan was a 43-year-old woman with three children and migrated to London 15 years ago with her husband. She said:

> since we first arrived my husband always worked outside of London. He left us in London, as we had other family members living in London and we had a house here. It has been years and years we lived like this. I got used to it. Actually it took me a quite long time to get used to living on my own. In the beginning I was really scared of staying alone in the night…It has been long long time I never turned the light off in the night.

Her husband visited his family once or twice a month, and devoted most of his time to his job.

In recognizing women's contributions to the ethnic business their role in freeing men from their responsibilities at home must be considered. Men's full devotion to work is only possible when women make further sacrifices from their lives and take up the male's role in their family lives. When male members are absent in the family, women become solely responsible for running the family and taking care of the children, which they say is a very large responsibility. Women usually consider their families as dysfunctional and fractured as men are away at work or totally absent working in another city. In this regard, women have been silently contributing to the expansion of family-based establishments in the Turkish ethnic economy in Britain. By offering their labour and time, and maintaining the social standing of their families in their communities they are building blocks for having a family-business in London. Keeping social ties and networks alive is important for all families, and it is important for men to leave their families within these networks even when they work in other cities. The existence and maintenance of the ethnic business is much more related to their position in their communities, and relations based on these ties and networks are at the centre of business. Family access to these networks is mostly secured by women's role in keeping their families together. As will be discussed in Chapter 7, families, childcare and marriages are used by women to make connections with their ethnic community and with the host society in which they live as migrants.

6.6 Women on work and employment: Between a rock and a hard place

The major shift in the economic activities of the Turkish community in London has had an enormous impact on women's approaches to paid work. Working in textile production used to be the main activity for almost all women until the early 2000s. Women not only made a large contribution to family income but also were the source of financial resources that were mostly invested in the ethnic economy. The older first generation women migrants worked in the textile industry without any exceptions. However, women's approaches to work have changed, due to the effects of the demise of the textile industry and the expansion of the ethnic economy. In fact, the inactivity rate rose among women, especially for those outside the ethnic economy circle, where the only access to income generating activities was through positions as wage-workers in the ethnic economy, which generated limited work opportunities for women. The families that run their own shop utilize their own family labour and mostly do not hire extra workers. A woman said that 'Nobody asks others to make a living in their business. Actually, it is understandable that their income is just enough for the family. If they hire someone else, they cannot make money from their own business. Their income is just enough for themselves.' Families unite their own labour to earn a living in a very competitive market, and cannot afford to hire extra workers.

The rising number of unemployed women has been a recent phenomenon in London. 'There used to be work in the factories but now there is no factory' said an informant who continued by saying 'now there are jobs paying 100 pounds a week.' The income earned in return for long hours of hard work is not sufficient for women, especially if they have small children. As one woman explains:

> Women get only 100 or 150 pounds a week. This amount is not sufficient if you need to put your kids into care. So working is not a good option for us. Paying what you earn to child carer is not logical and attractive. Because a week's care is almost 100 pounds so at the end what you have a zero sum.

For London's Turkish migrant women, they are only available to work after their children are grown up. They say that running a house and caring for children are difficult for women, and these duties come first. When the burden of domestic responsibilities is lightened after children are grown up, women may take up employment. In fact, women's priority is always to fulfil their maternal and domestic roles properly before they can even consider working. This is also an indication of how women's identity in Turkish society is built upon their domestic roles.

Recent approaches to work by first generation migrant women show a generational shift, as women's perspectives on migration, their settlement and future prospects in Britain have changed over time. The early migrant women's projection of their future in the host society, what can be named as guest worker ideology, was that they would return to their home country when they had enough savings to secure their livelihoods back in Turkey. This resulted in all members of families taking up employment, and their main aim was to earn money to secure lives back in Turkey when they returned home. However, this did not happen, as their stay was prolonged for various reasons, and eventually they all knew that they were not going back. In this regard, for the recent migrants, migration is permanent and there is no going back for good. This is a paradigmatic shift in the perspective of migrants towards their settlement, which may be the outcome of the earlier migrants' experience. Therefore, migration is no longer a temporary process, but is seen as permanent, and new settlers adjust their perspectives in this regard; when they arrive they know that their relocation is for good.

This shift has had an impact on women's perspectives on working and earning an income. In comparison with the early generation, the new settler women tend to focus more on their children and their future rather than earning cash to be used when they move back to Turkey. That is why their main concern isn't access to the labour market, although their options are quite limited. They are seen to be housewives who do not work. This perspective overlaps with the traditional patriarchal culture in which women's main societal role is to be a wife and mother. As will be discussed in Chapter 7, the Turkish community in London expects women to devote their time and energy solely to their family since the community suffers from the pain of a lost second generation.

The concerns about taking up a job are usually centred on the work women did in textile jobs, and women are aware that the only jobs available to them are informal and insecure ones in the ethnic economy. However, the main dilemma women face is the exchange between leaving their welfare benefits and taking up employment. They weigh up potential income against what they need to pay on top if they leave benefits. Women are left with a negative amount. According to one woman:

> In fact there is no work suitable for women. If you get an employment with English you have to leave your benefits. Then you have to pay your own rent, council tax and all other benefits. So, how am I supposed to support my expenses? What would I earn? It is only 100 pounds a week which is not enough to cover everything. Without benefits it is very difficult to meet all our needs just with the income comes from wages. Let me tell you something if there was no benefit and you had to live on wages no one would stay here. It would be just like Turkey!

Women consider other job opportunities such as working at Tesco, Somerfield or Sainsbury's, etc. However, their main concern is that their language ability would not be sufficient for this kind of employment. Thus, this formal employment seems closed to Turkish migrant women.

Formal employment channels are not considered, due to the risk of losing benefits and the lack of language skills.

Migrant women in the research did not mention anything about the domestic work opportunities available for women in London. It is a strong indicator that Turkish women did not consider working as domestic workers. In the literature, migrant women's domestic work is well studied and domestic workers constitute a large portion of today's migrant worker population. According to the ILO, 83% of domestic workers are women. London is a good destination for migrant women seeking domestic work. However, Turkish women did not even mention the availability of domestic work in their considerations of the job options available to them. This is a strong indicator of how women are completely isolated in their own community and have no intention of stepping outside it. In general, domestic work is seen as cleaning other people's dirt, and women are afraid of sexual abuse and of damaging their public image if they enter strangers' houses.

Women's evaluations of paid work opportunities are focused on jobs in the ethnic economy, hourly paid casual jobs at Tesco or Sainsbury's or the option of not working. Women weighted these jobs against the welfare benefits they would lose and the childcare costs they would need to pay if they took on formal work. They end up with a negative amount and so opt to be unemployed. In addition, women's evaluation of job opportunities in the ethnic economy is based on the view that they are only for family members. Immigrant women do not even consider taking up jobs such as domestic work, as it is seen as 'humiliating' and a manifestation of stepping out of the boundaries set for them in traditional patriarchal norms. Therefore, many non-working women feel that this market is not open to them.

6.7   Conclusion

This chapter has demonstrated that Turkish immigrant women have been silent contributors to the expanding family-based establishments of the Turkish ethnic economy in the UK. There are many categories of women involved in the ethnic business. Women contribute to the ethnic economy as mothers who are the main financers of ethnic shops, or as wives who offer their unpaid work or time as low waged casual workers. Some of these women work as unpaid family workers in family-owned businesses but some become low paid wage-workers to provide additional income for their families and children. Moreover, men married to the second generation of immigrant women utilize their wives' knowledge of the British system and language ability to run their businesses. However, women's contributions remain invisible, and they are classed as domestic work or reproductive activity in most cases. Another way that women make a contribution is in their role in social reproduction in which women expand their role in the private sphere to generate more time for men to work longer hours in the ethnic economy, or in their role in fostering the social ties and relations that are the very foundation of the Turkish ethnic economy. The role of women in maintaining the community networks and representing ethnic/national identity has been seen as essential in the establishment and success of the Turkish ethnic economy, which increased the emphasis on women's traditional gender roles as mothers and wives.

This chapter has also evaluated the major shift in women's economic activities in London. Women's invisible work in the ethnic economy has been compared to the textile work women used to do in the 1980s and 1990s in London. This shift occurred following the closure of textile workshops and the expansion of ethnic catering shops. This shift meant a move towards economic inactivity for a large number of women. The expansion of the Turkish ethnic economy, on the one hand, confined women into the domestic sphere, on the other hand, forced women to take up roles in ethnic shops to balance with their domestic roles as wives, mothers, sisters and daughters. This meant a reduction of the value of women's labour as their work in the ethnic economy is paid less compared with the value of their work in the days of textile production. Meanwhile, the value of women's work has significantly influenced the decision by women of whether to take up work or not. There is also greater emphasis in the Turkish community on women's roles as mothers and wives. Women's involvement in rearing children, and in social and religious practices, is seen as the primary role of women. Through strong emphasis on women's motherhood roles in the community, women not only care for their children, but are also representatives of their ethnic, religious and cultural identities. Moreover, these identities seem to set the foundation for the national culture on which the Turkish ethnic economy rests.

7
Zigzag Paths to Social Integration

A significant tension exists between discourses shaping integration policies in the West, with the increasing emphasis on the securitization of
immigrant polices post-9/11 and the demands on women by their own
communities to protect their local culture and heritage by keeping their
traditional roles intact. In the context of the UK, Kofman and Vacchelli
(2012) show that the main political discourse of social integration is
built on problems related to the lack of integration. Social exclusion
of minorities, ghettoization into segregated societies and lack of integration have resulted from the poor acquisition of the fundamentals
of British culture, i.e. its language and lifestyle. In particular, lack of
integration and social exclusion have been mostly ascribed to women
who have joined their husbands through family reunification, who usually do not speak English and hence put economic strain on existing
social services. For this reason, policymakers advocate an urgent need for
pre-entry tests, to ensure better economic integration through a better
knowledge of language and life in the UK (Kofman and Vacchelli 2012).
Therefore, this approach treats ethnic minority women as scapegoats for
non-integration and the representatives of non-Western values.

While the national discourse of social integration of immigrants has
been shifting towards restricting 'uneducated' and 'unskilled' women
whose entry into the UK undermines the British way of life, the Turkish
immigrant community in Britain has been focusing more on revitaliza-
tion of women's traditional roles, through the demands put on women
by the ethnic economy and community. Women's own families and ethnic communities require women to carry out their traditional duties and
fulfil their roles as representatives of their culture and ethnicity. While
women are drawn into maintaining their traditional roles as mothers
and wives through the demands of the ethnic economy, they are also

asked to strip themselves of these roles, which are seen to be preventing immigrant communities' integration by generating a vicious circle of ghettoization and exclusion. This is a major stress placed on immigrant women and there is no easy policy formula to solve this tension.

Moving beyond this impasse requires consideration of how first generation female migrants see their integration and how they give it meaning in their own world. This chapter aims to introduce Turkish women's views on integration. Women's integration to the host society follows a zigzag path in London's Turkish community. The Turkish ethnic economy is the only way for the Turkish community to construct their contribution to British society and women's work in the ethnic economy is therefore the most visible method of social contribution and integration. Thus, women's integration is not an individual affair, but paves the way for integration for the whole community as they are unseen contributors to the survival and business success of their communities through their roles as mothers and wives as well as workers in the Turkish ethnic economy. Women not only contribute to the ethnic economy through their labour, but they also have a major role in the construction and reproduction of national ideologies and identities. Since women are seen as the symbolic figuration of nation values and culture, they have an important role in constructing and reproducing particular notions of their specific culture. This can be done through women's involvement in rearing children, and in social and religious practices. Because of the increasing emphasis on how women fulfil their motherhood roles in the community, women not only care for their children, but also are representatives of their national and cultural identities. In fact, these identities seem to set the foundation of national culture on which the Turkish ethnic economy is built.

There are barriers that block women's efforts to integrate and generate their isolation in the Turkish community. In London, the expansion of the ethnic economy has resulted in women's withdrawal from the labour market to focus on their domestic roles as wives and mothers. There are many women who are unemployed and concerned more with raising children because the community has suffered the consequences of losing its second generation into gang culture. This is a new injury for the Turkish/Kurdish community in Britain, and women are generally blamed for not being 'proper mothers' and not paying sufficient attention to their children, which is seen to be the result of their work in the textile industry. Now, mothering has become a full-time occupation for many women. In fact, women see their motherhood and future prospects of their children as the only way of integrating into British society. Women see their role in the upbringing of their children as an important way of contributing to British society. In this regard, this chapter pays special attention to the experiences of migrant women, the ordeals to which they are subjected, but also their capacity to assume their destiny, to give it meaning and to represent it.

7.1   Facilitators of immigrant women's social integration

The portrayal of first generation Turkish women can be seen as a proto-type of non-Western women, who are the bearers of non-Western values and foster non-integration of their communities through their role in raising children. However, a close up on Turkish women shows their efforts to become a part of their host society. Contrary to the claims made in the policy discourse, Turkish women pay special attention to the ways in which their children are well integrated, so that they are not excluded. It is also true that women's individual social integration potential is very limited, due to their language ability, low education levels and the discrimination they face in the labour market. Even Turkish women locked in their traditional roles have developed alternative ways to integrate into their host society; social integration is achieved by the very traditional role of being a 'proper and devoted' mother. In the Turkish community, women consider motherhood as a full-time job, and protecting their children from gang culture and keeping them in school are the main occupations of these women in London. Therefore, women's integration is not a straight path but a zigzagged one, achieved through their children's integration.

7.1.1   Motherhood and mothering in the Turkish community

Motherhood has historically been seen as women's natural duty, to be performed in the private sphere. In contrast to women's motherhood roles, men were located in the public sphere performing political citizenship. Feminist scholars have argued, however, that women's motherhood activities contribute to political citizenship by producing citizens for the state. Women's unpaid reproductive and care work in the home is a way of subsidizing the welfare state and women's contribution to the public sphere and political domain (Pateman 1992). In Adrienne Rich's seminal work on motherhood, *Of Women Born: Motherhood as Experience and Institution,* a distinction is made between motherhood and mothering by focusing on motherhood's potential from its institutional construction. In feminist theory, distinctions are made between mothering as a practice and motherhood as an institution. In this regard, motherhood refers to an oppressive patriarchal institution for women, in which women are monitored and controlled for their mothering practices. On the other hand, mothering refers to the emancipatory practices women enjoyed during mothering (Rich 1976). In another vein, Goffman's (1961) theoretical framework of 'moral career' is an important one to conceptualize motherhood. Career refers to 'any social strand of any person's course through life'. Goffman (1961:119) argues that 'such a career is not a thing that can be brilliant or disappointing; it can no more be a success than a failure'. As Goffman (1961:119) puts it, the framework provides a 'two-sidedness' which links internal matters such as the image of self and self-identity with broader structures that include the 'publicly accessible institutional complex'.

Women's mothering practices in Turkey are rarely included in academic discussions, but are mostly taken for granted as women's primary role in Turkish society. In one of these rare studies, Deniz Kandiyoti's seminal work conceptualizing gender relations in Turkey, *Bargaining with Patriarchy*, focuses on women's strategies for gaining the love and sympathy of their sons to ensure their future security in a changing society which evolves from being rural based to urban. In her analysis, the classic patriarchal family appears to represent the structural arrangements of family life, even though it may vary in form and shape. It embodies the forms of control and subordination associated with the patriarchal family system in which women receive 'protection and security in exchange for submissiveness and propriety' and 'adopt inter personal strategies that maximise their security through manipulation of the affection of their sons and husbands' (Kandiyoti 1988:280). Women's devotion to their children, especially their sons, is structured from the perspective of the bargaining process, through which women secure their future and well-being in a setting where their only duty is to their reproductive activities in the domestic sphere.

This conceptual framework is a tool for understanding the value women attach to motherhood and mothering practices. It is evident that motherhood is the first priority for women migrants in London and other activities that they are engaged in are always in additional to the role they play as mothers. The love and care that women have for their children are maintained even when they are grown up. A woman was in tears when she mentioned that her son was leaving for Australia this summer for his gap-year. Her devotion to her children was beyond the putting her children before everything. She said:

> I wished that I had another kid who would be younger than these two. A kid keeps the family together. In the evenings, family members come together to pay with him or her so that you are together as a

whole family. Now in my family my kids are grown up now and my husband has the football couch role which keeps him busy all the time...I wish that I had another one.

In this regard, children are the glue of a good functional family and women live their lives through their full devotion to their children.

This conceptual framework also leads to an understanding in which women utilize their motherhood role to bargain with the community in which they live. Kandiyoti stresses that the bargaining process is between men and women in the household, whereas White, in her ethnographic study of low-income families in Istanbul, recognizes the importance of the relations taking place between women and the community. Therefore, women not only bargain with their immediate family members, but also negotiate with their communities. She writes:

> [Bargaining] could also primarily be seen as a bargain between the individual and the group, of which the conjugal family is a subset. In meeting the moral and labour requirements of her roles as wife, neighbour, mother, a woman signifies her willing to participate in the web of reciprocal obligations on which group stability and security rests.
>
> (White 1994:61)

In this regard, motherhood is a testimony of women's group membership and identity in one particular group. Turkish women in London also offer their mothering and motherhood in exchange for their group membership and in building their identity as a respectable wife and mother. Women also adapt to the changing demands of their community with regard to their mothering and working practices. The case of Turkish migrant women in London offers a good example of how these practices are changing and being adapted to the changing communal discourses of motherhood and mothering.

In the Turkish community in London, the expansion of the ethnic economy also resulted in women's withdrawal from the labour market to focus on their domestic roles. There are many women who are unemployed and concerned more with childcare. This was the result of two interrelated changes that took place in the Turkish community in London. During the high textile industry days, women were the main workers in the sector and it is claimed that their work resulted in the neglect of their motherly duties. The community leaders reported that there were many young people in prison or involved in gangs and drug use. This is a new consequence of the Turkish/Kurdish community in Britain and women are generally blamed for not being 'proper mothers' and not paying sufficient attention to their children. However, this blame is never put on fathers' shoulders, and women are seen as solely responsible for their children's upbringing and potential future successes. The working conditions forced on women to do long hours for small returns, with no future vision of their settlement in the UK, are not blamed either. Therefore, the simple conclusion reached is that women worked in textile workshops and did not spare enough time for their children, so they did not know what they were doing while they were working.

The looming trauma of the lost second generation has been on the minds of the community, since the heavy consequence of deaths and loss are being felt deeply, and this has influenced the roles of women in their families and community. This is confirmed by the high suicide rate among the Turkish youth in the UK. It is reported that 43 youngsters have died since 2008. In January 2012, there were three consecutive suicides and one of the youngsters left a note saying ten more of his friends would do the same (Habername 2012). Yusuf Çiçek, Enfield Councillor, declared:

> Turks in other European countries live in dispersed areas from each other, but in London Turkish speaking community lives together. Thus, kids grow up in streets with street and gang culture. The result is an epidemic of suicide, and many deaths in gang fights. These suicides have been seen as a family affair until recently, but now, it has been more public and we cannot stop it ... Those families whose children were committed suicide always say that their children were normal and had no problems. They desperately ask themselves why they committed suicide. The families desperately feel helpless in this regard.
>
> (Habername 2012)

Common concern is centred on the fact that families, namely women, have not cared enough for their children, but instead devoted all their time and energy to work and making money. One man, Ahmet, explained how his sister lost contact with her son who is believed to be involved with a drug gang. He says:

> there is no point in that you have homes and cars. She goes to Turkey every summer and collects her rent money but there is no way that

you can buy your son back. There is no compensation for this. People here are crazy to earn more and more, and they only calculate how much they can make. That's their main concern and they forget about children and their needs.

Ahmet was a cab driver and said that he does not want to end up with lost children, so he makes sure that he spares time for his family. He says: 'I don't work long hours as I am kind of my own boss and determine how many hours I can do. Everybody knows that after five o'clock Ahmet does not work.' For Ahmet, however, the main responsibility for maintaining a smooth running family is on women.

My wife is our internal affair minister. She runs everything...She is educated and attended many courses here in London and has a good level of English. But we never wanted her to take up a job as kids needed her at home. She makes sure that they go to school on time and safely get back. It is a full-time job...Maybe, in the future, when kids are grown up enough she can work.

The idea of lost children for the Turkish migrants is a heavy responsibility, and shapes women's role and place, as well as their mothering practices. A woman expressed her stress over these lost children in the following statement:

I feel like there is a gallows in Haringey and our children are hanging themselves one by one. This is an awful experience that our community is going through, and I am sure that nobody knows what to do. Everybody says that this is not going to happen to my children but I know that none of us is free of this tragedy. That's why our priority must be our children.

This not only has an impact on first generation women but also shapes the lives of second generation women who were born in London or brought to London when they were quite young. A young woman explained how she was married at a young age and now has two children.

My mother was working in a textile shop and she left quite early in the morning and came back late in the night. I was the oldest of my siblings and looked after them...I was a good student but when things started to happen with children of other families. They were

so scared that anything could happen to us and we got lost somehow...My parents decided to marry me off...Now I have my own
kids and trying to mother them. It is hard work and I now better
understand my parent's decision to marry me.

The older generation of mothers want to keep their children away from
trouble, whereas the younger ones are trying to raise their kids with
full devotion and care. It is certain that women's mothering practices
have dramatically changed and become a full-time occupation for many
women. Following children's schedules and other cultural activities also
shapes women's time and determines when they have time to work, if
they work at all. Sabahat was a divorced woman with a 12-year-old girl.
She earned her living by cleaning for other Turkish families. Sabahat was
the only woman engaged in cleaning work as this domestic work is not
popular among Turkish women in London. She explained how she jug-
gled her time and her daughter's schedule: 'I only work until the school
breaks. When she finishes the day at school I have to go and pick her
up. I always ask people I work for that I would only work until 3 pm latest. If they agree I do the work. Otherwise I don't.' Even when women
are working in their own shop they squeeze their working hours into
their children's school hours. Meryem explained her working schedule:
'After I drop children off at school, I go to our shop. I do pastry for lunch
time and do whatever must be done in the shop. Then I run to pick my
kids up.'

The new mothering discourse is built upon maintaining children's
interaction with their home culture, and ethnic and religious identity.
This was actioned by community organizations that offered different
courses and activities for kids and teenagers. Due to these developments,
community organizations became a meeting point for women as well,
and allowed them to socialize with other women with similar social
and cultural backgrounds. During weekends, community organizations
such as Cem-Evi and Day-Mer are full of kids and their mothers who
are waiting for their children to finish their activity, and they are able
to strengthen their social networks and friendships with other women.
Children attend a range of courses, from cultural activities to curriculum
supporting classes such as maths and English. In this regard, Sabahat
explains her effort for her daughters:

I must keep my hands on her all the time. I want her to be successful
and also busy so that she does not have time for other harmful stuff.

If I can give her a solid sense of her religion and culture and I also want to support her education and be successful. Otherwise it is easy for them to slip away from your hands.

This provides a two-sided benefit as children keep in touch with their home culture as well as receive extra support for their school work. Participating in these activities is the responsibility of women, as men are busy earning a living.

The discourse generated by the communal consensus on the issue of the lost second generation is based on women not being 'proper' mothers, and running after money rather than caring for their children and family. As a result of this consensus, women blamed for not being 'good' mothers should be full devotees to their children and familial responsibilities. Taking children to school or to their community organizations to attend different courses is done under the supervision of women. Women become a bridge for their children's integration and future life choices. Women are trying to be a bridge for their children between the new community they live in and their homeland culture and religious practices. Women take on this duty even if they have almost no understanding of the English language and their husbands are at work in another town or working long hours with almost no time and energy for their family and children.

7.1.2   Integration through children

The debate about motherhood has rarely been carried out in the conceptualization of migrant women's motherhood practices and it is often, in some public debates, referred to as migrant mothers' caring labour and its implications in fostering their children's integrations (Erel 2011). If motherhood is defined as the agent of integration or preservation of national identity, it is transmitted into the migration studies as an agent of integration. In this regard, migration research often views mothers as transmitting traditional, ethnically specific values and cultural resources to their children. Indeed, researchers and policymakers often investigate the extent to which migrant mothers' cultural orientation helps or hinders their children's integration into the country of residence. In current public debates in the UK, migrant women's mothering is being discussed in reference to how successful they are at fostering their children's integration (Erel 2011).

In her discussion, Erel (2011) questions how migrant mothers are central to the idea that 'bearing and rearing children "naturally" transmits ethnically bounded, homogeneous cultural capital to children which is the basis for ethnic or national belonging'. She continues:

> Recognizing migrant mothers as citizens raises the question of how plural ethnic identities can relate to citizenship identities. Migrant women are positioned near the boundary of citizenship. They can be construed either as potentially diluting or undermining the cultural and social cohesion of a citizen community or as revitalizing this very community by injecting 'new blood'.
>
> (Erel 2011:696)

An investigation of Turkish migrant women's mothering shows that mothering is a way for them to construct their own social integration as well as their children's multi-ethnic and cultural citizenship and identity. The unexpected consequence of living in the UK for the Turkish migrants has been the loss of contact with their children and now the community is trying to build a new approach to their method of integration by developing a new discourse of motherhood. The implications of this new way of raising children are immense for mothers, children and the Turkish community in London.

Most Turkish migrants in London are from a working-class background, with a low level of educational attainment. They want their children to break away from their working-class status by accepting the educational opportunities offered by the British state. Thus, first generation migrant women pin their hopes of social integration on their children's ability to enter into middle-class professional jobs in the future. A mother who was a cashier in an off-licence shop in north London was proud to say that her son was going to be a solicitor, and was about to finish law school. As she commented:

> I am very pleased that we got him to go through his education and he is going to be a lawyer. I feel like that I have completed my duty and managed to hold my family together. I also feel that his professional career is also a way for me to be a full member of this society.

In this setting, children are seen as the future of the community, and also of mothers. Filiz was the mother of three children and explained her expectations for them.

> My only dream is my children. My children are my future. Nothing in this life has importance for me than my children. Their success

and their ability to get good jobs in the future are my only desire. When they grow up, my dreams will be realised. That's why my life is devoted to them and I am trying to do everything for them.

Filiz's testimony is a strong one in emphasizing the link between children's integration and that of mothers. Another woman stressed her role in raising children in her testimony:

> I believe that I come this country late and missed out the financial opportunity offered by the textile production. I never worked outside home. But what I did instead that I looked after my kids. I could not have anything like property or money, nothing at all but my children won in the end. They now have good education and good jobs.

Social integration of immigrant women is being paved in their children's steps to integration. A mother's main concern is enabling her children's integration into decent professional jobs but also keeping them close to their home culture and religious values. This is why children's school achievement is sought through the courses provided in the community organizations in which children also participate in activities such as folk-dance and learning to play the *saz* (a local musical instrument, similar to the guitar). A woman explains this in her testimony:

> I want my girl firmly know her roots but well integrate into this society. Her one foot should be here with us and the other one in this society. She should have our culture and values but at the same time English ways of making a living. I think that in this way, she will be contributing to this society.

The Turkish women's integration strategy through raising socially integrated children contradicts the argument that migrant women raise children who are socially excluded and feed the vicious circle of migrants' social exclusion and non-integration. Turkish women's social value and contribution is measured by their children's success in their education and potential life paths. This measure is not only imposed on women by their families and community, but also by women themselves, who judge their own contribution through their motherhood and their children's success. Thus, the path women take to integration has implications in fostering migrant children's success in their future career and lives, which is in turn the route for women's zigzagged path to social integration and inclusion.

7.2   The barriers for integration: Language, de-skilling and discrimination

The ability of migrants to communicate in the language of the host country is a stepping stone for integration, and intersects with almost every dimension of migrant women's lives. Their legal status, long term residence and access to nationality, access to the educational system and formal vocational training, as well as access, insertion and positioning in the labour market are impacted by their language ability (Liapi and Vouyioukas 2009). According to Common Basic Principles 4 and 5 of the Framework for the Integration of Third Country Nationals in the EU4, a host society's language is indispensable to integration, although very few countries have a language learning policy targeted at migrants and even fewer make provision for integration courses. Moreover, migrant women have limited access to language courses. The only exceptions are migrant women with a study permit and *au pairs* employed in domestic work who are supposed to attend language courses during their stay (Liapi and Vouyioukas 2009).

Most first generation Turkish migrant women cannot speak English, and identify their lack of language skills as the main problem precluding their social integration and their ability to fully participate in the labour market by getting 'proper jobs'. However, men are better at English than women due to their stronger connections with the labour market within the larger society. Women often expressed poor levels of language proficiency, even when they had lived in London for ten years or more. One woman commented: 'I have been here for 15 years but I cannot even say kitchen in English.' Poor English language ability is generally explained by women's confinement to traditional gender roles and close community relations.

The fact that women cannot speak and understand English has a widespread effect on second generation women too. The most interesting finding was when I met two women who arrived in the UK when they were about 17 years old who did not learn English. One said:

> When I arrived I was 17 years old and I got married at quite young age. Then I had my kids... I got asthma, I should not have had kids at all but I had two. Having children kept me busy as my health is not good at all. So there was no time to learn English.

The other woman, who was 16 years old when she first came to London, told me that she also had little knowledge of English. Her case is more interesting, since she stayed with her brother who had an English wife, but she still has a poor level of English. She said that 'when I arrived I lived with my brother for a while. I used to speak some basic English with my sister-in-law. Later, I got married and then I had my own kids. In the end, I could never improve my English'.

The case of these women arriving at a young age but still not learning English is an interesting one, and sheds light on the degree of confinement of women to their traditional roles as mothers and wives, and into communal relationships. These traditional were also present in second generation women living in London and resulted in their early marriages which blocked their further integration into British society. When women's socialization takes place through these traditional roles, it is difficult for women to break from the role of housewife and improve their contact with the wider society. Without a sufficient level of language ability, women have fewer opportunities outside their community circle, and this precludes, especially first generation women's, social integration. Thus, the only option left for women is to marry and have children by following in the footsteps of their own mothers. In addition, if needed, women offer their labour for the ethnic economy run by the Turkish community, either in textile production or in the kebab catering business.

The need for women to have English language proficiency has changed as the community's main economic activity has shifted from textiles to the catering based ethnic economy. In textile generation, migration was perceived to be temporary and people expected to return home after staying for a while to financially secure their future back in Turkey. Thus, English was not needed in textile workshops where migrants only communicated with their own country fellows. However, the requirement to serve British customers in the Turkish ethnic economy has placed more emphasis on language skills and the ability to speak at least basic English. While men are more easily integrated into the requirements of the sector and so improve their English, women have been losing out in this process and so have been further confined to their traditional gender roles as mothers and wives. Women's inability to improve their English further pushes them out of the ethnic economy or channels their labour into more manual and marginal forms of work such as unpaid family or low-paid labour in which women do not need to speak English.

Women's willingness to learn English is low, as having poor English levels prevents them from seeking help to improve their language skills.

The older generation of women seemed to totally give up and did not bother to do anything about their language levels. However, younger female migrants may easily have learned English if they had been properly schooled and had some institutional guidance for their further education and language improvement. Many women complained about the pressure put on the public spending devoted to language education and some explained that they had to pay for their courses. Paid language education puts many off attending the courses. Even where women have a chance to attend a language course, there is hardly ever an opportunity in which they could practise their English. As one woman explained:

> I have been going those language courses for ages but I forget what I learn as soon as I leave the course. I think that I have so much in my mind that what I learn does not stay with me. Kids and domestic chores are big burdens. There is also no place that I can practice my English. Everyone I know around me is Turkish and we speak in Turkish…I must get a job to learn better English but in my current situation it is impossible as I have three kids to care.

Due to the nature of the expanding ethnic economy in which many Turkish people meet most of their needs without contact with the outside society, and the existence of close knit communal relations women are prevented from improving their English. Women emphasized the existence of large communal networks as an obstacle to practising their English.

> We shop from Turkish markets and eat in Turkish restaurants. We all have Turkish friends and relatives which whom we socialise. For our paper work, we go to Turkish organisations and get help for translations etc. When we need a solicitor or an accountant we go to Turkish ones. In what occasions can I speak English?

Around the areas of Haringey, Dolston and Hackney, there is a small Turkish town, in which Turkish migrants meet all their needs through the shops and services provided by Turkish migrants. Women's interactions with the wider society are so limited that they have no opportunity to practise the language of the host society.

Only a small number of first generation migrant women break the vicious cycle of living in family and community circles. Hasret was one of these women and aspired to be a dinner lady. She had attended a catering course at Hackney community college for two years and needed to do one more year to get her certificate. This involved classes ranging from hygiene to cooking, and her course was designed to be suitable for the needs of juggling her domestic responsibilities and course requirements. Hasret's English was just enough to follow the programme. Before she started, she had decided to attend the course. As time went by, her English improved. At the end of it, she would have a good level of English and a certificate. Therefore, attending the course improved her life in many respects. She tells her story as follows:

> I believe that the best for me is to be a dinner lady as I can look after my kids and work at the same time. When they are at school I will be working and during their breaks I will be also on break. This gives me the opportunity to be a mother and worker at the same time... If I worked for a Turkish shop you would have needed to work for 10 hours or more. Thus, it is very hard for a woman to work in those shops. The other option is to run your own shop but we don't have capital for it. So, I think that it is best for me to be a dinner lady.

Even when women have the inspiration to be involved in the mainstream labour market, their concern is still for the balance of family roles and working life. From women's own perspective, their main societal role is to be a mother and wife, and the other activities that they engage in are often additional and mostly seen as temporary. Women's efforts to learn language are mainly influenced by the options available for women to integrate themselves into the wider society and labour markets. This is usually the case for those few women like Hasret who are younger first generation migrants, with a relatively high educational background obtained in Turkey. The majority of first generation migrant women do not have much interest, or the opportunity, to improve their English, so their integration into the host society is mostly closed.

Women's inability to speak English is the most important obstacle in the handling of their children's school affairs, by which the second generation's school attendance and educational success is being shaped enormously. Poor English levels leave women unable to help their children with their school work. For example, it has an impact on how children follow their school routine and other school related social activities.

> One day, our kids had to start their day half-an-hour early. This information was orally delivered us when we went to collect our children.

The next day, I dropped my kid a little early and then I was on way back to home, I saw my neighbour, who was unaware of this announcement and taking her kid to school. Because she either did not understand what was told or her kid just forgot to tell her that they had to go to school an hour and a half earlier.

A woman informant told the above story to illustrate how women's English comprehension is important for children's education. As migrant women cannot speak English, and their own educational background is poor, they fall short in helping their children with their school work and assignments. Among the earlier migrants, children were left on their own to handle their school affairs. Since this resulted in a painful experience for the whole community of losing youngsters to gang culture, families now pay more attention to their children's education and community organizations have curriculum supporting courses for school age children. These courses are taken at the weekend to support children in their school work and assignments, and are a helping hand for families without sufficient English levels.

So far, this chapter has illustrated migrant women's incompetence in English, which has been the result of personal characteristics such as low education and the limitations put on women to perform their traditional patriarchal roles. It is, however, important to analyse the structural factors such as discrimination and de-skilling that prevent migrant women gaining access to the mainstream labour markets. This is mostly the case with those migrants who have better education levels. It is evident that skilled migrant women tend to experience disproportionate difficulties in finding a job commensurate with their education level and professional experience after relocating to a new country. Issues related to the recognition of foreign credentials, as well as labour market dynamics, often combine to limit migrant women's work in high-skilled occupations. Fatma was a classic example of how migrant women go through de-skilling of their qualifications that preclude their access to decent work and full employment. Fatma graduated from one of the prestigious dental schools in Turkey and was ready to practise her occupation. But she had to move to England as her husband got a good job as a computer engineer and she followed him. In the first years after arrival she tried to improve her English and then learnt that she had to go through a series of tests and examinations in order to become a practising dentist in England. Eventually, the couple was naturalized and became British citizens but Fatma's qualification still had to be approved by the General Dental Council. She took a written exam and passed it but whenever she took an oral and practise exam she failed. Here is her testimony explaining her situation:

> I am aware that there is a harsh discrimination practices in the exam I took. I believe that I answered all the questions right but I cannot somehow pass the exam … There are quotas every year they accept from those with foreign certificates and there is this tendency to accept Asians … Now I am working as a care worker and earning five pounds an hour which I think is unfair. There must be decent ways to integrate us into the practice. Instead of going through exams, we could be put through a course, in the end we could find qualified and unqualified as I am not sure how fair this exam system is!

There are also other categories of educated, skilled and qualified women who want to be integrated into the mainstream labour markets. Their main problem is the discrimination they face in each stage of finding decent employment. A woman complained about the Job Centre and its services for her. She wanted to be a maths teacher for adults but there were obstacles for her in gaining access to a training course to become a teacher for adult programmes.

> After a long deliberations with the Job Centre, I offered them that I can be a math teacher in your adult education programmes and asked them to pay my course fee for the training to get the teaching certificate but I got no respond … You know in this society we have very limited support to establish our own career paths. We want to work and we want to go to school but we cannot in the end. The only support we have is women just like us, our friends and neighbours.

Language qualifications are an important facilitator of migrant women's integration into the wider society. Women's options of having access to language courses or other training activities are shaped by their own attitudes as well as their families' but the structural factors such as availability of language courses and easy access to training activities shape women's efforts in learning language and gaining new skills. However, there are women whose qualifications and work experience gained in Turkey are not recognized as legitimate by potential employers and accreditation bodies. Therefore, they are pushed out of decent, full-time employment opportunities.

7.3 Women on integration

Women's testimonies strongly indicate that Turkish migrant women believe that integration is their contribution to British society. The discussion of integration is an unusual and extraordinarily strange issue for women, due to their feelings of isolation and exclusion. 'We are refugees no one expect us to be a part of this society. We cannot be integrated!' This is a statement from a woman informant in a group discussion on social integration. With a clear vision of their integration, women have, however, a clear sense of contribution to the Turkish community and the most common expression has been the success of the Turkish ethnic economy, which is used in reference to its contribution to the multicultural character of British society. The distinction made through their entrepreneurial endeavours and the hard work expressed in these establishments is evidence of the contribution to the Turkish community of London. Women mostly express the communal contributions of the Turkish community and achievements made together, rather than their own individual contribution and integration.

Even social integration is perceived as a communal act; women weight their life in London positively. In this regard, it is useful to present the findings of how women view Britain and what it represents for migrant women. Women see Britain as one of the most developed societies in the world. This issue was raised in more than one interview, and women were happy to be residents of that modern society. The modernity of Britain is perceived in contrast to the migrants' experience of Turkey and their life back there. Dilan was a Kurdish woman with three children who had been living in London for 15 years. Her husband was a kebab shop owner and worked in different cities in the UK. She says, 'Whenever we arrive back from Turkey I tell my children that this is how far civilisation gets and this is the ultimate. I cannot give you more...My husband is the same actually. When we approach to Dover each time he tells the kids that welcome to civilisation.' The perception of civilization by Dilan and her husband is based on a comparison of Britain with the 'backwardness' of Turkey as their view shows each time they return from their holidays in Turkey. Living in a modern society and having better living conditions are factors that make migrants feel good about their decisions to migrate to the UK.

Other areas where women think that the Turkish community in Britain makes contributions to the British society are paying taxes and the cultural diversity they bring to a multicultural society. Paying taxes and cultural diversity are the result of the activities of the Turkish ethnic economy, which many migrants feel is their main contribution to British society. In many testimonies, it is stated that the Turkish community helped the transformation of north London which is becoming one of the gentrified areas of London and serving middle-class settlers, in areas such as Green Lanes and Hackney. One man expressed the Turkish community's contribution to London in the following statement:

> When we first came to Hackney it was very run-down neighbourhood. Now have a look around the change it has gone through. I believe that we Turks have a part in this positive change.

Women's perception of their life in London also shows a zigzag path. In the initial conversations, women complained about their poor quality of life but later they concluded that their life has to continue here and would not have been better in Turkey. On the one hand, women say that their life in Britain is a precarious one that is has a feeling of temporariness. As one woman says, 'I feel that I am an idle person with no use. It feels like that one day will come and we will collect all our stuff and go back. I know that this is not true but I cannot help feeling like this.' The disparity between women's acknowledgment of their permanent settlement in the UK and their feeling of being temporary is an interesting one. On the other hand, women believe that their settlement in Britain will last a lifetime. One woman commented thus: 'Don't believe what other women talk about the fact that this is bad or they are very unhappy to be here. In the end we all know that we are in better state here. Nobody could go back to what they left back in Turkey.' Another woman echoed her thoughts of being in the UK in the following statement:

> Even from time to time I complain about being in London and how lonely gets our lives here. I know that we are here now and will be living whole my life here. Even if I wanted to go back to Turkey, my kids are British now. I cannot leave them.

These comments are not out of desperation because women do not have any other options, but rather they are content with their life in London and feel settled.

After all these explanations, the question that remains is how women judge their own social integration and contribution. Women define themselves as being 'idle', as people who have no positive contribution to offer. As discussed previously, their only contribution is their children. In one woman's words, 'If one day our children are grown up, independent people then this will be our contribution and our way of integration.' Therefore, women's views on their own contributions are generally bleak and negative. By making a direct connection between integration and contribution, women conclude that one has to make a contribution to be able to integrate. Contribution for women means having full-time employment. Since most women do not have a formal job, apart from those that work in their husbands' shops, they do not feel integrated. This view is similar to the traditional approach that links the notion of citizenship with labour market participation and paid work. Women's beliefs that contribution is linked having a paid job means that they don't feel integrated into British society and don't feel connected to it.

Another reason that women do not feel integrated is their dependency on welfare benefits to continue their lives in London and their refugee status. 'We are refugees and we will feel never integrated' was a testimony of a woman, Alev, who thought that the British society would never make them feel welcome as fully integrated citizens because they are refugees. Alev continued by saying:

> Even though I have a citizenship and all my family live here I still feel like that I am a half citizen who is not fully integrated and remained at the boarders of this country. Never inside but never outside! This is because we are aliens, foreign to this country.

The concept of 'half citizenship' is an interesting one. Alev's testimony indicates that she has a formal citizenship on paper but her integration in British society is not fully realized.

Women value their integration and contribution differently, and feel that they are making a contribution, but are not integrated. The integration has to be achieved through being a part of British life and in interaction with English people or being in the labour market which offers women a formal and decent paying job. In reality, women do not see themselves as integrated but they offset their sense of isolation and exclusion through being a 'proper' mother and raising children who can be a part of English life. Therefore, there are two ways in which women develop their integration, one is motherhood and the other is their work in the ethnic economy. Being a good mother/wife and working in the ethnic economy are the different spheres through which women offer their labour to their host society, thus resulting in a contribution. The contribution, on the one hand, is seen as a means of being useful, productive and a 'good woman'; on the other hand, the integration means being a part of British society and interacting with English people, not just living in their Turkish ghetto.

7.4 Brown envelopes: Interactions with the British state

On every door in Britain, there is a letter box. When the post arrives every morning the letter box makes a clink sound indicating the arrival of the post. In a Turkish home in London, until the post arrives a Turkish immigrant can live in their safe haven of the Turkish community. However, the post is the utmost interruption in this safe haven. At this point, the immigrant knows that s/he needs to seek help to know what is inside the letter. The arrival of the post marks the beginning of migrants' interactions with the institutions of the British state. The ways in which immigrants handle their relationships – through community organizations – with the state indicate an important aspect of social integration in the Turkish community, underlining the community's zigzag path of social integration, which is a fuzzy rather than straight line with a lot of other mediators involved.

Interaction with institutions such as the Home Office, the Job Centre, GPs, local councils, banks and schools, is a source of tension and stress for many migrant women. This is all new to them and for the first time in their lives they become an individual; the letters from the Home Office and the Job Centre are reminders of that individuality. Almost all women mentioned their unfinished correspondence with the Job Centre and each arriving letter gives them a scare. Women are not used to this type of communication since in Turkey most formal institutional relations are dealt with by face to face verbal communication with civil servants serving in different institutions. However, in the UK, the state's communication strategy, or any other institutions', is based on written correspondence and women need to be involved in this communication. This is an indication that this interaction is based on the perception of women's individuality and this is totally new for migrant women. Therefore, it generates a zone of alienation for women who are mostly seen as a member of the community, as mothers and wives, which usually makes little reference to women's individuality.

Dilek was one of the key informants in this research. She was a single mother, living with her daughter who was 12 years old. She arrived in London 15 years ago and met her husband there. When her daughter was five years old the couple decided to divorce. Since then Dilek has lived with her daughter. She says:

When Yaren turned 11 years old there are those rules that I had to work part-time to keep my benefits coming in. Then the Job Centre started to send me letters. Whenever I see these brown envelops in my mail, I get really scared. And I always asked myself what now?. I cannot really read English fluently Yaren helps me with these matters and then there are community organisations helping out with those letters. But they become nightmares for a while. I am Ok now. I sorted them out!

The best way to deal with brown envelopes is to take them to a community organization. In most community organizations the Turkish migrants organize help for immigrants to deal with the letters. They write a reply, or call a number if one is given in a letter. Therefore, community organizations act as advice bureaus for Turkish immigrants. For example, Day-Mer has two days a week allocated to replying to letters and bureaucratic matters that the migrants have with authorities. Saturday is one of these days and it is common to see women lining up waiting to be served. Each waits for her turn to see what the brown enveloped letter has to say. Even though most women are incompetent in English and unable to read and write in English, they are the family member responsible for responding to letters, which requires them to be familiar with the British state. Thus, women's relationship with the state takes place through letters in brown envelopes, and this takes women into a zone of the unknown based on their individuality.

Women's relations with state institutions are managed and mediated through community organizations. In this interaction women experience their individuality and are not able to perform this independently. Migration and life in a new society have changed women's perception of their own place in their family and society. Now, there is more emphasis on women as individuals whereas traditionally more emphasis was put on their identities as mothers and wives. Living in the 'brown envelope' society is a challenge and a discovery for women, in which they are considered as individuals; but women's responses to the process of this individualization are carried out through mediators such as community organizations. It is true that Britain is a new land for first generation migrant women, who are busy with domestic duties and childcare. Here again, women follow a zigzag path in their interactions with the host society in which they live. This is not only applicable to women; as a migrant community all Turks experience similar ways of communication and interacting in Britain.

7.5 Conclusion

Turkish women continue their journey in Britain as 'half citizens' who are contributors but not full participants. Many migrants believe that their status as refugees in the country precludes a positive outside view about them and they are socially stigmatized for their welfare dependency with no recognition of their contributions to British society. This results in feelings of exclusion and leads to women's isolation in the Turkish community. Women see integration constructed by having a 'decent' job and actively participating in the labour market, an aspect that Turkish women severely lacked

Women contribute to British society through their role in the Turkish ethnic economy and in raising the next generation of British citizens. Turkish women's path to social integration follows a zigzagged route and women utilize different mediators to facilitate their integration. Chapter 6 showed that women's contribution to the ethnic economy is the single most important method for social integration of the Turkish community in Britain. Therefore, women's integration is not an individual affair, but paves the way for integration of the whole community since they are unseen contributors to the survival and business success of their communities through their roles as mothers and wives, as well as being workers in the Turkish ethnic economy. Women not only contribute to the ethnic economy through their labour, but also play a major role in the construction and reproduction of national ideologies and identities.

Contribution to the ethnic economy is one of the major means of social integration, but women also developed a sense of integration and belonging through their role in mothering and raising children. Women value their contribution through their role in bearing and rearing children in which they want their children to have a solid connection with their ethnic and religious cultural heritage as well as with the British way of life and values. Therefore, it is possible to argue against the political discourse claiming that the first generation migrant women's method of child rearing is feeding into social exclusion and non-integration of the migrant community, as Turkish women are working hard for their children to be well integrated into their host society. Therefore, depicting first generation women as the source of non-integration is a false perception of how migrant women contribute to the well-being of their families and communities. Women not only contribute to their society through their major role in their children's well-being, but also through their role in the success of the expansion of the Turkish ethnic economy in London. Without any acknowledgment of these roles, women are blamed for the social exclusion of their communities.

There are barriers that block women's efforts to integrate and confine them to their ethnic community. The most important of them is their language ability as women see their English level as an obstacle in their efforts to be a part of British society. Women see their role in the upbringing of their children as an important method for their integration. Meanwhile, women are pulled and pushed in different directions by the demands on them from their families, their community and their host society. In one sense, women are obliged to be community members, good mothers and wives, with a strong emphasis on their communal roles rather than their individuality. In another sense, women are pulled into a zone of the unknown in their relations with the state and state apparatus. This tension is not easy to manage and is a difficult task to overcome for first generation women.

8
Conclusion

Work, Migrants and Social Integration began with two central questions: what is the nature of women's work in the Turkish ethnic economy in Britain and how has women's role in the ethnic economy facilitated their social integration into mainstream society? The increasing dominance of ethnically based fast-food catering businesses has contributed to making women's work highly invisible. Therefore, my aim has been to show the role of women in the ethnic economy, in order to indicate women's contributions not only as unpaid or low paid workers but also in terms of their domestic roles, which have enabled the maintenance of ethnic and social ties and networks that the ethnic economy heavily relies on. By focusing on the interrelations between ethnicity, gender and work, this book has shown that the Turkish community paved its integration path into the British society by keeping the home culture intact and establishing the Turkish ethnic economy and traditional gendered roles in which women were burdened with the roles of motherhood and wifehood.

This research was located within a specific line of literature that draws heavily on the interrelationship between the role of women in the ethnic economy and its possible impact on women's role in the family and society (Dhaliwal 1995, Phizacklea 1988, Anthias 1992, Struder 2003). There is a large consensus in the literature that even women play a major role in the success of ethnic businesses, and this little helps women to change their subordinate positions in their families and communities. Phizacklea (1988) shows that the utilization of social structures that enable subordinate female labour under patriarchal control is the essence of success of ethnic businesses that are predominantly controlled by men and are labour intensive in nature. Female immigrant labour is considered to be essential for maintaining a fresh labour supply in ethnic economies that usually operate on a small-scale basis (Portes and Sassen-Koob 1987, Anthias 1992). These studies have also identified how gender exclusion operates to keep women in a subordinate position in the ethnic economy. It is highlighted that men are the main beneficiaries of the ethnic economic activities. Women remain as contributors and helpers since their roles are defined primarily through their roles in the domestic sphere such as daughters, wives and mothers (Zhou and Logan 1989). A close examination of Turkish women's experiences in Britain show that women have adapted to changes in the economic activity of their community over time, and that social and cultural resources have shaped these adaptations. As the ethnic economy became the primary economic activity of the Turkish community, women have taken different roles in ethnic business but its family-based nature has resulted in the withdrawal of some women from income generating activities. Even though they are actively involved in their community's economic revival, Turkish migrant women continue their journey to Britain as 'half citizens' who are contributors, but not full participants. However, Turkish women have found their own ways of social integration through their unpaid contributions to the ethnic economy and their role in raising the second generation Turkish community in London. This book has also shown that depicting first generation migrant women as the source of social exclusion of their ethnic communities has no explanatory power in the case of Turkish women in London and does not appreciate how far migrant women contribute to the well-being of their families and communities.

8.1 The Turkish ethnic economy in London

The first objective of the book was to examine the structure of the Turkish ethnic economy in London and the ways in which the ethnic economy generates demand factors that condition women's ethnic work. The structure of the Turkish ethnic economy is a reflection of the migration patterns of Turkish groups and is highly influenced by the historical trajectory of that migration pattern. The groups who arrive earlier are better equipped with the financial and human resources to take advantage of expanding ethnic business, whereas the recent arrivals lack the means and resources to run their own business, but offer their labour as wage-workers to the ethnic economy.

The Turks' migration trajectory to Britain is different from the migration regime to mainland Europe, which was influenced by the guest worker regimes of post-World War II. Turkish migration to Britain was the result of socio-economic upheavals, conflicts and violence imposed upon certain groups who had hidden injuries because of their religious and ethnic identities. These injured communities of Turkey, Alevies, Kurds and political leftists, found a refuge in London and began a new life. What started as a refugee migration later turned into a chain migration as each migrant further encouraged their family members to join them, either by facilitating the emigration of their family members or marrying their children to other family members and relatives. This migratory trend was supported by the labour demand of textile production in London, and also attracted female migrant labourers from Turkey.

In recent years, Turks have emerged as self-employed entrepreneurs in almost all Western European countries, engaged in the *döner*-kebab business. The development of retail trade, mostly in the form of small-scale and family based establishments, had been based on the foundations of Germany-based wholesale suppliers of ethnic foods such as *döner* and other forms of kebab. The wholesale production in Germany has revolutionized the ways in which Turkish people engaged in the ethnic economy by enabling the easy engagement of Turkish migrants in the production and sale of *döner* takeaways all over Europe. This has resulted in the widespread of the Turkish shops all over Europe and the generation of great amount of employment opportunities for Turkish migrants in Europe. Since the early 2000s, the Turkish ethnic economy in the UK has become the main economic activity of Turkish migrants after the closure of garment workshops in London. The main feature of the Turkish ethnic economy is family-based operations in the form of off-license or *döner*-kebab shops run by pooling family labour and financial resources. The most of families running a shop usually utilized their own financial resources or borrowings from other family members or relatives living in London. Especially savings accumulated through their informal work during garment production was mentioned to be a main source of finance used to open their shops.

Running an ethnic shop requires working long hours and has been the reason for families forming partnerships with their close family members to share the heavy workload with someone who can be reliable. The degree of self-exploitation, coupled with harsh working conditions in the ethnic economy, is delegated wider to the community by the partnerships established between fathers and sons or close family members such as brothers or brothers-in-law. In almost all cases, the utilization of family labour and recruiting labour from the intimate circles of the ethnic community were central to the ethnic economy. The expansion of the community through new immigrants and students offers a fresh source of labour for the ever-increasing number of shops. The Turkish ethnic economy is a successful case of ethnic solidarity and economic cooperation in which human, social, cultural and financial capital is put into use for the advantage of a small group of shop owner, but for those living in the margins of British society it offers very small returns.

8.2 Turkish women's work in the ethnic business

The second objective of this research was to examine the nature of women's work in the Turkish ethnic economy in London, where Turkish women previously used to work heavily in the garment production industry until its demise in the early 2000s. Then, the community's main economic activity shifted to be in the ethnic economy and had a major impact on the use of female labour. Presently, most women work in the ethnic economy as unpaid family workers, 'helpers' or low-paid wage workers. This shift has also resulted in women's further subordination into domestic roles as well as the fact that women's work is built around their domestic roles such as wives, mothers, sisters and daughters.

The nature of economic activity that migrants engage in determines the gendered outcome of migratory flows. In comparison with the classic case of Turkish women's migration to Germany, the British case is well balanced in terms of the role of women in migration; and the popularity of women's labour in textile production in London pulled many Turkish female migrants to Britain. The result of the ethnographic study showed two main generations of women distinguished by their migration history and the type of economic activity they engaged in. The characteristics of these groups are differentiated not because their move to London took place in different time frames but because their access to economic activities is different. Those who arrived earlier in the 1980s worked in the textiles industry, which brought power and status for women in their families and community. The recent arrivals did not have the opportunity to work in textiles, but became unpaid family or low-wage workers in the Turkish ethnic economy. For some women, the expansion of the catering based family shops resulted in the withdrawal of women from paid work activities. This led women to return to their traditional roles as mothers and wives, and drop their income generating actives.

There are many categories of women involved in ethnic business. Women contribute to the ethnic economy as mothers who are the main financers of ethnic shops, or as wives who offer unpaid work or low-waged casual work. Some of these women are unpaid family workers in family-owned businesses, but some became low-paid wage-workers to provide additional income for their families and children. Moreover, men married to second generation immigrant women utilize their wives' knowledge of the British system and language abilities to run their businesses. This research has, therefore, shown that Turkish women are less economically active compared with their economic activity rate in the time of garment production. However, women continued to be an important source of labour for the ethnic business and their roles in the ethnic economy have been shaped in accordance with their domestic roles. They have contributed to the expansion and success of the ethnic business in a variety of ways including being mothers providing financial means to their children, or as wives acting as unpaid family workers, or casual workers offering lower-paid labour. It has also shown how traditional gender relations in conjunction with the labour demands of the industry keep many women in a subordinate position.

This book has evaluated the major shift in women's economic activities in London. Women's invisible work in the ethnic economy has been analysed in relation to the textile work women used to do in the 1980s and 1990s in London. This shift occurred through the closure of textile workshops and the expansion of ethnic catering shops. This shift, in fact, meant a move towards economic inactivity for a large number of women. The expansion of the Turkish ethnic economy, on the other hand, confined women to the domestic sphere, but on the other hand, forced women to take up roles in ethnic shops corresponding to their domestic roles, such as wives, mothers, sisters and daughters. What this shift meant for women was a reduction in the value of women's labour, as women's work in the ethnic economy is paid less compared with their work in the days of textile production. While the value of women's work has significantly reduced, the perception of whether a woman should take up work or not has also shifted dramatically. Accompanied with this change, there is greater emphasis in the Turkish community on women's roles as mothers and wives. Women's involvement in rearing children and in social and religious practices is seen as the prime role of women. By placing strong emphasis on women's motherhood roles in the community, women not only care for their children, but are also representatives of their ethnic, religious and cultural identities.

Women's contribution to the ethnic economy remains invisible, and is subsumed as domestic work or reproductive activity in most cases. Another form of women's contribution is their role in the area of social reproduction, in which women expand their role in the private sphere to generate more time for men to work longer hours in the ethnic economy or their role in fostering the social ties and relations that are the very foundation of the Turkish ethnic economy. Therefore, by further foster community networks, ethnic/national identity and cultural representation through their reproductive roles, women play an important role in the success of the Turkish ethnic economy

8.3 Migration and gender relations

The third objective of the book was to provide an understanding of the implications of expansion of the Turkish ethnic economy as the sole economic activity of Turkish migrants in London on gender relations and women's perceived place in the society as well as their sense of inclusion and integration. The implications of migration on gender relations and women's positions in society were explored. It was shown that in the Turkish culture, where social organization is heavily based on the family unit, family and marriage are important sources of identity and security, as well as economic support for women. Women mitigate patriarchal risk through marriage and complying with traditional gender roles and relations. By publicly voicing themselves through the roles of motherhood and wifehood, women can only gain status and decision making power to the extent that they assume those roles. Thus, the confinement of women to their roles as mothers and wives is the only way for women to attain power in both private and public spheres. Only through the manipulation of these relations can women effectively negotiate with their husbands, fathers and other members of their family and community. Within this context, this book shows how gender, work and women's domestic roles are entangled with each other and how changing the economic activity of the Turkish community had a long lasting effect on women's position in the community and has affected women's relationship to paid work, as well as of the way in which women set their priorities as 'the woman of the home'. This was the prevailing factor among the Turkish community in London, even in the way that women have had a long lasting history of participation in economic activity in London. Turkish women's migration to Britain was motivated by the available work opportunities in the textile production industry in which women were employed in high numbers. Since the early 1980s, Turkish migrants engaged in garment production in London influenced the trend of female migration, since it is thought that women are always better at garment making, and this helped to push up the number of women engaging in the production industry. Although Turkish women's migration to Europe is mostly evaluated as being due to family union and women are pictured as dependent migrants, the case of Turkish women in London indicates that they were never dependent members of their families but active economic agents of their families and communities. They were either industrial workers during the era of textile production, or informal service workers during the catering based ethnic economy period.

The gendered implications of migration were analysed in terms of the tendency to decompose and intensify existing forms of gender subordination and to recompose new forms of subordination. In some cases, migration helped women to decompose existing traditional roles by enabling them to escape abusive and violent relationships. The recomposition of gender subordination may be seen in the consolidation of women's roles as housewives or mothers. After the closure of textile workshops, women returned to their traditional roles and retired from labour market activities. The inactivity of women has been the result of the expansion of the male-dominated Turkish ethnic economy. Therefore, women lost their high income earning power in industrial production, and those in need only offer their labour for low-paying service jobs in the ethnic economy. This meant a step backwards for women whose earning potential was reduced, and a rise in female inactivity in the Turkish community. The Turkish women experience the intensification of gender subordination as a result of the increasing public policing of women's behaviour. The public discourse the that blaming women for not being 'good' enough mothers sees women's work in the garment production as the reason of the second generation's unsuccessful school records and their involvement in criminal activities. Therefore, women's motherhood is publicly scrutinized and watched over by the whole community and measured by their children's success in life. This confined women into a tight cage; not only were they expected to submit to the traditional gender roles but also their success was measured by their children's behaviour. This has resulted in the intensification of gender subordination among Turkish female migrants in London.

8.4   Migration, work and social integration

The final question of this book is: what could all these findings on Turkish women and community in London contribute to the existing body of literature on migration, ethnic economy and social integration in Western countries?

My study aimed to contribute to the analysis of the relationship between migrants' economics activities and their sense of social integration with a focus on women and gender. Departing from the case of the Turkish ethnic economy in London, it was shown that ethnic economies are not necessarily local activities of ethnic minorities but can be a well integrated regional economic activity of a particular group. The Turkish ethnic economy is a classic example of a regional ethnic economy run by Turkish migrants in different European countries, where Germany is its well functioning centre of manufacturers providing wholesale products to all over Europe. Having big manufacturers helps the *döner*-kebab business to be standardized and it became easier to manage a kebab shop. The result has been a European phenomenon of Turkish ethnic economy becoming widespread all over Europe and generating employment opportunities for many Turkish migrants who would otherwise have been unemployed. Therefore, the Turkish case helps us to move beyond the conceptualization of ethnic economy as marginal activities of ethnic groups, and to realize that it can be a regional multi-billion dollar business. In this regard, the Turkish ethnic economy is not simply serving the needs of a particular group, which is opposite to the view of the ethnic economy pictured by structural analysts in which the ethnic economy relied on their fellow immigrants' particular needs, thus creating a protected market, or only investing in sectors of the economy that were abandoned by native businessmen because of their demanding working conditions. The Turkish ethnic economy has, rather, become a part of European cuisine and fast-food culture, and diffused into a large clientele base.

The Turkish ethnic economy in London is a classic case of family-based establishments run by family members whose labour is self-exploited for the survival and success of ethnic shops that operate on a thin profit base. The hard working conditions and demands on labour are similar to those cases outlined in the literature and it is highly reliant on the ethnic capacity to organize itself and to mobilize ethnic solidarity. This is where female labour is so central to ethnic shops, in which women take up different roles and make diverse forms of contributions for the continuation of family businesses. To take a cursory look, London's Turkish ethnic economy is highly male dominated, while women's contribution is mostly invisible. Even their presence is not visible, and their contribution remains as a vital element of ethnic business. The first generation migrant women usually work as unpaid family workers in their husbands', sons' or fathers' shops. In London, the invisibility or seclusion of women's labour has affected the ways in which the Turkish ethnic economy operates in small shops on the first-floors on a high street, above which a family home is located. Thus, we see a blurred line between women's practices taking place in private and public spheres. Therefore, any attempt to understand the relationship between women's work and the ethnic economy needs to take into account these cultural, ethnic and local practices that influence the ways in which the ethnic business is conducted in each specific location and society.

Working either as unpaid family or low-paid wage-workers is women's path to social integration, through which women see their migrant lives as having meaning and sense in their host society. While women migrants construct their work in the ethnic economy as a means of social integration, the expansion of the ethnic economy as a dominant form of economic activity among the Turkish community has resulted in further expression of the traditional gender roles and relations for women. Motherhood and wifehood have been highlighted as the main roles of women, and the community and families demanded that women carry out these roles within a traditional manner in which women prioritize their domestic roles over their economic activities, and through these roles women express their group membership. As a result, many women in the Turkish community have withdrawn from economic activities compared with the textile days in London. The result is more women being economically inactive in London. It is evident that the catering business required fewer workers than the textile production industry and mainly utilized family members' labour. While women were concerned more with their domestic roles, these roles were also constructed as women's pathways to social integration as explained in the previous chapters.

What, then, does the example of Turkish migrant women tell us about the prevailing theorization of women's work in the ethnic economy, and its implications on women's social integration?

Turkish women's path to social integration is followed in a zigzag way, whereby women utilize different mediators to facilitate their integration. This book showed that women's contribution to the ethnic economy is the single most important method of social integration in the Turkish community in Britain. Therefore, women's integration is not an individual affair but paves the way for integration for the whole community since women are the invisible contributors to the survival and business success of their communities through their roles as mothers and wives, as well as being workers in the Turkish ethnic economy. Women not only contribute to the ethnic economy through their labour, but also play a major role in the construction and reproduction of national ideologies and identities. In this regard, women conceptualize their role in the upbringing of their children as an important method of their integration. Meanwhile, women are pulled and pushed in different directions by different demands placed on them from different sources, such as their own families, their community and their host society. In one direction, women are obliged to be community members, good mothers and wives, with a strong emphasis on their communal roles rather than individuality. In another direction, women are pulled into a zone of the unknown in their relation with the state and state apparatus. This tension is not easy to manage, and is a difficult task to overcome for first generation women.

Women construct their social integration through their contribution to the ethnic economy, through which women also developed a sense of integration and belonging. Women also feel their social integration through their role in mothering and raising children. When their children have a solid connection with their ethnic and religious cultural heritage as well as with the British way of life and values, this is a way for women's social integration. This book argued that the current political discourses of social integration have a tendency to blame the first-generation migrant women's method of child rearing as the reason of migrant communities' social exclusion. This is only helping to further stigmatize migrant women as the Turkish women are working hard for their children to be well integrated into their host society. The future well-being of the children is the single way in which women visualise their social integration into the British society. Turkish women migrating to Britain as refugees have been through a major life changing experience that has not only affected women's roles in their families, but also their economic activities. Shortly after migrating to London, most women found themselves working in the textile sweatshops, in the hope of securing their lives and saving enough cash if they were to return soon. However, most stayed longer than they anticipated in the beginning and built a life in London. When the catering based ethnic economy became the dominant form of economic activity Turkish, women became less actively involved than in the days of the textile industry. Women's work in the ethnic economy is established as an extension of their domestic roles, rather than as a mere reflection of earning a living. In this regard, women exchange their labour in the ethnic economy with community membership and identity in London.

In particular, women's work as unpaid family workers is strongly tied to their domestic roles as mothers, wives and daughters. Even Turkish women in Britain have always been a part of the ethnic economy and women often make an extra effort to show that their priority is always given to their domestic identities. Their productive activities might be unrecognized, but their dedication is socially rewarded by labelling themselves as 'good women' and 'good mothers', not as workers.

The prevalent state of the Turkish ethnic economy in London, women's work in the ethnic economy and the ways in which women are able to construct their social integration and contribution pose an important question about how women challenge and negotiate prevailing gender ideologies. Even though there are public demands put on women to carry out the traditional roles and remain within the confines of those roles, there are ways in which women's internalization of traditional gender roles and identities allow them to feel integrated into their host society without losing the social protection and security offered by their own community and families. Women are able to negotiate effectively with patriarchal structures about what they see as their best advantage, and to redefine the terms and conditions for when the next round of negotiations take place. The avenues of initialization and protection offered by the British state to Turkish immigrant women are an important point for women to take up gender negotiations more effectively. Therefore, it is important to remember that these women are not merely passive victims of the immigration process, the working conditions of the ethnic economy and patriarchy, but active players who attempt to utilize the opportunities created by the immigration process and socio-economic changes brought about through restructuring of ethnic economic activities.

The socio-economic changes brought about through the migration process, coupled with the changing economic activities of the Turkish community in Britain, have offered new avenues for women to negotiate the traditional gendered roles and relations in their own community as well as to construct their social integration into the British society. The communal demands put on women to carry out the traditional roles may be pulling women into the domestic sphere, but this does not mean that Turkish women are the source of social exclusion in their community. Rather, women pave their own path into social integration through their roles as mothers, and through the social integration of the second generation Turkish migrants. These dynamics underlying the societal position of the first generation of Turkish women in Britain may present an excellent opportunity to begin challenging current gender arrangements and to improve women's positions in the Turkish community. Only some of the possible avenues of inquiry have been introduced here by my exploratory study of a limited number of Turkish women in London. Further research on Turkish women's daily struggles and practices in Britain is clearly needed.

Notes

3   The Ethnic Economy and the Turkish Ethnic Economy in London

1. http://britishkebabawards.co.uk/2013/04/20/doner-kebab-manufacturers/ (accessed on 14 November 2013).

4   Migratory Trends and the 'Turkish' Community in London

1. The term *gurbetçi* is used in Turkish to describe people that left their homeland and went abroad to look for better work opportunities. *Gurbet* is the place where people leave their homeland (*memleket*) and is also often used in the context of domestic migration of the rural population. Later, it began to be used to describe people migrating to Germany to get work.
2. The Maraş massacre was the massacre of over 100 civilians, mostly Alevi Kurdish slum dwellers, living as migrant workers in shanty towns, in the industrial heart of Turkey. It was an attack by rightists on leftists, Turks on Kurds, Sunnis on Alevis.
3. *Hemşehri* is used to define people who have the same village of origin, such as people from Maraş and Kayseri who call each other *hemşehri*. When rural people moved to cities in the 1960s and 1970s they started to develop informal connections with their *hemşehries* and it was used as an informal network in which immigrants exchanged information, resources and help, as well as formed solidarity networks. Similar exchanges based on *hemşehri* relations have also been brought to London.

5   Turkish Immigrant Women in London

1. Worship house of Alevi people. It is the only Cemevi and is a very vibrant place for people's gatherings. It serves lunch everyday. It was used not only for worship but also for social and cultural activities.
2. Almancı is a term used to refer to Turkish migrants in Germany. In some cases it depicts such individuals as being rich, eating pork, having a comfortable life abroad, losing their Turkish identity and becoming increasingly 'Germanized' (King and Kilinc 2013:9).
3. The children of first generation migrants are not considered to be the first generation even though they are not born in the UK, due to the fact that they followed their parents and to some degree they were educated in the UK.
4. About 17% of all women were aged between 25 and 30, while 45% were in their 30s, 23% in their 40s and the rest over 50 years.

5. Finishing high-school takes 12 years in Turkey, after which pupils can sit the university entrance exam.
6. About 78% of all migrant women in the sample were legally married with children, only 15% were divorcees and the rest were widowed.

6 Women's Work in London's Turkish Ethnic Economy

1. In the Turkish language there is no distinction between the words textile and garments. Textile is used to cover all activities related to textiles and ready-made clothing production. Therefore, in this section, the word textile is usually used to mean garment making, and it is used interchangeably with garments.

Bibliography

Abadan-Unat, N. (1980) 'International labour migration and its effects upon women's occupational and family roles: A Turkish view', in N. Abadan-Unat (ed.), *Women on the Move: Contemporary Changes in Family and Society*, pp. 133–158. (Paris: UNESCO).

Abadan-Unat, N. (2006) *Bitmeyen Göç: Konuk İşçilikten Ulus-Ötesi Yurttaşlığa* (Unending Migration: from Guest-worker to Transnational Citizen). (Istanbul: Istanbul: Bilgi University Press).

Agarwal, B. (1994) *A Field of One's Own: Gender and Land Rights in South Asia*. (Cambridge: Cambridge University Press).

Akgündüz, A. (2008) *Labor Migration from Turkey to Western Europe, 1960–1974: A Multidisciplinary Analysis*. (Aldershot and Burlington: Ashgate).

Aldrich, H., R. Ward and R. Waldinger. (1990) *Ethnic Entrepreneurs: Immigrant Business in Industrial Societies*. (London: Sage Publications).

Altinay, L. and E. Altinay. (2008) 'Factors influencing business growth: The rise of Turkish entrepreneurship in the UK', *International Journal of Entrepreneurial Behaviour and Research*, 14(1), pp. 24–46.

Anderson, B. (2000) *Doing the Dirty Work? The Global Politics of Domestic Labour*. (London and New York: Zed Books).

Anderson, B. (2006) *A Very Private Business: Migration and Domestic Work*, COMPAS Working Paper No. 28. (Oxford: University of Oxford). http://www.compas.ox.ac.uk/fileadmin/files/Publications/working_papers/WP_2006/WP0628_Anderson.pdf.

Anderson, B. and B. Rogaly. (2005) *Forced Labour and Migration*. (TUC: London).

Andeson, B. and B. Rogaly. (2005) *Forced Labour and Migration to the UK*. (COMPAS and TUC). http://www.compas.ox.ac.uk/fileadmin/files/Publications/Reports/Forced%20Labour%20TUC%20Report.pdf, date accessed 14 January 2014.

Anderson, K. and D. Jack. (1991) 'Learning to listen: Interview techniques and analysis', in S.B. Gluck and D. Patai (eds), *Women's Words: The Feminist Practice of Oral History*, pp. 11–26. (London: Routledge).

Anthias, F. (1992) *Ethnicity, Class, Gender, and Migration: Greek Cypriots in Britain*. (Aldershot: Ashgate).

Anthias, F. (1992) *Ethnicity, Class, Gender, and Migration: Greek Cypriots in Britain*. (Avebury: Ashgate).

Anthias, F. and M. Cederberg. (2006) *State of the Art Theoretical Perspectives and Debates in the UK*, Integration of Female Immigrants in Labour Market and Society. Policy Assessment and Policy Recommendations, WP4. http://www.femipol.uni-frankfurt.de/docs/working_papers/state_of_the_art/UK.pdf, date accessed 10 February 2012.

Anthias, F. and N. Mehta, Nishi. (2003) 'The intersection between gender, the family and self-employment: The family as a resource', *International Review of Sociology*, 13(1), pp. 105–116.

Anthias, F. and N. Yuval Davis. (1989) 'Introduction', in N. Yuval Davis and F. Anthias (eds), *Woman, Nation, State*, pp. 1–15. (Basingstoke: Macmillan).

Atay, T. (2010) ' "Ethnicity within ethnicity" among the Turkish-speaking immigrants in London', *Insight Turkey*, 12(1), pp. 123–138.

Auster, E. and H.E. Aldrich. (1984) 'Small business vulnerability, ethnic enclaves, and ethnic enterprise', in R. Ward and R. Jenkins (eds), *Ethnic Communities in Business: Strategies for Economic Survival*, pp. 39–54. (Cambridge: Cambridge University Press).

Bastina, T. (2007) 'From mining to garment workshops: Bolivian migrants in Buenos Aires', *Journal of Ethnic and Migration Studies*, 33(4), pp. 655–669.

Basu, A. and E. Altinay. (2003) 'Family and work in minority ethnic business in the UK', Joseph Rowntree Trust, *Findings*, No. 13. http://www.jrf.org.uk/sites/files/jrf/jr154-family-ethnic-work.pdf, date accessed 1 June 2012.

Bayar, A. (1996) 'Ethnic business among Turkish immigrants in Europe', *Forum*, 3(4), pp. 1–7.

Baysan, A. (2011) 'Revitalizing the myth or return? German-Turkish exchange students going to Turkey: Motives, decision-making and future career plans, Istanbul Bilgi University'. http://eu.bilgi.edu.tr/docs/JM/Revitalization_of_the_myth_of_return_german_turkish_exchange_students_going_to_turkey_by_Alper_Baysan.pdf, date accessed 12 January 2014.

Bilgili, Ö. (2012) Turkeys multifarious attitude towards migration and its migrants, European University Institute, Robert Schuman Centre for Advanced Studies, Migration Policy Centre, Analytical and Synthetic Note No: 2012/01. http://www.migrationpolicycentre.eu/docs/MPC%202012%20EN%2001.pdf

Bonacich, E. (1988) 'Social cost of immigrant entrepreneurship', *Amerasia Journal*, 14(1), pp. 119–128.

Bonacich, E. and J. Modell (eds). (1980) *The Economic Basis of Ethnic Solidarity: Small Business in the Japanese American Community*. (Berkeley: University of California).

Borland, K. (1991) 'That is not what I said: Interpretative conflict in oral narrative research', in S.B. Gluck and D. Patai (eds), *Women's Words: The Feminist Practice of Oral History*, pp. 63–76. (London: Routledge).

Borooah, V.K. and M. Hart. (1999) 'Factors affecting self-employment among Indian and Black Caribbean men in Britain', *Small Business Economics*, 13(2), pp. 111–129.

Bottomley, G. M. de Lepervanche and J. Martin (eds). (1991) *Intersexions: Gender, Class, Culture, Ethnicity*. (Sydney: Allen and Unwin).

Boyd, M. (1989) 'Family and personal networks in international migration: Recent developments and new agendas', *International Migration Review*, 23(3), pp. 638–670.

Boyd, M. and E. Grieco. (2003) *Women and Migration: Incorporating Gender into International Migration Theory.* http://www.migrationinformation.org/Feature/print.cfm?ID=106, date accessed 31 January 2014.

Brettell, C.B. (2007) 'Immigrant women in small business: Biographies of becoming entrepreneurs', in L.P. Dana (ed.), *Handbook of Research on Ethnic Minority Entrepreneurship: A Co-evolutionary View on Resource Management*, pp. 30–41. (Cheltenham, Northampton: Edward Elgar).

Brubaker, R. (2001) 'The return of assimilation? Changing perspectives on immigration and its sequels in France, Germany, and the United States', *Ethnic and Racial Studies*, 24(4), pp. 531–548.

Buchan, J., R. Jobanputra, P. Gough and R. Hutt. (2006) 'Internationally recruited nurses in London: A survey of career paths and plans', *Human Resources for Health*, 4(14). http://www.ncbi.nlm.nih.gov/pmc/articles/PMC1526449/, date accessed 21 July 2012.

Castles, S. and M.J. Miller. (1993) *The Age of Migration: International Population Movements in the Modern World*. (London: Macmillan).

Chamberlayne, P. and M. Rustin. (1999) *From Biography to Social Policy: Final Report of the SostrisProject*, Centre for Biography in Social Policy, Department of Sociology, University of East London.

Charles N. and H. Hintjens. (1998) *Gender, Ethnicity and Political Ideologies*. (London: Routledge).

Chin, M. (2005) *Sewing Women: Immigrants and the New York City Garment Industry*. (Columbia University Press).

Commission of the European Communities. (2005) *A Common Agenda for Integration: Framework for the Integration of Third Country Nationals in the European Union*. COM: 389. Brussels. http://europa.eu/legislation_summaries/justice_freedom_security/free_movement_of_persons_asylum_immigration/l14502_en.htm, date accessed 3 April 2012.

Cornell, S. (1996) 'The variable ties that bind: Content and circumstance in ethnic processes', *Ethnic and Racial Studies*, 19(2), pp. 265–289.

Council of Europe. (1995) *Immigrant Women and Integration*, Community Relations, Directorate of Social and Economic Affairs. http://www.coe.int/t/dg3/migration/archives/Documentation/Series_Community_Relations/Immigrant_women_and_integration_en.pdf, date accessed 14 February 2012.

Dallalfar, A. (1994) 'Iranian women as immigrant entrepreneurs', *Gender and Society*, 8(4), pp. 541–561.

D'Angelo, A., O. Galip, N. Kaye and M. Lorinc. (2013) Welfare needs of Turkish and Kurdish Communities in London: A Community based research project, SPRC Middlesex University and Day-Mer. (London). http://sprc.info/wp-content/uploads/2012/07/Welfare-Needs-of-Turkish-and-Kurdish-Communities-in-London-A-community-Based-Research-project.-Preliminary-report.pdf, date accessed 10 February 2014.

Dedeoglu, S. (2011) 'Garment ateliers and women workers in Istanbul: Wives, daughters and Azerbaijani immigrants', *Middle Eastern Studies*, 47(4), pp. 663–674.

Dedeoglu, S. (2012) *Women Workers in Turkey: Global Industrial Production in Istanbul*. (London and New York: IB Tauris).

De Haan, A. and S. Maxwell. (1998) 'Poverty and social exclusion in north and south', *IDS Bulletin*, 29(1), pp. 1–9.

Delaney, C. (1987) 'Seeds of honor: Fields of shame', in D.D. Gilmore (ed.), *Honor and Shame and the Unity of the Mediterranean*, Special Publication No: 22, pp. 35–48. (Washington: American Anthropology Association).

DeVault, M.L. (1996) 'Talking back to sociology: Distinctive contributions of feminist methodology', *Annual Review of Sociology*, 22, pp. 29–50.

Dhaliwal, A. (1995) 'Gender at work: The renegotiation of middle-class womanhood in a South Asianowned business', in Wend L. Ng, Soo-Young Chin, James

S. Moy and Gary Y. Okihiro (eds), *Reviewing Asian America: Locating Diversity*, pp. 75–86. (Pullman, WA: Washington State University Press).

Düvell, F. (2010) *Turkish Migration to the UK*, Centre on Migration, Policy and Society (COMPAS), Oxford. http://www.compas.ox.ac.uk/fileadmin/files/Publications/Reports/6_Turks_UK.pdf, date accessed 11 February 2014.

EFMS INTPOL Team. (2006) *Integration and Integration Policies: IMISCOE Network Feasibility Study*, European Forum for Migration Studies. http://www.efms.uni-bamberg.de/pdf/INTPOL%20Final%20Paper.pdf, date accessed 19 January 2011.

Ehrenreich, B. and A. Hochschild. (2003) *Global Woman: Nannies, Maids, and Sex Workers in the New Economy*. (New York: Metropolitan Books).

El-Kholy, H.A. (2002) *Defiance and Compliance: Negotiating Gender in Low-Income Cairo*. (New York and London: Berghahn Books).

Elson, D. (1999) 'Labour markets as gendered institutions: Equality, efficiency and empowerment issues', *World Development*, 27(3), pp. 611–627.

Elson, D. and R. Pearson. (1981) 'Nimble fingers make cheap workers', *Feminist Review*, 7, Spring, pp. 87–107.

Enneli, P., T. Modood and H. Bradley. (2005) *Young Turks and Kurds: A Set of Invisible Disadvantaged Groups*. (York: Joseph Rowntree Foundation).

Erdemir, A and E. Vasta. (2007) *Differentiating Irregularity and Solidarity: Turkish Immigrants at Work in London*. (Oxford: Compass).

Erder, S. (2007) ' "Yabancısız" kurgulanan ülkenin "yabancıları" ', in F. Aylan Arı (ed.), *Türkiye'de Yabancı İşçiler: Uluslar arası Göç, İşgücü ve Nüfus Hareketleri*, pp. 5–56. (İstanbul: Derin Yayınları).

Erel, U. (2011) 'Reframing migrant mothers as citizens', *Citizenship Studies*, 15(6–7), pp. 695–709.

Espiritu, Y.L. (1999) 'Gender and labor in Asian immigrant families', *American Behavioral Scientist*, 42(4), pp. 628–647.

Espiritu, Y.L. (2005) 'Gender, migration, and work: Filipina health care professionals to the United States', *Revue Européenne des Digrations Internationals*, 21(1), pp. 55–75.

European Commission. (2005) A Common Agenda for Integration Framework for the Integration of Third-Country Nationals in the European Union, Brusells. http://eur-lex.europa.eu/legal-content/EN/TXT/PDF/?uri=CELEX:52005DC0389&from=EN

European Foundation for the Improvement of Living and Working Conditions. (1995) Public Welfare Services and Social Exclusion: The Development of Consumer Oriented Initiatives in the European Union. (Dublin: The Foundation).

Faist, T. (1997) 'The crucial meso-level', in T. Hammar, G. Brochmann, K. Tamas and T. Faist (eds), *International Migration, Immobility and Development*, pp. 187–217. (Oxford: Berg).

Faist, T. (1998) 'Transnational social spaces out of international migration: Evolution, significance, and future prospects', *Archieves of European Sociology*, 39(2), pp. 213–247.

Faist, T. (2000) *The Volume and Dynamics of International Migration and Transnational Social Spaces*. (Oxford: Oxford University Press).

Fantasia, R. (1988) *Cultures of Solidarity: Consciousness, Action and Contemporary American Workers*. (Berkeley and London: University of California Press).

Faugier, J. and M. Sargeant. (1997) 'Sampling hard to reach populations', *Journal of Advanced Nursing*, 26, pp. 790–797.

Fregetto, E. (2004) 'Immigrant and ethnic entrepreneurship: A U.S. perspective', in H.P. Welsch (ed.), *Entrepreneurship: The Way Ahead*, pp. 253–268. (New York: Routledge).

Gallie, D. (1999) 'Unemployment and social exclusion in the European Union', *European Societies*, 1(2), pp. 139–167.

Giddens, A. (1990) *The Consequences of Modernity*. (Stanford: Stanford University Press).

Gilbertson, G.A. (1995) 'Women's labor and enclave employment: The case of Dominican and Colombian women in New York City', *International Migration Review*, 29(3), pp. 657–670.

Great London Authority (GLA). (2005) *London – The World in a City: An analysis of the 2001 Census Results*. (London: Greater London Authority Data Management and Analysis Group Briefing 2005/2006).

Great London Authority (GLA). (2009) *Turkish, Kurdish and Turkish Cypriot Communities in London*. (London: Greater London Authority).

Glaser, B.G. and A. Strauss. (1968) *The Discovery of Grounded Theory: Strategies for Qualitative Research*. (London: Weidenfeld and Nicolson).

Gluck, S.B. and D. Patai (eds). (1991) *Women's Words: The Feminist Practice of Oral History*. (New York: Routledge).

Goffman, E. (1961) *Asylums: Essays on the Social Situation of Mental Patients and Other Inmates*. (Harmondsworth, Middlesex: Penguin Books).

Goulbourne, H. and J. Solomos. (2000) 'Families, ethnicity and social capital', *Social Policy and Society*, 2(4), pp. 329–338.

Goulbourne, H., T. Reynolds, J. Solomos and E. Zontini. (2010) *Transnational Families. Ethnicities, Identities and Social Capital*. (London: Routledge).

Habername. (2012) *Türk Gençleri Arasında İntihar Salgını*, 8 February 2012. http://www.habername.com/haber-londra-ingiltere-intihar-alevi-kultur-merkezi-turkiye-stk-70796.html

Hagan, J.M. (1998) 'Social networks, gender and immigrant incorporation', *American Sociological Review*, 63(1), pp. 57–67.

Hammersley, M. and P. Atkins. (1995) *Ethnography: Principles in Practice*, 2nd Edition. (London and New York: Routledge).

Harbison, S.F. (1981) 'Family structure and family strategy in migration decision making', in G.F. DeJong and R.W. Gardner (eds), *Migration Decision Making*, pp. 225–251. (New York: Pergamon).

Hart, G. (1995) 'Gender and household dynamics: Recent theories and their implications', in M.G. Quibria (ed.), *Critical Issues in Asian Development*, pp. 39–74. (Hong Kong: Oxford University Press).

Hillmann, F. (1999) 'A look at the "hidden side": Turkish women in Berlin's ethnic labour market', *International Journal of Urban and Regional Research*, 23(2), pp. 267–282.

İçduygu, A. (2006) 'The labour dimesions of irregular migration in Turkey', *CARIM Research Report*, 2006/2005. http://cadmus.eui.eu/dspace/handle/1814/6266, date accessed 11 June 2012.

İçduygu, A. (2008) 'Circular migration and Turkey: An overview of the past and present – some demo-economic implications', *CARIM Research Report*, 2008/2010. http://cadmus.eui.eu/dspace/handle/1814/8331, date accessed 24 March 2012.

İçduygu, A. (2010a) 'Türkiye'de Uluslararası Göçün Siyasal Arkaplanı: Küreselleşen Dünyada Ulus-Devlet İnşa Etmek ve Korumak', in B. Pusch and T. Wilkoszewski (eds), *Türkiye'ye Uluslararası Göç: Toplumsal Koşullar- Bireysel Yaşamlar*, pp. 3–24. (Istanbul: Kitap Yayınevi).

İçduygu, A. (2010b) *Europe, Turkey, and International Migration: An Uneasy Negotiation*, Robert Schuman Centre for Advanced Studies, EUI. http://www.eui.eu/ Documents/RSCAS/Research/MWG/201011/01-26-Icduygu.pdf, date accessed 23 May 2012.

İçduygu A. and K. Kirişci. (2009) 'Introduction: Turkey's international migration in transition', in A. İçduygu and K. Kirişçi (eds), *Land of Diverse Migrations: Challenges of Emigration and Immigration in Turkey*, pp.8–34. (Istanbul: Istanbul Bilgi University Press).

İçduygu A. and D. Sert. (2009) 'Country Profile: Turkey', Focus Migration, No: 5, (Hamburg: Hamburg Institute of International Economics (HWWI)). http:// focus-migration.hwwi.de/uploads/tx_wilpubdb/CP_05_Turkey_2009.pdf

IOM. (2003) World Migration Report 2003. (Geneva: International Organization for Migration).

IPPR. (2007) *Britain's Immigrants: An Economic Profile*. http://www.ippr.org/ publication/55/1598/britains-immigrants-an-economic-profile, date accessed 3 January 2014.

Ireland, P. (2004) *Becoming Europe: Immigration, Integration and the Welfare State*. (Pittsburgh: University of Pittsburgh Press).

Jones, T. and D. McEvoy. (1986) 'Ethnic enterprise: The popular image', in J. Curran, J. Stanworth and D. Watkins (eds), *The Survival of the Small Firm*, pp. 197–219. (Gower: Aldershot).

Jordan, B. and F. Düvell (2002) *Irregular Migration: Dilemmas of Transnational Mobility*, (Aldershot: Edward Elgar).

Kabeer, N. (1994) *Reversed Realities*. (London: Verso).

Kabeer, N. (2000) *The Power to Choose: Bangladeshi Women and Labour Market Decisions in London and Dhaka*. (London and New York: Verso).

Kadıoğlu, A. (1997) 'Migration experiences of Turkish women: Notes from a researcher's dairy', *International Migration*, 35(4), pp. 537–557.

Kandiyoti, D. (1988) 'Bargaining with patriarchy', *Gender and Society*, 2(3), pp. 274–290.

Kandiyoti, D. (1989) 'Women and Turkish state: Political actors or symbolic pawns?' in N. Yuval-Davis and F. Anthias (eds), *Women-Nation-State*, pp. 126–150. (New York: St.Martin's, Press).

Kandiyoti, D. (1995) 'Patterns of patriarchy: Notes for an analysis of male dominance in Turkish society', in Ş. Tekeli (ed.), *Women in Modern Turkish Society*, pp. 312–338. (London: Zed).

Kandiyoti, D. (1997) 'Gendering the modern: On Missing dimensions in the study of Turkish modernity', in S. Bozdoğan and R. Kasaba (eds), *Rethinking Modernity and National Identity in Turkey*, pp. 113–156. (Seattle: University of Washington Press).

Kandiyoti, D. (1998) 'Gender, power and contestation: Rethinking bargaining with patriarch', in C. Jacson and R. Pearson (eds), *Feminist Visions of Development: Gender Analysis and Policy*, pp. 135–151. (London and New York: Routledge).

King, R. and N. Kilinc. (2013) *'Euro-Turks' Return: The Counterdiasporic Migration of German-Born Turks to Turkey*, Willy brandt series of Working Papers in international migration and ethnic relations, Malmö University, 2/13. http://www.mah.se/upload/Forskningscentrum/MIM/Publications/WB%2013.2.pdf

Kofman, E. (1999) 'Female "Birds of Passage" a decade later: Gender and immigration in the European Union', *International Migration Review*, 33(2), pp. 269–299.

Kofman, E. and E. Vacchelli. (2012) *National Discourses on the Migration-Integration Nexus During a Period of Electoral and Political Change in the United Kingdom*, Work Package 2, Promoting Sustainable Policies for Integration (PROSINT). http://research.icmpd.org/fileadmin/Research-website/Project_material/PROSINT/Reports/UK_WP2_Frame_Analysis_Final.pdf, date accessed 19 January 2014.

Kofman, E., S. Saharso and E. Vacchelli. (2013) 'Gendered perspectives on integration discourses and measures', *International Migration*, IOM. http://onlinelibrary.wiley.com/doi/10.1111/imig.12102/pdf, date accessed 19 January 2014.

Kofman, E., A. Phizacklea, P. Raghuram and R. Sales. (2000) *Gender and International Migration in Europe: Employment, Welfare and Politics*. (London and New York: Routledge).

Kontos, M. (2009) 'Executive summary', in M. Kontos (ed.), *Integration of Female Immigrants in Labour Market and Society: A Comparative Analysis: Summary, Results and Recommendations*, EU-Project: Integration of Female Immigrants in Labour Market and Society. Policy Assessment and Policy Recommendations (FeMiPol), pp. 28–34. http://www.femipol.uni-frankfurt.de/docs/femipol_finalreport.pdf, date accessed 25 December 2012.

Koser, K. (1998) 'Out of the frying pan into the fire: A case study of illegality among asylum seekers', in K. Koser and H. Lutz (eds), *The New Migration in Europe: Social Constructions and Social Realities*, pp. 185–198. (Basingstoke: Macmillan).

Küçükcan, T. (2004) 'The making Turkish-Muslim diaspora in Britain: Religious collective identity in a multicultural public sphere', *Journal of Muslim Affairs*, 24(2), pp. 243–258.

Lee, R.M. (1993) *Doing Research on Sensitive Topic*. (London: Sage).

Leung, M. (2002) 'From four-course peking duck to take-away Singapore rice: An inquiry into the dynamics of the ethnic Chinese catering business in Germany', *International Journal of Entrepreneurial Behaviour & Research*, 8(1/2), pp. 134–147.

Levitas, R. (1998) *The Inclusive Society? Social Exclusion and New Labour*. (Basingstoke: Macmillan).

Liapi, M. and A. Vouyioukas. (2009) 'Language skills, educational qualifications and professional skills', in M. Kontos (ed.), *Integration of Female Immigrants in Labour Market and Society: A Comparative Analysis: Summary, Results and Recommendations*, EU-Project: Integration of Female Immigrants in Labour Market and Society. Policy Assessment and Policy Recommendations (FeMiPol), pp. 28–34. (Frankfurt: The Goethe University). http://www.femipol.uni-frankfurt.de/docs/femipol_finalreport.pdf, date accessed 19 January 2014.

Light, I. (1972) *Ethnic Enterprise in America: Business and Welfare among Chinese, Japanese and Blacks*. (Berkeley: University of California Press).

Light, I. (2000) 'Globalisation and migration networks', in J. Rath (ed.), *Immigrant Businesses. The Economic, Political and Social Environment*, pp. 162–181. (Basingstoke: Macmillan Press).

Light, I. (2007) 'Global entrepreneurship and transnationalism', in L.P. Dana (ed.), *Handbook of Research on Ethnic Minority Entrepreneurship: A Co-evolutionary View on Resource Management*, pp. 3–15. (Cheltenham, Northampton: Edward Elgar).

Light, I. and P. Bhachu (eds). (1993) *Immigration & Entrepreneurship: Culture, Capital and Ethnic Networks.* (London: Transaction Publishers).

Light, I. and S. Gold. (2000) *Ethnic Economies.* (San Diego: Academic Press).

Light, I.H. and E. Bonacich. (1988) *Immigrant Entrepreneurs: Koreans in Los Angeles, 1965–1982.* (Berkeley: University of California Press).

Lister, R. (2004) *Poverty.* (London: Polity Press).

London Chamber Office. (2003) *Ethnic Minorities*, Information Centre Guide http://www.londonchamber.co.uk/docimages/149.pdf, date accessed 3 October 2012.

Lowndes, V. (2000) 'Women and social capital: A comment on hall's "Social Capital in Britain" ', *British Journal of Political Science*, 30(3), pp. 533–540.

Lummis, T. (1987) *Listening to History: The Authenticity of Oral Evidence.* (London Hutchinson Education).

Luts, H. (2008) *Gender in the Migratory Process*, Conference on Theories of Migration and Social Change, (Oxford: St. Ann's College), 1–3 July 2008. http://www.imi.ox.ac.uk/pdfs/helma-lutz-gender-in-migratory-processes

Lutz, H. (2004) 'Life in the twilight zone: Migration, transnationality and gender in the private household', *Journal of Contemporary European Studies*, 12(1), pp. 47–55.

Mahler, S.J. and P.R. Pessar. (2006) 'Gender matters: Ethnographers bring gender from the periphery to the core of migration studies', *International Migration Review*, 40(1), pp. 27–63.

Marchand, H.M. and A.S. Runyan. (2000) 'Introduction: Feminist sightings of global restructuring: Conceptualisation and reconceptualisations', in H.M. Marchand and A.S. Runyan (eds), *Gender and Global Restructuring: Sightings, Sites and Resistances*, pp. 1–22. (London and New York: Routledge).

Martin, C. (1996) 'French review article: The debate in France over "social exclusion" ', *Social Policy and Administration*, 30(4), pp. 382–392.

Martin, J. (1991) 'Multiculturalism and feminism', in G. Bottomley, M. de Lepervanche and J. Martin (eds), *Intersexions: Gender, Class, Culture, Ethnicity*, pp. 110–131. (Sydney: Allen and Unwin).

Martin, P. (2012) 'Turkey-EU migration: The road ahead', *Perceptions*, 17(2), pp. 125–144.

Massey, D.S., R. Alarcon, J. Durand and H. Gonzalez. (1987) *Return to Aztlan: The Social Process of International Migration from Western Mexico.* (Berkeley: University of California Press).

Masurel, E., P. Nijkamp and G. Vindigni. (2004) 'Breeding places for ethnic entrepreneurs: A comparative marketing approach', *Entrepreneurship & Regional Development*, 16(1), pp. 77–86.

McLean, S.L., D.A. Schultz, M.B. Steger (eds) (2002) *Social Capital. Critical Perspectives on Community and Bowling Alone.* (New York and London: New York University Press).

Mehmet Ali, A. (1985) 'Why are we wasted?' *Multi-Ethnic Education Review*, 4(1), pp. 7–12.

Mehmet Ali, A. (2001) *Turkish Speaking Communities and Education. No Delight.* (London: Fatal Publications).

Menjivar, C. (1997) 'Immigrant kinship networks and the impact of the receiving context: Salvadorans in San Francisco in the early 1990s', *Social Problems*, 44(1), pp. 104–123.

Menjivar, C. (2000) *Fragmented Ties: Salvadoran Immigrant Networks in America.* (Berkeley: University of California Press).

Metso, M. and N. Le Feuvre. (2006) *Quantitative Methods for Analysing Gender, Ethnicity and Migration.* (York: University of York). http://www.york.ac.uk/res/researchintegration/Integrative_Research_Methods/Metso%20and%20Le%20Feuvre%20Quantitative%20Methods%20April%202007.pdfESSE

Moore, H. (1994) *A Passion for Difference.* (Cambridge: Polity Press).

Morokvasic, M. (1984) 'Birds of passage are also women', *International Migration Review*, 18(4), pp. 886–907.

Moser, C. (1993) *Gender Planning in Development Theory: Practice and Training.* (London and New York: Routledge).

Mushaben, J.M. (2006) 'Thinking globally, integrating locally: Gender, entrepreneurship and urban citizenship in Germany', *Citizenship Studies*, 10(2), pp. 203–227.

Narayan, D. and M.F. Cassidy. (2001) 'A dimensional approach to measuring social capital: Development and validation of a social capital inventory', *Current Sociology*, 49(2), pp. 59–102.

Nicholson, L. (1994) 'Interpreting gender', *Signs*, 20(1), pp. 79–105.

Paine, S. (1974) *Exporting Workers: The Turkish Case.* (Cambridge: Cambridge Univesrity Press).

Panayiotopoulos, P. (2010) *Ethnicity, Migration and Enterprise.* (London: Palgrave Macmillan).

Panayiotopoulos, P.I. (1996) 'Challenging orthodoxies: Cypriot entrepreneurs in the London Garment industry', *Journal of Ethnic and Migration Studies*, 22(3), pp. 437–60.

Panayiotopoulos, P.I. (2006) *Immigrant Enterprise in Europe and the United States.* (London: Routledge).

Parekh, B. (2004) 'Redistribution or recognition? A misguided debate', in M. Stephen, T. Modood and J. Squires (eds), *Ethnicity, Nationalism and Minority Rights*, pp. 199–213. (Cambridge: Cambridge University Press).

Pateman, C. (1992) 'Equality, difference, subordination: The politics of motherhood and women's citizenship', in G. Bock and S. James (eds), *Beyond Equality and Difference: Citizenship, Feminist Politics, Female Subjectivity*, pp. 17–31. (London: Routledge).

Pecoud, A. (2002) 'Weltoffenheit schafft jobs: Turkish entrepreneurship and multiculturalism in Berlin', *International Journal of Urban and Regional Research*, 26(3), pp. 494–507.

Pecoud, A. (2004) 'Entrepreneurship and identity. Cosmopolitanism and cultural competencies among German-Turkish businesspeople in Berlin', *Journal of Ethnic and Migration Studies*, 30(1), pp. 3–20.

Pecoud, A. (2010) 'What is ethnic in an ethnic economy?' *International Review of Sociology*, 20(1), pp. 59–76.

Penninx, R. (1982) 'A Critical review of theory and practice: The case of Turkey', *International Migration Review*, 16(4), pp. 781–818.

Penninx, R. and M. Martiniello. (2004) 'Integration processes and policies: State of the art and lessons', in R. Penninx, K. Kraal, M. Martiniello and S. Vertovec, Steven (eds), *Citizenship in European Cities. Immigrants, Local Politics and Integration Policies*, pp. 139–165. (Aldershof: Ashgate).

Pessar, P. (1986) 'The role of gender in Dominican settlement patterns in the United States', in J. Nash and H. Safa (eds), *Women and Change in Latin America*, pp. 273–294. (South Hadley, MA: Bergin & Garvey Publishers).

Pessar, P.R. (1984) 'The linkage between the household and workplace in the experience of Dominican immigrant women in the United States', *International Migration Review*, 18(4), pp. 1188–1211.

Pessar, P.R. and S.J. Mahler. (2003) 'Transnational migration: Bringing gender', *International Migration Review*, 37(3), pp. 812–846.

Phillips, A. and S. Saharso. (2008) 'The rights of women and the crisis of multiculturalism', *Ethnicities*, 8(3), pp. 291–301.

Phizacklea, A. (ed.). (1983) *One Way Ticket:Migration and Female Labour*. (London: Routledge and Kegan Paul).

Phizacklea, A. (1988) 'Entrepreneurship, ethnicity and gender', in S. Westwood and S. Bhachu (eds), *Enterprising Women: Ethnicity, Economy and Gender Relations*, pp. 20–33. (London: Routledge).

Phizacklea, A. and M. Ram. (1996) 'Being your boss: Ethnic minority entrepreneurs in comparative perspective', *Work, Employment & Society*, 10(2), pp. 319–339.

Portes, A. and J. Borocz. (1989) 'Contemporary immigration: Theoretical perspectives on its determinants and modes of incorporation', *International Migration Review*, 23(3), pp. 606–630.

Portes, A. and L. Jensen. (1987) 'What's an ethnic enclave? The case for conceptual clarity', *American Sociological Review*, 52(3), pp. 768–771.

Portes, A. and S. Sassen-Koob. (1987) 'Making it underground: Comparative material on the informal sector in Western market economies', *American Journal of Sociology*, 9(3), pp. 30–61.

Portes, A., C. Escobar and R. Arana. (2008) 'Bridging the gap: Transnational and ethnic organisations in the political incorporation of immigrants in the United States', *Ethnic and Racial Studies*, 31(6), pp. 1056–1090.

Putnam, R.D. (2000) *Bowling Alone: The Collapse of America's Social Capital*. (New York: Simon and Shuster).

Ram, M., D. Smallbone and D. Deakins. (2002) *Access to Finance and Business Support by Ethnic Minority Firms in the UK*. (London: British Bankers Association).

Rath, J. (ed.). (2000) *Immigrant Businesses. The Economic, Political and Social Environment*. (Houndmills: Macmillan).

Rath, J. and R. Kloosterman. (2000) ' "Outsiders" business. Research of immigrant entrepreneurship in the Netherlands', *International Migration Review*, 34(3), pp. 656–680.

Rath, J. and R. Kloosterman. (2003) 'The Netherlands: A Dutch treat', in R. Kloosterman and J. Rath (eds), *Immigrant Entrepreneurs: Venturing Abroad in the Age of Globalisation*, pp. 123–146. (Oxford: Berg Publishers).

Razin, E. (2002) 'The economic context, embeddedness and immigrant entrepreneurs (Conclusion)', *International Journal of Entrepreneurial Behaviour & Research*, 8(1/2), pp. 162–167.

Rich, A. (1976) *Of Woman Born: Motherhood as Experience and Institution.* (New York: W.W. Norton).

Robins, K. and A. Aksoy. (2001) 'From spaces of identity to mental spaces: Lessons from Turkish-Cypriot cultural experience in Britain', *Journal of Ethnic and Migration Studies*, 27(4), pp. 685–711.

Sahgal, G. and N. Yuval-Davis. (1992) *Refusing Holy Orders. Women and Fundamentalism in Britain.* (London: Virago).

Sassen, S. (1996) *Losing Control?: Sovereignty in an Age of Globalization.* (New York, NY: Columbia University Press).

Sen, A. (2000) *Social Exclusion.* (Manila, Asian Development Bank). http://housingforall.org/Social_exclusion.pdf

Sharma, U. (1986) *Women's Work, Class, and the Urban Household: A Study of Shimla, North India.* (London: Tavistok).

Silvey, R. (2006) 'Geographies of gender and migration: Spatializing social difference', *International Migration Review*, 40(1), pp. 64–81.

Şimşek, D. (2012) *Identity Formation of Cypriot Turkish, Kurdish and Turkish Young People in London in a Transnational Context.* City University London, Unpublished Doctoral Thesis.

Spencer, S. (2006) *Social Integration of Migrants in Europe: A Review of the European Literature 2000–2006*, COMPAS. (Oxford: University of Oxford). https://www.compas.ox.ac.uk/publications/reports-and-other-publications/spencer-oecd-literature-review/, date accessed 24 March 2012.

Spenner, D. and F.D. Bean. (1999) 'Self-employment concentration and earnings among Mexican immigrants in the US', *Social Forces*, 77(3), pp. 1021–1047.

Spencer, S. and A. Rudiger. (2003) *Social Integration of Immigrants and Ethnic Minorities, Policies to Combat Discrimination*, OECD and European Commission. http://www.oecd.org/els/mig/15516956.pdf, date accessed 1 December 2012.

Spicker, P. (1997) 'Exclusion', *Journal of Common Market Studies*, 35(1), pp. 133–143.

Strüder, I.R. (2003) 'Self-employed Turkish-speaking women in London: Opportunities and constraints within and beyond the ethnic economy', *International Journal of Entrepreneurship and Innovation*, 4(3), pp. 185–195.

Takenaka, A. (2009) 'How diasporic ties emerge: Pan-American Nikkei communities and the Japanese state', *Ethnic and Racial Studies*, 32(8), pp. 1325–145.

TAVAK. 2013 'Avrupalı Türklerin Büyük Başarısı – İşçi olarak geldiler ama artık ekonomiye fayda sağlıyorlar', *A Report by Türk-Alman Eğitim Bilimsel Araştırmalar Vakfı* (İstanbul). http://www.brandday.net/arastirmalar/avrupali-turklerin-buyuk-basarisi-isci-olarak-geldiler-ama-artik-ekonomiye-fayda-sagliyorlar-h481.html, date accessed 11 January 2014.

Thomson, M. (2006) *Immigration to the UK: The Case of Turks*, Sussex Centre for Migration Research. (Brighton: University of Sussex).

Thomson, M., N. Mai, J. Keles and R. King. (2008) ' "Turks" in the UK: Problems of definition and the partial rlevance of policy', *Journal of Immigrant and Refugee Studies*, 6(3), pp. 423–434.

Tolciu, A., A.J. Schaland and T. El-CherkehTolciu. (2010) *Migrant Entrepreneurship in Hamburg: Results from a Qualitative Study with Turkish Entrepreneurs,* Hamburg Institute of International Economics (HWWI). Hamburg. http://www.hwwi. org/uploads/tx_wilpubdb/HWWI_Research_Paper_3-22.pdf, date accessed 11 November 2012.

Ünlütürk-Ulutaş, Ç. (2013) '"Almanya'yı temizliyorum": Almanya'da göçmen, kadın ve temizlikçi olmak', *Çalışma ve Toplum,* 2013/37, pp. 235–257.

Verdaguer, M.E. (2009) *Class, Ethnicity, Gender and Latino Entrepreneurship.* (New York and London: Routledge).

Volery T. (2007) 'Ethnic entrepreneurship: Theoretical framework', in L.P. Dana (ed.), *Handbook of Research on Ethnic Minority Entrepreneurship: A Co-evolutionary View on Resource Management,* pp. 30–41. (Cheltenham, Northampton: Edward Elgar).

Wahlbeck, O. (1999) *Kurdish Diasporas: A Comparative Study of Kurdish Refugee Communities.* (Basingstoke: Macmillan).

Waldinger, A., H. Aldrich and R. Ward (eds). (1990) *Ethnic Entrepreneurs: Immigrant Business in Industrial Societies.* (Newbury Park, London and New Delhi: Sage Publications).

Waldinger, R., D. McEvoy and H. Aldrich. (1990b) 'Spatial dimensions of opportunity structures', in R. Waldinger, H. Aldrich and R. Ward (eds), *Ethnic Entrepreneurs: Immigrant Business in Industrial Societies,* pp. 106–130. (London: Sage).

Waldinger, R., H. Aldrich and R. Ward. (1990a) 'Opportunities, group characteristics and strategies', in R. Waldinger, H. Aldrich and R. Ward (eds), *Ethnic Entrepreneurs: Immigrant Business in Industrial Societies,* pp. 13–48. (London: Sage).

Ward, R. and R. Jenkins (eds). (1984) *Ethnic Communities in Business: Strategies for Economic Survival.* (Cambridge: Cambridge University Press).

Werbner, P. (1999) 'Global pathways: Working class cosmopolitans and the creation of transnational ethnic worlds', *Social Anthropology,* 7(7), pp. 17–35.

Westwood, S. and P. Bhachu (eds). (1988) *Enterprising Women: Ethnicity, Economy, and Gender Relations.* (London: Routledge).

White, J.B. (1994) *Money Makes us Relatives: Women's Labor in Urban Turkey.* (Austin: University of Texas Press).

Wilford, R. and R. Miller (eds). (1998) *Women, Ethnicity and Nationalism.* (London: Routledge).

Wolf, D. (ed.). (1996) *Feminist Dilemmas in Fieldwork.* (Boulder: Westview Press).

Yuval-Davis, N. (1997) *Gender and Nation.* (London: Sage).

Yuval-Davis, N. and F. Anthias. (1989) 'Introduction', in N. Yuval Davis and F. Anthias (eds), *Woman, Nation State,* pp. 1–15. (Basingstoke: Macmillan).

Zetter, R., D. Griffiths, N. Sigona, D. Flynn, T. Pasha, R. Beynon and D. Flynn. (2006) *Immigration, Social Cohesion, and Social Capital: What are the Links?,* The Joseph Rowntree Foundation. (Oxford: Oxford Brookes University). http://www.jrf.org.uk/sites/files/jrf/9781899354440.pdf, date accessed 15 July 2012.

Zhou, M. (1992) *Chinatown: The Socioeconomic Potential of an Urban Enclave.* (Philadelphia: Temple University Press).

Zhou, M. (2004) 'Revisiting ethnic minority entrepreneurship: Convergencies, controversies and conceptual advancements', *International Migration Review*, 38(3), pp. 1040–1074.

Zhou, M. and J.R. Logan. (1989) 'Returns on human capital in ethnic enclaves: New York City's Chinatown', *American Sociological Review*, 54, pp. 809–820.

Zimmer, C. and H.E. Aldrich. (1987) 'Resource mobilization through ethnic networks: Kinship and friendship ties of shopkeepers in England', *Sociological Perspectives*, 30(4), pp. 422–455.

Index

Printed and bound by CPI Group (UK) Ltd, Croydon, CR0 4YY